COLLECTING LINCOLN

STUART SCHNEIDER

4880 Lower Valley Road, Atglen, PA 19310

Library of Congress Cataloging-in-Publication Data

Schneider, Stuart L.
    Collecting Lincoln/Stuart Schneider.
        p. cm.
    Includes bibliographical references and index.
    ISBN 0-7643-0270-1
    1. Lincoln, Abraham, 1809-1865--Collectibles. II. Title.
E457.65.S35   1997
973.7'092--dc21   97-9849
                                                   CIP

Published by Schiffer Publishing Ltd.
4880 Lower Valley Road
Atglen, PA 19310
Phone: (610) 593-1777; Fax: (610) 593-2002
E-mail: Schifferbk@aol.com
Please write for a free catalog.
This book may be purchased from the publisher.
Please include $2.95 for shipping.
Try your bookstore first.

We are interested in hearing from authors
with book ideas on related subjects.

Designed by "Sue"

ISBN: 0-7643-0270-1
Printed in Hong Kong

CONTENTS

ACKNOWLEGMENTS

In an undertaking as broad and inclusive as this, one person's knowledge or collection, no matter how great, is not enough. The fields were diverse and many collectors had pieces that were available nowhere else. Because this is a collector's book, I did not want to use pieces from museums, as they are usually off the market forever. Money alone can not make a good collection. These people have spent thousands of hours putting together their collections or obtaining their material. The non-collector cannot grasp the years of work it takes to assemble a good collection.

The author wishes to thank the following people who graciously agreed to allow photography of parts of their collections or contributed information and advice. Without that help, this book would not have been possible. Thank you (in alphabetical order): Donald Benham, Christies Auction House, Frank Coburn (Lincoln Memorial University), Colgate-Palmolive Co., Chris Coover, George Craig (President of the Lincoln Group of New York), Currency Auctions of America, Robert DeLorenzo, Cary Demont, George Fischler, Barry Frank, Joseph & Diana Garrera, Leonard Glazer, Howard Hazelcorn, Jean S. Hoefer, Harold Holzer, Tony Hyman, The Lattimer Family, Joe Levine (Presidential Coin & Antique Company), Chuck Levitan, The Lincoln Group of New York, Jonathan Mann, Kenneth Newman (The Old Print Shop, Inc.), Linda Offutt, Lloyd Ostendorf, Gregory & Lynn Romano, Grant Romer, Richard Sloan (past-President of the Lincoln Group of New York), Daniel Weinberg (Abraham Lincoln Book Shop), Frank & Virginia Williams.

These peoples' and organizations' hospitality, love of Lincoln, desire to make this a great book and their superb collections added significantly to the quality of this book.

INTRODUCTION

Lincoln is the most fascinating president of the 19th century (and many would argue, the 20th century as well). There are thousands of "collectors" of Lincoln. My personal interest in Lincoln began in 1959 when I started collecting Civil War items, just prior to the Civil War centennial. Among the remarkable things that I found were photographs of soldiers and an occasional photograph of Abraham Lincoln. These were carefully stored away without much study. After college, beginning work as a professional photographer rekindled my interest in the history of photography. Later, I went to law school and became an attorney. From this background in photography and law, my interest grew in collecting original photographs of Lincoln. As good photos were difficult to find, I studied other items having to do with Lincoln. I learned of and joined *The Lincoln Group of New York* in hopes of finding kindred souls to share information and possibly trade Lincoln photographs.

Membership in the Lincoln Group was an eye opening experience. The members showed me numerous ways to collect Lincoln. One couple liked to travel to places where Lincoln stayed or visited; another collected books about Lincoln; another liked to replay Lincoln's involvement in the battles of the Civil War; several dressed, spoke and looked like Lincoln; while another recreated part of the presidential box at Ford's The-

ater, where Lincoln was shot, in his home. I desperately wanted to write about Lincoln collecting, but with the seemingly endless variety of interests, I thought that it was impossible to write such a book. The old adage, "When eating an elephant, take one bite at a time" put the book in perspective. Start with photography, interview the collectors and show what they collect.

In preparing this book, I have stayed with collectors, purposely staying away from museum collections. Most of the time, when a piece goes into a museum it is off the collector's market forever. I wanted to seek out items that collectors owned. The pieces herein are all from private collections. Each collection has its own personality reflecting the interests of its owner. These pieces bring Lincoln alive to them. I hope you enjoy this way of looking at Lincoln and the influence that he had on our society. For convenience, the book is broken down into categories which collectors have concentrated on. While it is impossible to show everything available to collectors, this book endeavors to show representative examples of the pieces that a collector might find. An attempt was made to show only items made before 1935, but a few interesting or unusual items, made after that date, begged to be included. Some reproductions are also shown so that the collector can see what they look like.

1. LINCOLN COLLECTORS

Collecting items associated with Lincoln is not a new hobby. It has been popular since the time of Lincoln's death. There were noted, wealthy collectors who searched for the possessions of Lincoln, book collectors who sought out the rarest of Lincoln books, autograph collectors attracted to Lincoln's letters, and the list goes on. Lincoln collectors became active even as Lincoln lay dying. Here is a short look at Lincoln collectors of the past.

One of the earliest collectors, who located, wrote about, and exhibited Lincoln relics was Osborn Oldroyd. Oldroyd began collecting "Lincolniana", as the collector's term came to be known in the 1870s. Among the items he found were the Lincoln family bible and the chair in which Lincoln was sitting when he was shot. Around 1883 he moved into Lincoln's house in Springfield and turned it into a museum. Robert Todd Lincoln, who owned the home, gave it to the state of Illinois and Oldroyd became its curator. In 1893, Oldroyd was "displaced" from his Lincoln home (allegedly because he had items associated with Booth and the assassination on exhibit in the house, which offended Robert) and moved to Washington, taking his collection with him. He began exhibiting the collection at the Peterson House (across from Ford's theater) where Lincoln died. Eventually, Oldroyd became the curator of the Peterson House Museum. During these years, he wrote several books about Lincoln and reprinted one of Lincoln's last campaign speeches. In 1926, the government, which owned the Peterson House, purchased Oldroyd's collection for $50,000.

The exhibition of Lincoln items was immensely popular. This was obvious to the planners of the World's Fair of 1893, where one of the most popular exhibits (besides the first Ferris Wheel and the first ice cream cone) was the Lincolniana exhibit. It included Lincoln's law books, his law office table, his fee books, and autographed letters. The collection was sold a year later.

Collector Andrew Zabriski sought out Lincoln medals. In 1873, he published a catalog of 189 medals. By 1893, he had cataloged 350 medals. The medals produced during the 1909 centennial alone would have overwhelmed him.

Frederick Hill Meserve was among the first to collect Lincoln photographs. He was fascinated by Lincoln's face and traveled the country to locate photos of Lincoln. His greatest find was a cache of Brady's original negatives. One hundred photographs of Lincoln were photographically printed and tipped into a limited edition book which Meserve published in 1911. The book is a collector's item in itself. A later edition printed the images mechanically rather than photographically.

There were hundreds of books and pamphlets published after Lincoln's death. Judge Daniel Fish sought out the books about Lincoln and in 1906 published a bibliography of those books. In 1930, his collection went to the Lincoln National Life Insurance Company of Fort Wayne, Indiana (which hired Louis A. Warren, a great Lincoln authority, to head its Lincoln Historical Research Foundation), to start their research library. Other early Lincolniana collectors were William Lambert (books and manuscripts), Charles McLellan (books, pamphlets, engravings and sheet music), Judd Stewart (books and autographs), Joseph Oakleaf (books and pamphlets which went to Indiana University), J.P. Morgan (autographs) and Thomas Emmet (autographed material which sold in 1896 for $50,000). Ida Tarbell, Lincoln author (*The Life of Abraham Lincoln* and other books) and journalist (McClure's Magazine), was also a Lincoln collector. She sold the rights to produce a play from one series of articles to Charles "Chic" Sale who later played Lincoln in a movie (A. *Lincoln-The Perfect Tribute*).

In 1886, Oliver Barrett began collecting Lincolniana. He occasionally went door to door in Springfield, looking for Lincoln material and found many Lincoln documents. His collection was eventually sold at auction by Parke-Bernet. The sale has become legend and the auction catalog itself is a collector's item.

Another collector, Henry Hill, became the Illinois Governor in 1933 and brought his collection of Lincoln books, broadsides and pamphlets with him to the governor's house. He made sure that funds were available to preserve Lincoln properties in the state. He eventually gave his collection to the Illinois Historical Society which has one of the best current day collections (well cared for and displayed) of Lincolniana.

The first price guide to Lincoln collectibles appeared in 1906. Lincoln material had become very popular and with the coming of the 1909 Lincoln Centennial, it became more so with the prices increasing dramatically.

An interesting collector was Valentine Bjorkman of Newark, New Jersey. Starting shortly after the turn of the century, he began collecting books that Lincoln had read. He moved on to collecting books about Lincoln, engravings & lithographs, statues & busts, newspaper accounts about Lincoln in the early 20th century, different newspapers of April and May 1865, and numerous other pieces. To quote Bjorkman about his Lincoln collecting, he said, "A hobby steadys the nerves, refreshes the mind, stimulates the imagination and dispels the worries and irritations incidental to everyday life. ... It has been my purpose from the beginning to accumulate a collection that would be of real value to the student and historian." His collection was given to a college in 1939 and then the worst thing, from the perspective of a collector-historian, happened. The college began to run out of money and neglected caring for the collection. Pieces collected over a lifetime were left to languish in less than ideal storage. Luckily, a Lincoln collector purchased the collection and is busy restoring, recataloging, and caring for these irreplaceable pieces.

Malcom Forbes, another great collector (with some wonderful Lincoln pieces, although only a few are on display), once said about his collection that he wanted it sold rather than given to a museum after he was gone. He had enjoyed the hunt to find and purchase the pieces that made up his collection and other collectors should have the same pleasures. Most museums would disagree with this approach. Many collectors may be better caretakers of Lincoln memorabilia than museums that have numerous collections and can only afford to show and care for a portion of those collections. This is not a condemnation of all museums—there are a few that have done a wonderful job of preserving and displaying Lincolniana.

Today's collector can have a general or specific interest in Lincoln. They may collect anything with his image or associated with him, or they may collect only one area, such as autographs, Lincoln pennies, books about Lincoln, the assassination, political items, etc. Some collectors mentally collect Lincoln. They are fascinated by the man and his deeds, but not interested in owning Lincoln items. They read books about him, second guess his motives and reasoning and delight in visits to places where he may have stayed or visited. Regardless of the type of interest in Lincoln, collectors should join some type of Lincoln group to help them learn more about Lincoln and about what they collect.

In the quest for Lincoln items, the collector will probably go on wild goose chases looking for good material. The people who helped with this book had stories of great finds or interesting people that they met in their quest for Lincoln pieces. My own quest for Lincoln material has lead to many dead ends and also to several lucky finds. The most memorable, but unsuccessful, chase was started by a call from the editor of a Civil War collector's newspaper telling me that a "large collection" was about to be offered in upstate New York. An appointment was made to see the collection.

I flew up, rented a car and then drove to the home where I was greeted by three rooms filled with a thirty-year collection of Lincoln "stuff." Dreamingly I thought of the wonderful pieces that would be added to my collection. In looking through the numerous boxes, shelves, closets, and drawers, I was greeted by every souvenir and knick-knack ever made mentioning Lincoln. There were small "Land of Lincoln" license plates, restaurant paper place mats from Illinois, plastic Lincoln statues, current Gettysburg gift shop souvenirs, Lincoln on drinking glasses, walls covered with hundreds of framed, recent reprints of Civil War and Lincoln photographs, school-type books about Lincoln, and hundreds of other inexpensive things that mentioned or showed Lincoln. In the many years of amassing, this collector of Lincoln items had failed to buy even one original Lincoln photograph, so I came away with nothing. Over time, I began to feel that his effort was a tribute to the appeal of Lincoln and his collectiblity, regardless of budget. Lincoln has a magical allure. Many collectors want a piece of Abraham Lincoln, whether it is rare or common. This demand for the rare and older Lincoln pieces has driven up the prices, to levels unimaginable twenty or even ten years ago.

Valuing Lincoln Items

Valuing Lincoln items is difficult in this quickly escalating collecting field. There are auctions, mail order dealers, antique dealers, private collectors, and other places where pieces may be purchased. Since many of the pieces are unique, prices for one piece may not reflect prices for a similar item. Prices on good items have at least doubled over the last few years. On rare Lincoln autographed letters with good content, prices have gone up four or more times in the same period. "Nice" Brady CDV photos of Lincoln were $35 to $65 twenty years ago. The same images sell for $450 to $2,500 currently and demand outstrips supply, so the prices will continue rising. A simple Lincoln signature might cost $2,000 to $4,000, up from $300 twelve years ago. Autographed Lincoln CDVs have recently sold for $20,000 to $39,000 at auction.

As high as prices may seem, money alone can not put together a good collection. Some pieces may be one of four or five known and the collectors who own those pieces want to hold on to them until they die. They are often not for sale at any price. Even if you have millions to spend, you may still need lots of time, effort, or personal contacts to be there when a piece comes on the market.

Auctions may be the best way to obtain good Lincoln pieces. They are often the market setters. Auctions are able to offer pieces that would otherwise be unavailable elsewhere. Interestingly, your competition at an auction may not be whom you would expect. One Lincoln collector attended an auction to buy a specific item and found himself bidding against another determined bidder. The price went higher than usual, but he finally got the item and then went over to speak to the under bidder to discuss Lincoln collecting. The under bidder, it turned out, was not a Lincoln collector and knew nothing about the piece that he was bidding on. He just liked it, had the money and thought that it would be nice to have on his wall. Competition for good Lincoln items may come from collectors and non-collectors alike. New collectors are entering the field and some people are buying for investment rather than to add items to their collection.

Prices will vary and will depend upon how broadly you search for Lincoln items. Political items shows may charge little for centennial pieces or memorial pieces. Gun shows may turn up good photographs. Vintage photography shows may offer more common Lincoln photographs very reasonably. Antique shows may be the place to find Lincoln bookends and statues—they are often heavy and the dealer may not want to carry them back home.

The same pieces will sell higher at an auction or catalog dedicated only to Lincoln. Time is money. So, the biggest benefit of buying from a Lincoln catalog or at a Lincoln auction is that you can do all your "shopping" in one place rather than chase down individual pieces at ten auctions, a photo show, a gun show, and nine antique shows.

It is suggested that you seek out the better pieces and pay what they are worth to you. Some long time collectors sometimes get stuck in a rut. They paid less in the past and they refuse to pay "such a high price" now. They are missing the boat. It might be more practical to think of purchases in the Wall Street term of "price averaging". Pay a little for one, pay a lot for another and the real cost is somewhere in the middle for the two pieces. Expensive Lincoln items of the past look inexpensive by today's prices and are often currently unavail-

able at any price. You will only regret the pieces you missed, not the pieces that you obtained.

Values in this book are given in ranges and I have tried to give values that reflect collector demand and supply available. It is believed that these are the fair ranges that the piece will trade in. The person that you deal with may not follow these "rules" or the rules may change as more collectors discover Lincolniana. **Note: All items, except as noted, Are Valued In Very Fine to Excellent Condition**, regardless of the condition in the photograph. If it is not Very Fine to Excellent, it may be worth less. If it is in Mint condition, it may be worth more.

Occasionally, when I am hesitant to spend what I think is a great deal of money on a Lincoln piece, I put Lincoln in perspective with prices that other antiques and collectibles are bringing today. Jackie Kennedy's possessions brought mind staggering prices. Madonna's outfit for a single video sold for over $10,000. Nice, hard to find tobacco tins, from the 1920s and 30s, can make it into the thousands and outer space toys from the 1950s and 60s can bring more than $500. Will these items still demand premium prices 100 years from now? Lincoln will still be a most amazing and popular President and Madonna's name will only elicit blank stares. Lincoln's memory has value. Lincoln is enduring.

It is often said that a price guide is out of date the moment that it is published. Do not let that affect your use of a value guide. A value guide is comparative. It allows you to compare two items to determine if they are of comparable value. It is useful in buying and trading and it can help give you a feel for the rarity of a piece.

Remember, two is a coincidence, three is a collection. Happy hunting!

2. BRIEF LINCOLN HISTORY

There are so many good books on the history of Lincoln, that the attempt here is to put some of the collected items in the context of Lincoln's life, rather than offer any sort of comprehensive history. Learn about Lincoln and it will hone your skills to know what could exist at a particular time in history.

Abraham Lincoln's parents, Nancy Hanks and Thomas Lincoln, were both originally from Virginia but had moved to Kentucky where they met. They were married in 1806, had a daughter, Sarah, and on February 12, 1809, a son—Abraham. In 1816, the Lincolns moved to Indiana. When Abe was ten, Nancy Lincoln died. A year later, Thomas went back to Kentucky to find a wife. He met and married Sarah Bush Johnson, who Abe Lincoln always thought of as his true mother. In 1826, Abe's sister married and died a year and a half later in childbirth. In 1830, the family moved to Illinois. The following year, Abe left home to strike out on his own. He moved to New Salem where he lived for six years. There, he worked in a store, did all kinds of labor to survive, and made many lifelong friends.

In 1832 he signed up as a militiaman in the Black Hawk Wars for several months. Also in that year, he ran for state legislature and lost. In 1833 he became postmaster of his town. In 1834 he again ran for the state legislature as a Whig candidate, won and took up the informal study of law. He was licensed to practice law in 1836 and he moved to the new state capital in Springfield where he joined John Todd Stuart in the practice of law in 1837. His involvement in politics led to his becoming one of the leaders of the Whig party. Stuart basically stopped practicing law and Lincoln went on to become the law partner of Stephen T. Logan in 1840.

Lincoln married Mary Todd in 1842. They were married in Ninian Edwards' house. Their first child, Robert Todd Lincoln, was born in 1843. As a lawyer, Lincoln was very successful in gaining clients and winning cases. He and Logan amicably parted ways in 1844. He asked his law clerk, William Herndon, to become his partner and the firm of Lincoln & Herndon was started. In August of 1846, Lincoln ran and was elected to Congress starting in December 1847. He and his family moved to Washington, D.C. In 1849, his stint as congressman was over and they moved back to Springfield where he picked up the law practice again. In 1855, Lincoln ran and hoped to become a U.S. Senator, but Lyman Trumbull was

chosen instead. He stayed in politics and in 1857 joined the new Republican party.

Lincoln ran for Senator against Stephen Douglas, a Democrat, in 1858, generating the great Lincoln-Douglas debates. He lost again, but was recognized as a rising star in Western politics. He decided to run for President in the coming 1860 elections and spent the next few years quietly cementing his political power and influence. The other leading Republican contenders were Senator William H. Seward, Simon Cameron, Salmon P. Chase, and John C. Fremont. Lincoln accepted an invitation to speak in New York in February 1860 and had his photo taken at Mathew Brady's studio. His speech, at the Cooper Union, centered on the government's involvement with slavery. Lincoln was introduced by William Cullen Bryant and at the end of his speech, the crowd stood and cheered. The newspapers took notice.

Slogans were important in political campaigns, since images, not words, affected the majority of illiterate voters. Lincoln became "The Rail Splitter" or "Honest Abe" and received the Republican nomination. Hannibal Hamlin, a former Democrat from Maine, balanced the ticket and the race for President (against Stephen Douglas and others) was on. Numerous biography booklets were published to answer questions about the candidate. Photographs were printed to show what Lincoln looked like. Songbooks were created and Wide Awake Clubs were formed to parade and bring Lincoln's name before the public. The campaign was successful with Lincoln receiving 1,866,452 votes to Douglas' 1,376,957. Breckinridge received 849,781 votes and Bell only got 588,879 votes.

Lincoln began growing a beard in late November 1860. Within a month of the election, every state in the lower South started moving toward succession. He needed to form a cabinet, get up to speed in running the government and try to keep the South from seceding. William Seward, with his vast experience, was asked to be Secretary of State; Salmon Chase, a bitter rival of Seward, was chosen as Secretary of the Treasury; Gideon Wells was appointed Secretary of the Navy; Edward Bates accepted the Attorney General's position.

Lincoln began a train ride to Washington, D.C. Word soon arrived that as the train passed through Baltimore, men planned to assassinate Lincoln. Lincoln took another train in disguise and safely made it to Washington. Cartoons soon appeared making fun of Lincoln in a kilt and tam hat disguise, since he was disguised by the Scotsman, Allan Pinkerton.

The new president was at once hit with the problem of Fort Sumter. It was under blockade by the Confederacy. Lincoln had to order evacuation or order reinforcement to save the lives of the men. If he chose evacuation, the Confederacy would look strong and the Federal government weak. If he chose reinforcement, the South would secede and a Civil War would begin. After much discussion and advisement, he chose to notify the Confederacy that he would resupply the fort with only food and medicine. When the ships appeared, the Confederacy started the bombardment, the fort fell and the war was begun.

Northern newspapers said that the war would only last ninety days due to the superiority of the North's resources. Lincoln knew better. He had to raise an army, train it, clothe it, feed it and house it. The South had a similar task. In 1861, the North met the South at Bull Run (as known in the North and "Manassas" as it was known in the South). The Federal troops came in strong and were winning until the Southern troops were reinforced by General Johnston's forces. The Northern lines broke and retreated. Bull Run was considered a defeat. George B. McClellan was brought in to rebuild the army. After several months, the aged military leader Winfield Scott was replaced by McClellan. So began Lincoln's attempt to find the right military leader to defeat the Confederate army.

The Union forces were trained and ready. After several months, however, McClellan's troops were still in place. No battles were planned and the Confederates were still at Manassas. McClellan believed that the Confederate forces were great in number and he called for more troops. Lincoln replaced Secretary of the Army, Simon Cameron, with Edwin Stanton. Lincoln constantly urged McClellan to move. After about seven months of inaction, some battles were fought by the troops in the west under the leadership of George Thomas and Ulysses Grant. The Lincolns threw a formal ball on February 5, 1862. Their son, Willie, died on February 20. The Monitor and the Merrimack did battle on March 9 and the Union Monitor was the winner. Lincoln kept meeting with McClellan to move on the South's army. McClellan reluctantly moved to Manassas but the Confederates had left. It became obvious that McClellan had way overestimated the number of Confederate forces that had been encamped at Manassas.

In April 1862, the Western Union forces defeated the Confederates at Shiloh, at a cost of 13,000 Union lives. McClellan began to advance on Richmond in May with 135,000 troops. Confederate forces attacked part of his force and stopped him. After Confederate General Joseph Johnston was wounded, Robert E. Lee took over command of the Southern army in June. McClellan was still getting ready to attack Richmond at the end of June when Lee attacked his forces. McClellan retreated. On July 11, Lincoln replaced McClellan with John Pope as head of the Army of Virginia and made General Henry Halleck head of the Army of the Potomac. Pope attacked and was defeated at the second battle at Bull Run.

The army was demoralized and McClellan was reluctantly reinstated as the head of the Northern forces. Lee invaded Maryland. McClellan won the battle at Antietam on September 17 and about a week later, Lincoln announced the Emancipation Proclamation freeing the slaves as of January 1, 1863. Timing was important as Great Britain and France were about to lend total support to the Confederate States and the Proclamation freeing the slaves stopped them from doing so. In October, Lincoln visited McClellan again. McClellan still would not follow Lincoln's orders to get moving and was removed again in November 1862. Ambrose Burnside took his place. Burnside was replaced by Joseph Hooker in January 1863. Hooker was replaced by George Meade in June 1863. In July, the battle at Gettysburg was won, but Meade failed to chase and destroy Lee's army on several opportunities. The holiday, Thanksgiving, was created to occur on the last Thursday in November. In November 1863, Lincoln gave his Gettysburg Address.

In February 1864, two photographs of Lincoln were taken that eventually became the Lincoln portrait on the penny and the Lincoln portrait on the $5 bill. Meade was replaced by Ulysses Grant in February 1864. Lincoln had finally found a general who would fight and he could more fully concentrate on getting re-elected. In June, Lincoln won his party's re-nomination for president. His new running mate was Andrew Johnson. Former General McClellan was nominated in August by the Democrats as their Presidential candidate. Nevada was admitted into the Union as the 36th state in October. In November, Lincoln was re-elected President.

At the end of January 1865, the House voted (the Thirteenth Amendment) to totally abolish slavery. On April 9, 1865, Lee surrendered to Grant at Appomattox and the great war between the states was over. On the evening of April 14, 1865, Lincoln went to Ford's Theater to see a play, *Our American Cousin*, and was shot by John Wilkes Booth. He died the following morning.

3. PHOTOGRAPHS

Lincoln lived during a period when more than five types of photography were used. His portrait can be found on Daguerreotypes, Ambrotypes, Tintypes, Salt Prints, Albumen Prints, and Silver or Platinum Prints. In the Daguerreotype (collectors call them "Dags") process, 1839 to about 1855, each photo was unique (but there were always photographers who photographed other photos since it was the only way to make a copy at that time, so duplicate dags are seen occasionally). Dags of Lincoln are scarce with values estimated in the hundreds of thousands of dollars. Each year brings out a new "Lincoln" daguerreotype find. The owner often has "documentation" showing that it truly is a photo of Abraham Lincoln. None of these recently found dags have convinced a majority of experts and have, for the most part, faded into obscurity. Advice for the collector— Don't hold your breath waiting to find one. The Ambrotype (about 1855-1865) and Tintype (about 1860-1900s) processes were similarly unique—a single photo was made on a wet plate in the camera—glass for the Ambrotype and Japanned (black enameled) tin for the tintype. The Lincoln tintypes or ferrotypes are most common in the political "badges" of 1860 and 1864 and most are copies from other photographs. To make the campaign badges, a multi-lens camera took multiple tiny photos of a photograph of Lincoln (Lincoln did not sit for these tiny photos) on one large tintype plate. The plate was cut apart and each little photo was put into a brass shell or sold as a Gem (about 1 x .75 inches) or larger tintype. Tintypes were popular and many exist. They are often dark and sometimes show rust damage.

Ambrotypes are rarer. Ambrotype political photos of Lincoln exist for his first presidential campaign and are actively sought. There are some originals and copy photos of Lincoln known in the ambrotype medium. Again, a presently unknown, original ambrotype of Lincoln would be worth tens of thousands of dollars. There are two types of ambrotypes. One is on dark red glass and the other is on clear glass. A dark red glass ambrotype photo was a complete photo after developing. With the clear glass ambrotype, the glass had to be backed with black for the photo to be visible. Backings could be black paint on the back of the glass, a black painted piece of metal, or a piece of black velvet. The Ambrotype was held in a sandwich of cover glass, then a decorative brass mat, then the ambrotype and backing, all held in a "preserver" or thin copper or brass wrap-around frame.

AUTOGRAPHED PHOTO, ca. 1858. An autographed photo taken by Roderick Cole of Peoria, Illinois, or possibly by Preston Butler. This particular example was given by Lincoln to a neighborhood child named Mary Simonds. It was passed down through the family and obtained from her granddaughter. 5.5 x 7.5 inches. *Courtesy of Lloyd Ostendorf.*

In the 1850s, using the wet plate process, photographers began making negatives on glass. Positives were printed onto paper that was treated in a "salt" solution. These are called Salt Prints. Multiple prints could be made and some of the beardless photographs of Lincoln are salt prints. Beardless Lincoln salt prints have a sort of light brown or tan softness to them and lack luster or gloss. The photo is deeper into the paper rather than on the surface of the paper as with an albumen print.

AUTOGRAPHED PHOTO, ca. 1858. A centerpiece of the
collection, this autographed photo taken by Roderick Cole of Peoria,
Illinois, or possibly by Preston Butler. Here is the young Abraham
Lincoln. He liked this photo and signed more than three of them. 5.5 x
7.5 inches. *From the Frank & Virginia Williams Collection of Lincolniana.*

By 1860, the albumen print was the print of choice. The coating on the paper was made from an egg white base (albumen) and the photo was on the albumen surface of the paper. Mathew Brady and Alexander Gardner's photos of Lincoln and the Civil War were made this way. Albumen prints were richer and glossier than salt prints, but with time, many have faded, giving a much softer image. The printing process in the 1860s was usually by contact print (laying the negative on sensitive paper and exposing it to light for a photo as large as the negative).

Most CDVs—Cartes de Visite (Which refers to a photo 2.25 x 3.75 inches on a card—2.5 x 4 inches. Pronounced "Cart Di [as in "didn't"] Vizeet") were albumen prints. The CDV was invented in France in 1854 and made its appearance in the United States about 1860. It is said that over 100,000 CDVs of Lincoln were made for his 1860 presiden-

PHOTO, 1858. This photograph was taken by William Judkins Thomson on October 11, 1858, in or near Galesburg, Illinois. The original was an ambrotype. The reverse side of the photo states the photo was taken in Galesburg on October 8, 1858, right after the Lincoln-Douglas debate that took place there. It is on a cabinet card mount from a photographer named George Harrison whose studio was in Galesburg. Harrison obtained the original photo and copied it about 1876 or so. *From the Frank & Virginia Williams Collection of Lincolniana.* Value $500-$650.

PHOTO, 1858. This unusual photograph was taken by T.P. Pearson on August 26, 1858, in Macomb, Illinois. The original was an ambrotype (on glass). This photo (which is reversed, note the mole on Lincoln's cheek) appears on a cabinet card by A. H. Beck of Washington. The cabinet card is an 1880s or later format (8.75 x 6.5 inches). The shiny surface and the cabinet card format are give-a-ways that the photo was printed well after Lincoln died. At auction, these beardless Lincolns on cabinet cards consistently bring over $500. Value $500-$650.

tial campaign. CDVs were produced from 1860 to 1885. Those from the 1860s are usually on a thinner card stock than those of the 1870s. Many 1860s CDVs have a two line border around the edge for a framing effect and CDVs bearing tax stamps on the back are from the period September 1, 1864, to August 1, 1866.

Very little enlarging was done during this time, so larger prints are rarer. Most of the Lincolns "from life" are found in the CDV format and offer the greatest variety and price range. Some are rare and some are not so rare.

CDV cameras often had four lenses which were sequentially uncapped and then capped to give four images on one plate. If two, side by side, were uncapped together, they yielded a Stereo photograph. Stereo views were twin photos mounted on a rectangular card taken by a camera with two lens which were about 2.5 inches apart. The slightly different perspective of each lens gives a three-dimensional effect when viewed through a stereo viewer.

PHOTO, ca. 1859. A salt print by Samuel Fassett. The photo was taken on October 4, 1859, and printed about that time. It is 6.5 x 7.5 inches. Value $7,500-$8,500.

CDV, ca. 1859. A CDV by Samuel Fassett. The photo was taken on October 4, 1859. Fassett reprinted this as a CDV about 1860 or 1861. It is rare as a CDV with Fassett's backmark. From *the Frank & Virginia Williams Collection of Lincolniana*. Value $2,500-$3,000.

Lincoln's image was printed on stereo cards while he was living and after his death. Earlier cards are usually worth more than later cards. Here are some tips for dating the cards. The original early cards, between 1854 and 1861, were square cornered (sometimes they became slightly rounded with use) and usually white or ivory with a high luster. Between 1859 and 1861, one could also find cards with a high luster gray. From 1862 to 1872 the cards were mostly yellow with earlier cards being a lighter yellow and later cards a deeper chrome yellow. Starting in 1866, several makers began using colors such as purple or pink and then green. About 1868, the cards were made with rounded corners. Earlier cards contained two mounted photos. Larger cards were made in the late 1870s and after. Then they were made with one wide photo containing the two images. Tax stamps indicate the same date range as CDVs.

Probably the best known photographer of Lincoln is Mathew Brady, although Alexander Gardner took more photos of Lincoln. Brady CDVs were marked with his studio imprint on the front or back of the photo. They were printed by the thousands during Lincoln's life and printed by the Brady studio or by Edward Anthony and then E. & H.T. Anthony. Many people wanted to see what Lincoln looked like (newspapers could not reproduce photographs until well after the Civil War). Anthony ran a photographic supply house and as the demand for Lincoln photos was greater than the Brady studio could handle, Anthony took over the printing and sale of the photos. These were printed from the original Brady negatives and are considered to be 1st generation photos.

There are also 2nd and 3rd generation paper photos of Lincoln, where one photographer took a photo of another photographer's image and then sold it as their own (2nd generation) and the same process could be continued down the line for 3rd or later generation photos. They are usually worth less than a 1st generation photo. Tips for spotting these later generation photos are: 1) they show more contrast and the photo's midtones are often lost and 2) they are "known" photos by known photographers, yet the imprint is that of another photographer or there is no photographer's imprint.

Photographs of lithographs and prints were also very popular. Lithographs and engravings, mechanical printing processes, were made in CDV and larger sizes. Look at the photo under a magnifying glass to see if there are engraving lines in the clothing or shaded areas. There should be no halftone dots in any Civil War period print or photo. The halftone process came about after the war. Some people believe that the lithographs and engravings are original Lincoln photos and you can turn blue in the face trying to convince them otherwise. These lithos and photos of lithos are fairly common and usually sell for $15 to $40.

Photos were made in larger sizes, many after Lincoln's death. Cabinet cards (which refers to a photo 3.75 x 5.5 inches on a card that is 4.25 x 6.5 inches) were introduced in 1867 and made until just after the turn of the century. In the late 1880s, Silver and Platinum prints began to appear. The detail and tonal range of the photographs changed again. By way of example, a negative can reproduce 256 tonal variations from black to white. Once the negative is printed, an albumen or silver print only reproduces 12 tonal variations at best. A platinum print reproduces more than 200, yielding a richer photograph. Some of the nicest of these later photos are the "Ayres' Lincolns". Ayres' platinum photographs are commanding a premium over other "reprinters" works. Ayres was an artist in the printing medium and his work is of the highest quality.

CDV, 1860s. Two variations of Brady studio mounts. The one on the left is later than the one on the right. These are just two of several Brady studio back marks that can be found.

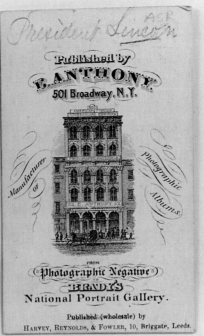
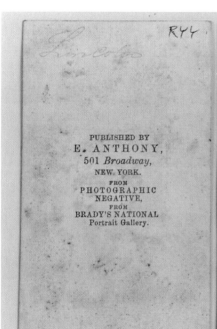

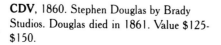

CDV, 1860. A strong photograph of Stephen Douglas taken by the Brady Gallery. Value $125-$150.

CDV, 1860s. Four variations of Anthony/Brady mounts found on the back of Lincoln photographs. The tax stamp helps to date one mount as being used between September 1, 1864, and August 1, 1866. During 1863, E. Anthony became known as E. & H.T. Anthony.

CDV, 1860. Stephen Douglas by Brady Studios. Douglas died in 1861. Value $125-$150.

CDV, 1860. The famous Cooper Union Photo taken by the Brady Gallery on February 17, 1860. Lincoln said it was this photograph that put him in the White House. These are getting hard to find. Value $450-$750.

The Ayres Photograph

Springfield, Illinois, photographer Alexander Hessler took several photographs of a beardless Lincoln in 1858 and 1860. The photos were used in the campaign for president, but were in little demand once Lincoln became President and grew a beard. Publishers wanted pictures of the new president with a beard. In 1865 Hessler retired and sold his Chicago studio and supplies to photographer, George Ayres. Ayres ran the studio for two years, during which time, he recycled the silver and glass of the studio's old glass negatives. While digging among Hessler's negatives, Ayres came upon several glass negatives of Lincoln which he set aside. He moved to Buffalo in June 1867 taking his equipment and the negatives. Five weeks later, Hessler's former studio burned down. Ayres resurrected the negatives in 1886 and printed the photo that was used as

the frontispiece for Hay and Nicolay's history of Lincoln. The photo appeared in *The Century Magazine* November 1886 issue. Ayres made copy prints for his friends over the next few years. In 1893, with the countrywide interest in Lincoln revived, Ayres began to reprint and sell the photographs from the original negatives.

He made prints in three forms—a silver print, where the tones are similar to a modern black and white photo; an albumen print where the tones are light to medium browns; and a toned platinum print where the tones are dark, rich browns. The silver prints are not too popular, while albumen prints are actively sought and platinum prints are the most wonderful of the Lincoln prints. The detail and tonal quality is rich and full. Ayres made the prints in several sizes, 6" x 8" or larger, and usually marked his prints on the front or back. He did not mark them all. If the photo is mounted on heavier paper, the mark may still be on the back of the photo itself. Or it is possible that the photo is a further copy print made by someone else in the 1890s. A photographer named Rice obtained at least one of Alexander Gardner's negatives and reprinted photographs of Lincoln from 1869 to the 1890s. Rice claimed that he had taken the photograph.

Photographers often copied earlier photos. There are Cabinet Cards and other Victorian period photos that show an early beardless Lincoln or a later bearded Lincoln. They have value, as attested by current auction prices, but realistically, the earlier prints, printed while Lincoln was living, are worth much more than the later prints.

PHOTO, ca. 1860. A large albumen photograph of Lincoln, Willie, and Tad (behind the corner post) standing in front of their home. It was taken by J. A. Whippel of Boston. The boys below Lincoln are unidentified but may be Isaac Diller and another neighbor. 12 x 14 inches. *From the Frank & Virginia Williams Collection of Lincolniana.* Value $4,000-$6,000.

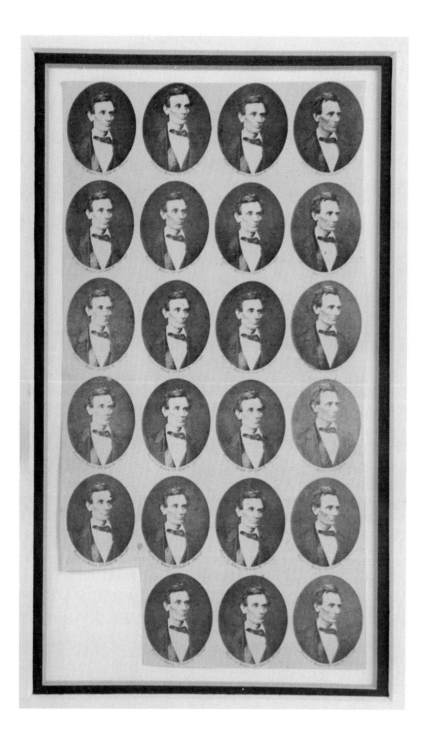

GROUP OF PHOTOS, 1860. Twenty-three small photographs created as political photos, probably to be attached to ribbons. Each is .75 inches x 1 inch and marked "Photo by Hesler, 113 Lake St., Chicago". There are two poses and the photos were not taken with a multi-lens or Wing style camera. They were taken by Alexander Hesler on June 3, 1860. The session was arranged by Chicago Republicans in anticipation of the huge demand for photographs of Lincoln expected after he was nominated at the Republican National Convention in May, 1860. These were given to Lincoln who gave them to Robert Lincoln who gave them to F.H. Meserve in 1917 and from whose collection they came, along with a letter from Meserve. Value $8,500-$9,500 as a group.

Robert T. Lincoln sent these to me July 20. 1917 and wrote "Mr. Nicolay wrote these were probably made in June or July 1860."
F.H. Meserve

PHOTO, 1860. A wonderful platinum print photo, taken by Alexander
Hesler on June 3, 1860. George B. Ayres bought Hesler's studio and
reprinted the photo in the 1880s and 1890s. See the text for the details.
Size is 9.125 x 7 inches. Also shown is Ayres' autograph on the reverse.
Value (Platinum). $900-$1,250, (Albumen print) $750-$1,000, (Silver
print) $300-$400.

PHOTO, 1860. A large albumen photograph of Lincoln standing in front of his home taken in the summer of 1860 by John Adams Whippel of Boston. The mat of the photo is mis-marked, "Abraham Lincoln At Home— Farewell address to his old neighbors, Springfield, February 12, 1861". As the close-up shows, Lincoln is beardless and the trees are with leaves. The boy whose body is blurred beneath Lincoln is Isaac Diller, a playmate of the Lincoln boys. He ran over to get in the picture and then, at the moment the photo was taken, he moved. Only his socks and shoes are in focus. The photo was published by Charles DeSilver, Philadelphia, in 1865. About 8 x 13 inches. *From the Joseph Edward Garrera collection.* Value $4,000-$6,000.

CDV, 1861. One of a series of photos taken by Gardner at the Brady studio on February 4, 1861. Value $750-$1,200.

ABRAHAM LINCOLN

CDV, 1861. Two variations of a seated view of Lincoln taken at Brady's studio on February 24, 1861, on Anthony/Brady mounts. Note the slight variations in image color and detail. Value $750-$1,200.

CDV, 1861. Two variations of a seated view of Lincoln taken at Brady's studio on February 24, 1861, on Anthony/Brady mounts. If you look carefully at the pedestal behind Lincoln and the legs of the table at the right side of the photo, you will see a slight divergence of angle which occurred when the photo was taken through a two or four lens camera. Value $750-$1,200 each.

CDV, 1861. Two variations of a seated view of Lincoln taken at Brady's studio on February 24, 1861, on Anthony/Brady mounts. Note the slight variations in image color. Value $750-$1,200 each.

CDV, 1861. Two variations of a seated view of Lincoln taken at Brady's studio on February 24, 1861, on Anthony/Brady mounts. Note the variations in image color and detail. Value $750-$1,200 each.

CDV, 1861. Two variations of a view of Lincoln taken by C.D. Fredricks or James McClees or more likely W.L. Germon in the spring of 1861. The left photo is on a McClees' mount and the right photo is on a Fredrick's mount. The Fredrick photo has been retouched. Note the added pleats in Lincoln's shirt. Are these two different photos, with Lincoln looking down in the left photo and him looking up in the right? It may be the effect of the retoucher. Value $450-$550 each.

CDV, ca. 1861. Vice President Hanibal Hamlin. Photo by the Brady studio. *From the Frank & Virginia Williams Collection of Lincolniana.* Value $125-$175.

Lincoln Look-a-Likes

There are "discoveries" of new, formerly unknown Lincoln photographs that crop up from time to time. Unfortunately, most of these photographs only look like Lincoln, rather than are Lincoln. There are actually collectors of Lincoln look-a-like photographs. One type is the Lincoln impersonator or recreator. As with current day presidents, there were actors who made a living looking and sounding like Lincoln. Another is the inadvertent look-a-like or someone who just looked like Lincoln, while another is a photograph that may not look much like Lincoln, but someone claims is actually a young beardless Lincoln. Lincoln collectors live in perpetual hope of finding a formerly unknown Lincoln photograph.

CDV, ca. 1861. Secretary of the Interior Caleb Smith on a Brady/Anthony mount. Smith served less than two years and then resigned. He died in January 1864. *From the Frank & Virginia Williams Collection of Lincolniana*. Value $100-$125.

Composites

There are several kinds of composite photographs of Lincoln that are collectible. One is the group of photos, such as the President and Cabinet, The Peace Commissioners, or Lincoln's death bed scene that are pasted up and re-photographed as a group shot. Another is a photograph (or print) where Lincoln's head is grafted onto someone else's body. It was an easy way to show or sell new images of Lincoln by putting his head in an already existing picture.

Provenance—the documentation of the history of the item—is helpful...sometimes. Many photos come with a story about how a relative received the photo from Lincoln himself, or someone on his staff. Some believe that the name "Abraham Lincoln" written below or on the back to identify the photo, was written by Lincoln himself. A tip: believe nothing you hear and half of what you see. Many photos of Lincoln were saved and through time, the simple act of saving the photo turns into an exaggerated story of personal contact with the man himself.

CDV, ca. 1861. Secretary of the Treasury Salmon P. Chase by Charles Frederick's studio. Chase was very effective in running the country's finances. He helped to establish a stable Federal currency. His political aspirations included his replacing Lincoln as President, but Lincoln's brilliant handling of the man only made Lincoln's position stronger. *From the Frank & Virginia Williams Collection of Lincolniana*. Value $300-$400.

Collectors should have some of the reference books, listed in the back of this book, in their library. For the newer Lincoln photograph collector, be warned that there are some modern reproductions that appear on the market. Frederick Hill Meserve located Brady's original negatives and reprinted Lincoln photos (usually CDV size) in the 1930s. Time-Life reprinted some of these in the 1970s and they look great. One civil war dealer sold reprints of many Lincoln photos in the 1970s. If you have not handled many civil war period photos and don't know when "something is not right," you may be fooled. As always, if you are new to this field, deal with reputable dealers that will guarantee the authenticity of your purchase for life. Years ago, when the typical Lincoln photo cost $35.00, there was very little incentive to forge an "original". Now that the price is 10 to 50 times higher, a good photographer with a bad attitude and a darkroom has an incentive to produce new "originals".

CDV, ca. 1861. A young looking Secretary of State, William Seward, took a group of foreign ministers to the Watkins Glen area of New York for an outing probably in the autumn of 1861. Seward is on the right side of the photo. *Also illustrated, but never before identified, is Mathew Brady in the white suit in the center of the photo.* The photo bears the registration of W.J. Baker in 1863. *From the Frank & Virginia Williams Collection of Lincolniana.* Value $600-$750.

CDV, ca. 1861. A photograph of Mrs. Stephen Douglas taken by Charles Fredericks. She is dressed in mourning clothes as Stephen Douglas died on June 3, 1861. *From the Frank & Virginia Williams Collection of Lincolniana.* Value $50-$65.

CDV, 1862. One of a series of photos taken by the Brady studio. Value $750-$1,200.

PHOTO, October 3, 1862. A photo taken by Gardner that was backmarked and sold by Brady's Gallery. This is a smaller and different photo than the one published in *Gardner's Photographic Sketchbook Of The War*. Lincoln stands in front of a tent flanked by his officers. The seated man is Ward Hill Lamon, Lincoln's personal bodyguard. 3.125 x 4.5 inches on a mount about 4.5 x 6 inches. Value $3,500-$4,500.

Incidents of the War.

PRESIDENT LINCOLN ON BATTLE-FIELD OF ANTIETAM.

October, 1862.

A. GARDNER, Photographer.

PHOTO, October 3, 1862. A photo taken by Gardner and published in 1865 and 1866, in two volumes called, *Gardner's Photographic Sketchbook Of The War*. The earlier printing says, "Incidents of the War". Gardner's studio printed each photograph separately. Then the photographs were tipped into the book. Lincoln stands in front of a tent flanked by his officers—(from left to right) Col. Sacket, Capt. Monteith, Lt. Col. Sweitzer, Gen'l. Morell, Col. Webb, Gen'l. McClellan, Scout Adams, Dr. Letterman, unknown, Lincoln, Col. Hunt, Gen'l. Porter, Joseph Kennedy, Col. Locke, Gen'l. Humphreys, Capt. George A. Custer. The photo is 7.875 inches x 8.875 inches on a mount about 10 inches x 12 inches. Value $8,500-$10,500.

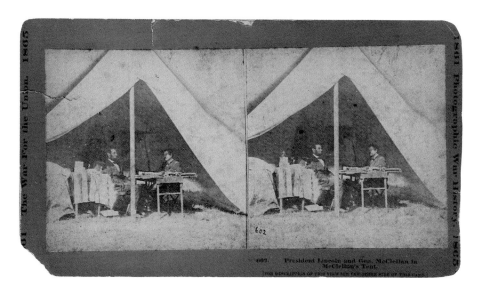

STEREO VIEW, 1862. This stereo photograph was taken by Gardner on October 4, 1862. It shows Lincoln meeting with McClellan near Antietam, Maryland. In the late 1870s, Taylor & Huntington reprinted a series of the original negatives, calling it *The War for the Union Photographic History, 1861-1865.* It is on an oversized mount with rounded corners, typical of the 1870-1880 stereo views. *From the Frank & Virginia Williams Collection of Lincolniana.* Value $400-$500.

CDV, 1862. Seward by Brady Studios. Value $150-$200.

CDV, ca. 1862. Secretary of War, Edwin M. Stanton as taken by Brady's studio. *From the Frank & Virginia Williams Collection of Lincolniana.* Value $175-$225.

CDV, ca. 1862. Secretary of the Treasury, Salmon P. Chase by Brady's studio. Chase was very effective in running the country's finances. He helped to establish a stable Federal currency. His political aspirations included his replacing Lincoln as President. *From the Frank & Virginia Williams Collection of Lincolniana*. Value $300-$350.

CDV, ca. 1862. Attorney General, Edward Bates as taken by Brady's studio on an Anthony mount. Bates served until the end of 1864 and was replaced by James Speed. *From the Frank & Virginia Williams Collection of Lincolniana*. Value $300-$350.

CDV, ca. 1862. President Lincoln's secretary, John Nicolay. This CDV is autographed by Nicolay. Nicolay began working for Lincoln when he was President-elect and acted as secretary, confidant, go-between, and protector and documentor of the President's public life. *From the Frank & Virginia Williams Collection of Lincolniana*. Value $300-$350 with autograph.

CDV, 1862. Two variations of a contemplative view of Lincoln taken at Brady's studio in 1862 on Anthony/Brady mounts. Value $750-$1,200.

CDV, 1862. A seated profile view of Lincoln taken at Brady's studio in 1862 on a Brady mount. Value $750-$1,200.

CDV, 1862. A typical photographer and his wet plate camera, the type with which Lincoln would be familiar. Photos of the men who took the photographs are very rare. Value $500-$700.

CDV, 1862. Lady Liberty photographs. During the war, these patriotic Ladies photographs were often sold to raise money for hospital supplies to care for wounded soldiers. Value $70-$90.

CDV, ca. 1862. A photo of a print with Lincoln's head on John C. Fremont's body. The head is a reversed Cooper Union Brady image. The lamp on the table has replaced a globe that appeared in the Fremont image originally engraved by J.C. Buttre. Lincoln's head can be found on Martin Van Buren's, Andrew Jackson's, Francis Blair's, Henry Clay's and John C. Calhoun's bodies. Value $65-$85.

CDV, 1863. A standing view of Lincoln taken by Thomas LeMere at Brady's studio on April 17, 1863, on an Anthony/Brady mount. Value $750-$1,200.

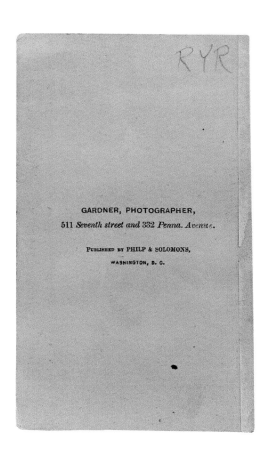

CDV, 1863. An Alexander Gardner CDV mount found on the back of a Lincoln photo.

CDV, 1863. A seated view of Lincoln taken at Gardner's studio on August 9, 1863. Value $750-$1,200.

CDV, 1863. A seated view of Lincoln taken at Gardner's studio on August 9, 1863, on an Gardner mount. Value $750-$1,200.

CDV, 1863. An autographed photo taken on August 9, 1863, by Alexander Gardner. This was part of an autograph album and sold by Christies Auction House on May 20, 1994. *Courtesy of Christies.* Value $20,000-$25,000.

CDV, 1863. A photograph published by John Sowle, from a photograph by J.P. Soule, issued in celebration of the emancipation proclamation. Value $40-$60.

CDV, ca. 1864. Secretary of War Simon Cameron. Cameron was an ineffective Secretary of War. Lincoln was finally able to replace him, after allegations surfaced that Cameron had been taking graft. He was replaced by Edwin Stanton, but remained a staunch supporter of Lincoln and later, the widowed Mary Lincoln. *From the Frank & Virginia Williams Collection of Lincolniana.* Value $300-$350.

CDV, ca. 1864. Secretary of War Edwin M. Stanton. Stanton replaced Simon Cameron in January 1862 after allegations that Cameron had been taking graft. *From the Frank & Virginia Williams Collection of Lincolniana*. Value $150-$175.

CDV, 1864. Lincoln on a 36 star flag. This may be a political piece as the photo was taken on January 8, 1864. Value $450-$700.

CDV, 1864. A photo taken January 8, 1864, by the Brady studio of Lincoln standing with his left arm behind his back. It can be found with a New York or Washington front mark. Value $750-$1,200.

CDV, 1864. A seated view of Lincoln taken at Brady's studio on January 8, 1864, on an Anthony/Brady mount. Lincoln looks right into the camera and looks like the man in charge of the country. Value $750-$1,200.

CDV, 1864. Two variations of seated three-quarter views of Lincoln taken at Brady's studio on January 8, 1864, on Brady mounts. Value $750-$1,200.

STEREO VIEW, 1864. A rare stereo photograph taken by Brady's studio on January 8, 1864. It is on an E. & H.T. Anthony card. Through a stereo viewer, you see a three-dimensional Abraham Lincoln. *From the Frank & Virginia Williams Collection of Lincolniana.* Value $1,750-$2,500.

PHOTO WITH AUTOGRAPH, 1864. A February 9, 1864, photo by the Brady studio that has been autographed by Mary Lincoln. This is generally known as the $5 view since it was used to create the Lincoln image on the five dollar bill. The mount has been trimmed to 12 x 9 inches and the photo is 6.125 inches wide by 8 inches tall. Value $9,500-$11,000 with autograph.

CDV, 1864. Brady's $5 view of Lincoln taken by Anthony Berger at Brady's studio on February 9, 1864, on a Brady mount. Value $750-$1,200.

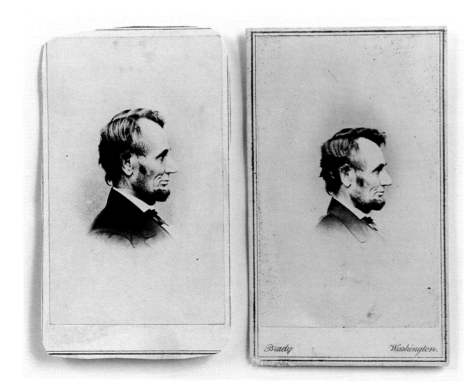

CDV, 1864. Two variations of a profile view of Lincoln taken at Brady's studio on February 9, 1864, on a no-name mount and a Brady mount. This is the view that appears on the Lincoln penny. Note the variations in image color. Value $750-$1,200.

CDV, 1864. Two views of Lincoln taken by Anthony Berger at Brady's studio on February 9, 1864. The left photo is a gem size (about 1 inch high) photo glued to an embossed CDV card. The right photo is a reversed gem tintype set into an embossed CDV card. Value (L-R) $85-$110, $300-$375.

CDV, 1864. An autographed photo taken on February 9, 1864, by Anthony Berger of the Brady studio. This example was sold by Christies at their May 20, 1994, auction. *Courtesy of Christies.* Value $20,000-$25,000.

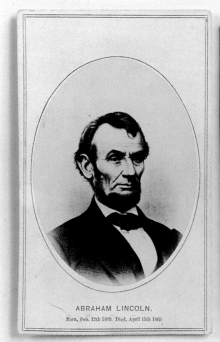

CDV, 1864. A common photo of an engraved view of Lincoln based upon the photo taken at Brady's studio on February 9, 1864. Clues that it is an engraving are the bow tie and clothing textures when looked at under magnification. Value $30-$50.

CDV, 1864. Two popular photos of engraved views of Lincoln based upon the photo taken by Brady's studio on February 9, 1864. Again, clues that they are engravings are the bow tie and clothing textures. These are especially nice examples and sell for a slight premium over more common examples. Value $50-$75.

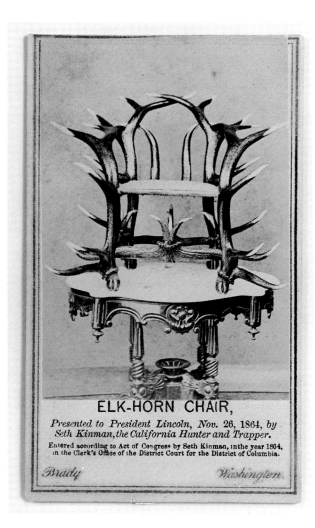

ELK-HORN CHAIR,

Presented to President Lincoln, Nov. 26, 1864, by Seth Kinman, the California Hunter and Trapper.

Entered according to Act of Congress by Seth Kinman, in the year 1864, in the Clerk's Office of the District Court for the District of Columbia.

Brady   *Washington.*

CDV, 1864. There are no back markings. The original was taken by Wendroth & Taylor in 1864. Value $350-$450.

SETH KINMAN,

California Hunter and Trapper, who presented President Lincoln with the Elk-Horn Chair.

Entered according to Act of Congress by Seth Kinman, in the year 1864, in the Clerk's Office of the District Court for the District of Columbia.

CDV, ca. 1864. Seth Kinman, a California hunter and trapper, gave Lincoln an elk-horn chair. The gift was reported in the newspapers and the public wanted to see what Kinman and the chair looked like. Both went to Brady's studio in Washington and had their photo made. Value $350-$450 for the pair.

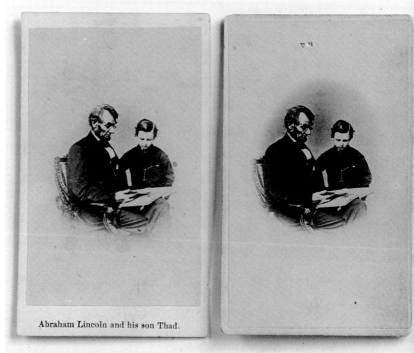

CDV, 1864. Lincoln and Tad second generation or later (copy) photographs printed when Lincoln was President. Identifiable as second generation or later photographs, as there are no back markings on these Brady photos and the features are contrasted. These are particularly good examples of this photo, which is more commonly found as a photo of an engraving. In the engraving, Lincoln's sleeve and pants show engraving marks. Value $100-$150.

CDV, 1864. A composite of Lincoln and his "Peace Commissioners" on one CDV. Value $60-$90.

CDV, ca. 1864. Photograph of a print based upon the Brady photo of Lincoln and Tad. *From the Robert DeLorenzo collection.* Value $30-$40.

CDV, ca. 1864. Andrew Johnson. The back of the CDV has a tax stamp on it. *From the Frank & Virginia Williams Collection of Lincolniana.* Value $100-$125.

CDV, ca. 1865. President Lincoln's secretary, John Hay. John Nicolay recruited Hay in 1861 when the volume of work became too great. This CDV was probably taken shortly after the death of Lincoln. Together Nicolay and Hay wrote a book, *Abraham Lincoln: A History*, published in 1890. *From the Frank & Virginia Williams Collection of Lincolniana.* Value $300-$350.

CDV, 1864. A composite of Lincoln and senators on a CDV in a period gutta percha frame. Value $50-$70 without frame.

PHOTO, 1865. This crisp photo was taken by Alexander Gardner on February 5, 1865. It appears on a cabinet card by R. Goebels. The cabinet card is an 1880 or later format (8.75 x 6.5 inches). Value $500-$650.

CDV, 1865. The crew cut Lincoln photo is especially difficult to find. The photo was taken by Lewis E. Walker and published by E. & H.T. Anthony. Value $1,200-$2,000.

STEREO VIEW, 1865. This is one of two "crew cut" views of Lincoln, on an E. & H.T. Anthony card. Through a stereo viewer, you see a three-dimensional Abraham Lincoln. You can almost reach out and touch him. A very rare view. Value $1,500-$2,500.

PHOTO, 1865. One of the last photographs of Lincoln. It was taken on the balcony of the White House on March 6, 1865. The photographer, H.F. Warren, could not gain entrance to the president's home to photograph Lincoln. He went outside and photographed Tad Lincoln riding his favorite pony. Returning the next day, he showed the finished photos to Mrs. Lincoln and gave them to her as a gift. She asked what she could do in return and Warren asked her to arrange for him to photograph the president. You can see that Lincoln is not pleased with the imposition. Warren took three photos and published them for sale the next day. When Lincoln died in April, Warren continued to sell the photos but changed the caption from "The Latest Photograph of President Lincoln" to "The Last Photograph of President Lincoln". The photos are found in sizes from a CDV to an 11 x 14 inch photo. This photo is 6 x 8 inches on a mount of 10 x 13.5 inches. Value (of this size and marking) $3,000-$4,500.

CDV, ca. 1865. Photograph of a print showing all of the important people visiting Lincoln as he lay dying. *From the Robert DeLorenzo collection.* Value $40-$60.

STEREO VIEW, 1865. Lincoln's funeral hearse on its procession through Philadelphia. Each city had a different funeral hearse which helps to identify the city. Stereo cards give a three-dimensional appearance when viewed through a stereo viewer. Value $250-$325.

CDV, 1865. A composite of several Brady photos of Lincoln on one "In Memory" CDV. Value $100-$150.

STEREO VIEW, 1865. A nice close-up view of Lincoln's coffin on display in New York City. Through a stereo viewer, you can see everything in great detail, including the decorations on the catafalque. Value $250-$325.

STEREO VIEW, 1865. The Funeral of President Lincoln in New York City, on an E. & H.T. Anthony card. Value $250-$325.

STEREO VIEW, 1865. The Funeral of President Lincoln in Springfield on an E. & H.T. Anthony card. Value $250-$325.

CDV, 1865. The catafalque which carried Lincoln's body in Washington, D.C. *From the Frank & Virginia Williams Collection of Lincolniana.* Value $250-$300.

CDV, ca. 1865. Lincoln's horse dressed in mourning in front of Lincoln's home. Value $100-$135.

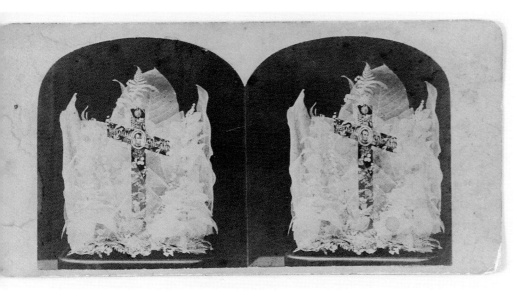

STEREO VIEW, 1868. Lincoln—desiccated leaves, on an E. & H.T. Anthony card. A popular but unexciting still life with Lincoln's picture surrounded by desiccated leaves. Value $35-$45.

TINTYPE, ca. 1862. This sixth plate (about 2 inches x 2.5 inches) photograph in a patriotic, Civil War mat bears a resemblance to Lincoln. Value $75-$90.

CDV, ca. 1865. An unknown Lincoln look-a-like. There were Lincoln impersonators as well as people who just looked like Lincoln. It helps to know what the look-a-likes looked like to identify or exclude a previously "unknown" Lincoln photograph that may be found. Value $100-$150.

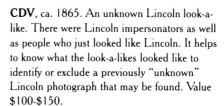

PHOTO, 1891. Moses P. Rice obtained Alexander Gardner's November 8, 1863, photo negative of Lincoln. He and his gallery began reprinting it in 1869 and continued to reprint it and create objects such as prints and tiles into the turn of the century. Rice claimed to have taken the original photo, which is untrue. Rice's reprints are very popular and are actively sought. The photo can be found in many sizes and even printed on a textured rice paper. 4 x 5.25 inches. *From the Joseph Edward Garrera collection.* Value $400-$650.

CDV, ca. 1865. A Lincoln look-a-like who also looks like Ulysses S. Grant. Perhaps his name was Ulysses Lincoln or possibly Abraham Grant. This sort of photograph turns up from time to time and the owner often has a story about how it was given to the great-grandfather by Lincoln himself or some such provenance. A wise man once said, "Believe nothing you hear and half of what you see". Value $20-$35.

4. POLITICAL ITEMS FOR LINCOLN'S CAMPAIGN

POLITICAL RIBBON, ca. 1858. Small photograph taken by Alexander Hesler (1 x 1.25 inches) attached to a red silk ribbon. A political ribbon for Lincoln's 1858 run for the Senate against Stephen Douglas or perhaps an early Presidential campaign item. Value $3,000-$3,500.

CAMPAIGN BUTTON, 1860. Tintype campaign buttons, 24 mm in diameter. Lincoln's photo is on the front and Hanibal Hamlin is on the reverse. The words "Abraham Lincoln—1860" are stamped on the brass shell. The original photo is the Cooper Union Photo. The second button is the Stephen Douglas version of a tintype campaign button with his Vice-Presidential running mate, Herschel Johnson, on the reverse. Value (Lincoln) $500-$650, (Douglas) $350-$450.

CAMPAIGN BUTTON, 1860. A political "button", 24 mm in diameter. Lincoln's photo (tintype) is on the front and Hanibal Hamlin is on the reverse. The words "Union of the States—1860" are stamped on the brass shell. The original photo was probably taken by Roderick Cole of Peoria, Illinois, in 1858. Value $500-$700.

CAMPAIGN BUTTON, 1860. Tintype campaign buttons, 24 mm in diameter. Lincoln's photo is on the front and Hanibal Hamlin is on the reverse. The original photo on the left is the 1858 Cole image, while the one on the right is a slimmed down version of the Cooper Union Photo by Brady. Value $500-$650 each.

CAMPAIGN PIN, 1860. Tintype campaign button, 25 mm in diameter. Stephen Douglas with his Vice-Presidential running mate, Herschel Johnson, on the reverse. Value $350-$450.

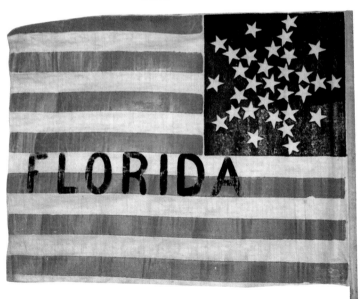

CAMPAIGN BUTTON, 1860. Tintype campaign button, 19 mm in diameter. Stephen Douglas' photo is on the front and Herschel Johnson is on the reverse. Value $350-$450.

FLAG, ca. 1860. This Florida flag identified the delegates from Florida at the Republican convention at the WigWam in 1860. It was found with a group, from several states, that had been used at the convention and saved. 12 x 16 inches. *From the Howard Hazelcorn Collection.* Value $400-$650.

ENVELOPE, 1860. A political envelope offering Abraham Lincoln, the rail splitter, for President and Hannibal Hamlin for Vice-President. Collectors pay a premium for envelopes that were postally used versus those not used. Value $150-$175.

ENVELOPE, 1860. A political envelope— Lincoln and Hamlin. Value $100-$125.

ENVELOPE, 1860. A political envelope offering Abraham Lincoln for President and Hannibal Hamlin for Vice-President. Value $125-$175.

ENVELOPE, 1860. A political envelope showing Abraham Lincoln. Value $80-$100.

ENVELOPE, 1860. A political envelope showing Abe Lincoln. Value $80-$100.

ENVELOPE, 1860. A political envelope showing Stephen Douglas. Value $45-$60.

48

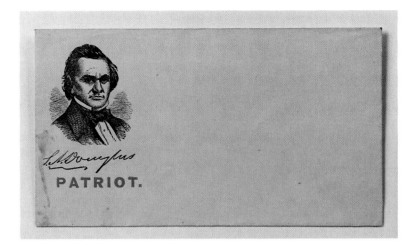

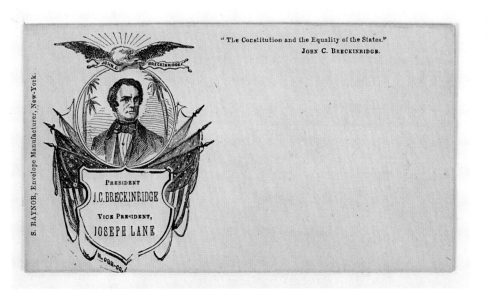

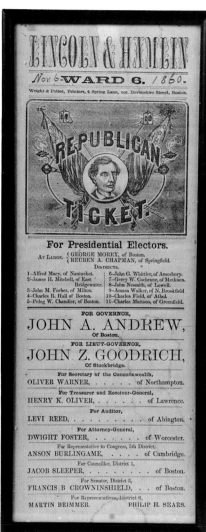

ENVELOPE, ca. 1860. A political envelope showing Douglas. Some of these political envelopes are tremendously undervalued at present. *From the Frank & Virginia Williams Collection of Lincolniana.* Value $100-$135.

ENVELOPE, 1860. A political envelope showing J. C. Fremont. Value $45-$60.

ENVELOPE, 1860. A political envelope showing J. C. Breckinridge. Value $55-$70.

BALLOT, 1860. A Lincoln-Hamlin Republican ticket listing the candidates. 4.5 x 12 inches *From the Frank & Virginia Williams Collection of Lincolniana.* Value $550-$700.

TOKEN, 1860. A gilded brass token "Millions for Freedom, Not One Cent For Slavery 1860" on the front and "Success for Republican Principles" on the reverse. This is sometimes called "Bramhall's Token", struck in Waterbury, Connecticut, and was one of the early campaign tokens. 25 mm. Value $45-$60.

TOKEN, ca. 1860. "Abraham Lincoln" and his birth date are on front, "Wide Awakes", "Abra-ham Lin-coln", and "Honest Abe of the West" are on back. White metal, 18 mm. Value $65-$90.

MEDALET, 1860. A 26 mm medalet promoting The Rail Splitter of the West, brass, dies by Ellis, made in Waterbury, Connecticut. It can be found in copper, brass, nickel, white metal, gold plated white metal, and silver plated brass. Value $100-$140.

TOKEN, 1860. A token made for the Hartford, Connecticut, Wide Awake organization. Both sides show marchers in their uniforms. The Hartford Wide Awake Club was one of Lincoln's earliest supporters. 28 mm. Value $100-$125.

MEDALET, 1860. A 38 mm in diameter token for Hon. Abraham Lincoln—The Rail Splitter of The West, for President. Note the "Becker" stamp on the reverse side. This copy was made in 1960 and is called the Becker copy. It was made by Ralph Becker, a political items collector, who eventually donated his collection to the Smithsonian Institution. Value $20-$30.

MEDALET, 1860. This very well worn campaign medalet says, "For President Abraham Lincoln of Illinois" on the front. The reverse shows an eagle and thirteen stars. This was found on the battlefield at Gettysburg, possibly used as a good luck charm by a soldier. 38 mm in white metal. It can be found in other metals. The dies were cut by Benjamin F. True of Cincinnati. The metal was restruck in 1928 and as late as 1950. Value $30-$45 (as is).

MEDALET, 1860. A brass medalet for Stephen Douglas, "The Champion of Popular Sovereignty 1860". Dies by R. Lovett, 28 mm, can be found in different metals. Value $85-$145.

CAMPAIGN BUTTON, 1860. Tintype campaign button 28 mm in diameter. John Bell's photo is on the front and Edward Everitt is on the reverse. The images are dark which is often the case with these early tintype photos. Value $350-$450.

CAMPAIGN BUTTON, 1860. Tintype campaign button 20 mm in diameter. John C. Breckinridge's photo is on the front and Joseph Lane is on the reverse. *From the Frank & Virginia Williams Collection of Lincolniana.* Value $375-$475.

MEDALET, 1860. A white metal medalet for Stephen Douglas, "Democratic Candidate 1860". 28 mm, can be found in different metals. Value $85-$145.

CAMPAIGN BUTTON, 1860. Tintype campaign button in the "doughnut" style, 31 mm in diameter. The doughnut style has rounded edges rather than flat edges and available in at least 5 or 6 sizes. This size is the most readily found. Lincoln's photo is on the front and Hanibal Hamlin is on the reverse. The words "Abraham Lincoln" are stamped on the brass shell. The original photo is the Cooper Union Photo. Value (with both images in nice shape) $550-$750.

FLAG, 1860. A thirty-three star flag announcing the candidates for president. 11.5 x 16.5 inches. *From the Howard Hazelcorn Collection.* Value $4,500-$6,000.

FLAG, 1860. A great Wide Awake banner used in the Wide Awake parades. *From the Howard Hazelcorn Collection.* 17 x 38 inches. Value $18,000-$22,000.

POSTER, 1860. "The Republican Banner For 1860" by Currier & Ives announcing the Republican candidates for president. 10 x 14 inches. Value $1,500-$2,500.

BROADSIDE, 1860. A 13 x 18 inch broadside announcing the Republican candidates for president. Value $1,750-$2,500.

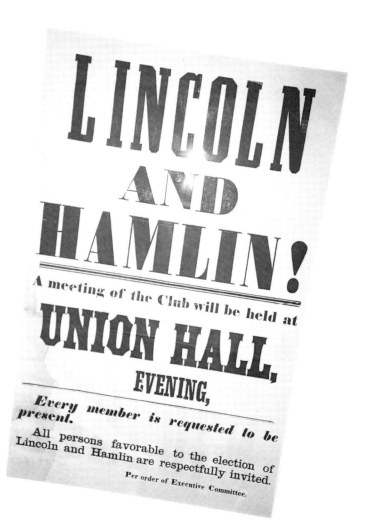

POSTER, 1860. "Promie Des Hochnoechters" meaning Prize of the Wide Awakes. A German Wide Awake poster showing the Republican candidates for president. These were distributed in German speaking neighborhoods. 19 x 24 inches. Value $1,000-$1,500.

RIBBON, 1860. A rare Wide Awake Club ribbon illustrating Lincoln. 2.5 x 4.5 inches. *Courtesy of Rex Stark.* Value $2,300-$2,500.

FLAG, 1860. A cotton muslin flag showing Lincoln surrounded by thirteen stars. 11 x 15 inches. Value $5,500-$7,500.

RIBBON, 1860. A Shawnee Wide Awake Club ribbon in an off-white color. 1.5 x 4.5 inches. *Courtesy of Rex Stark.* Value $850-$950.

RIBBON, 1860. A silk ribbon showing Lincoln and Hamlin, "The People's Choice". Both candidates shown together are called "jugate". 2.25 x 7 inches. Value $2,200-$3,500.

RIBBON, 1864. A silk ribbon showing Lincoln and Johnson. Both candidates shown together are called "jugate". One of only two designs of 1864 jugate ribbons. 2.5 x 4 inches. Value $3,000-$4,000.

BANNER, ca. 1864. An unusual banner with a great image of Lincoln. At first glance it is obviously a political piece, but then the beard and the date seem slightly at odds. Most likely it is a re-election banner. Many re-election pieces used the beardless photo of Lincoln or the date of his election. 22 x 35 inches. *From the Frank & Virginia Williams Collection of Lincolniana.*

POSTER, 1864. A Currier & Ives poster showing the candidates for president. An almost identical poster was available for McClellan and Pendleton. *From the Howard Hazelcorn Collection.* 12 x 17 inches. Value $1,500-$2,500.

RIBBON, 1864. A great political ribbon for Abraham Lincoln for President and Andrew Johnson for Vice-President. Value $2,000 $2,200.

RIBBON, 1864. An unlisted 3 x 6 inch delegate's ribbon for an 1864 political convention in Cleveland. Value $300-$450.

FLAG, 1864. A large cotton flag showing Lincoln and Johnson used at rallies, parades, or campaign headquarters. This is the only known 1864 flag showing both candidates. 3.5 x 5.5 feet. Value $30,000-$35,000.

BROADSIDE, ca. 1864. This broadside lists Maj. Gen. Geo. B. McClellan as the candidate for President. It is uncommon to find McClellan items in color. 27 x 35 inches. *From the Howard Hazelcorn Collection.* Value $3,750-$4,250.

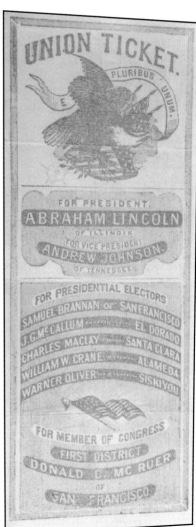

BALLOT, ca. 1864. This Union Ticket lists the President, Vice-President, and other candidates. The reverse side shows the battle between the Monitor and the Merrimac. 3 x 7.5 inches. *From the Howard Hazelcorn Collection.* Value $225-$275.

BALLOT, ca. 1860. This Democratic Ticket lists the candidates for President, Vice-President, and others. It is uncommon to find Douglas' portrait on the front of the ballot. 3 x 6 inches. *From the Howard Hazelcorn Collection.* Value $250-$400.

CAMPAIGN PIN, 1864. A political pin, 12 mm in diameter. Lincoln's photo is a tintype. The original photo was taken by the Brady studio in 1864. Value $550-$650.

CAMPAIGN BUTTON, 1864. A political "button", 18 mm in diameter. Lincoln's photo (tintype) is on the front and Andrew Johnson is on the reverse. In this case, Lincoln's image is badly damaged with flaking of the emulsion due to rusting of the tin plate. Value (in damaged cond.) $200-$250.

CAMPAIGN BUTTON, 1864. A political button, 25 mm in diameter. Lincoln's photo is a tintype and his name appears above his photo, same with Johnson on the reverse. A small loop is at the top. *From the Howard Hazelcorn Collection.* Value $550-$650.

CAMPAIGN BUTTON, 1864. A political "button", 16 mm in diameter. Lincoln's photo is a tintype. Value $550-$700.

CAMPAIGN BUTTON, 1864. A political button, 25 mm in diameter. George McClellan's photo is a tintype and his name appears above his photo, Pendelton's photo is on the reverse. A small loop is at the top. *From the Howard Hazelcorn Collection.* Value $550-$650.

CAMPAIGN BUTTON, 1864. A "Gault" style political button, 25 mm in diameter. Gault was the designer of this type of brass shell. John C. Fremont's photo is a tintype, Vice presidential candidate John Cochrane's photo is on the reverse. *From the Howard Hazelcorn Collection.* Value $950-$1050.

CAMPAIGN BUTTON, 1864. A "Gault" style political button, 25 mm in diameter. Gault was the designer of this type of brass shell. Lincoln's photo is a tintype, Vice presidential candidate Andrew Johnson's photo is on the reverse. *From the Howard Hazelcorn Collection.* Value $1250-$1750.

CAMPAIGN BADGE, 1864. Tintype campaign "badge" with cloth flag and tin eagle 2.5 inches in length. These have become very difficult to find. *From the Frank & Virginia Williams Collection of Lincolniana.* Value $1,000-$1,400.

CAMPAIGN STICKPIN, 1864. A political "button" or possibly an 1865 mourning piece, 2.75 inches in length. Lincoln's photo is an albumen photograph. Value $500-$650.

CAMPAIGN BUTTONS, 1864. A group of donut style political buttons, 23 mm in diameter. The presidential candidate's photo is on the front and the vice presidential candidate's photo is on the reverse. *From the Howard Hazelcorn Collection.* Value $550-$800 each.

RIBBON, 1864. A political ribbon marked "War of 1861" with an 1864 Lincoln albumen photo in a .75 inches high gold broach. 1.75 x 4.5 inches. Value $1,250-$1,600.

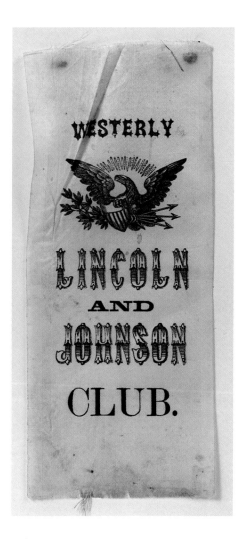

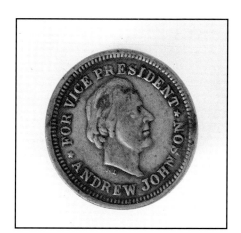

RIBBON, ca. 1864. A difficult to find Rhode Island political ribbon for the second presidential campaign of Lincoln. 3 x 7 inches. *From the Frank & Virginia Williams Collection of Lincolniana.* Value $2,500-$3,000.

TOKEN, 1864. A Lincoln political token with a portrait of Lincoln on one side and Johnson on the other. 22 mm. Value $50-$65.

RIBBON, ca. 1864. A political ribbon for the second presidential campaign of Lincoln. 2 x 6.5 inches. *From the Frank & Virginia Williams Collection of Lincolniana.* Value $2,250-$2,750.

TOKEN, 1864. An 1864 campaign piece with the words, "Lincoln and Liberty" on the front and the reverse shows an axe splitting wood with the words "Good for another Heat". It plays on the riddle "How does wood heat you twice?" Answer, "First when you split it and again when you burn it." 18 mm. Always found with the hole drilled in it. Value $80-$115.

MEDALET, 1864. A 32 mm medalet promoting Lincoln & Johnson Union Candidates, white metal, made by W.H. Key, Philadelphia. Value $135-$175.

MEDALET, 1864. A 28 mm medalet promoting Abraham Lincoln Prest. of The U.S., white metal, made by W.H. Key, Philadelphia. Value $135-$175.

MEDALET, 1864. A 34 mm medalet promoting Honest Old Abe, white metal. Value $135-$175.

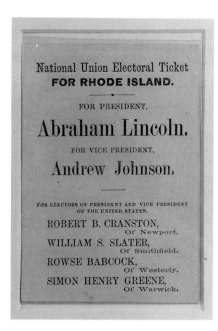

BALLOT, 1864. A paper ballot from Rhode Island. *From the Robert DeLorenzo collection.* Value $75-$110.

BOOKLET, 1864. An unusual campaign songster booklet. It is an 1864 songbook but pictures a beardless Lincoln on the cover. Some of the songs inside are for Lincoln and Johnson. It may have been made to appeal to those who supported Lincoln in his first run for president. Value $125-$225.

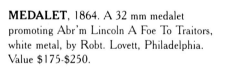

MEDALET, 1864. A 32 mm medalet promoting Abr'm Lincoln A Foe To Traitors, white metal, by Robt. Lovett, Philadelphia. Value $175-$250.

MEDALET, 1864. A 34 mm inch medalet promoting Abm Lincoln, Rep. Candidate for President, white metal, by Robt. Lovett, Philadelphia. Value $120-$145.

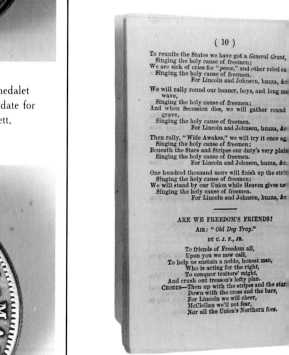

MEDALET, 1864. A brass medalet written in German. Possibly a Whist counter. 26 mm. Value $35-$45.

LINCOLN CAMPAIGN BADGE, 1860

During the 1860 presidential campaign, candidate Abraham Lincoln was referred to as "Honest Abe" and "The Rail-Splitter." This miniature axe, worn by his supporters, bears both terms.

Original in the Lincoln Museum, Washington, D.C. Authentic, copyrighted reproduction in metal, brass-plated by Alva Museum Repilcas, Inc., New York.

This COLLECTION of LINCOLN MEMENTOS contains:
- Authentic replica of Lincoln's Campaign Badge
- Reproduction of Lincoln's favorite photograph by Alexander Hesler, Chicago, 1860 (above)
- Three of Lincoln's most famous speeches:
  FAREWELL ADDRESS AT SPRINGFIELD, ILL.
  GETTYSBURG ADDRESS
  SECOND INAUGURAL ADDRESS

POLITICAL PIN. 1.25 to 1.5 inch pins in the shape of an axe with the words, "Honest Abe, The Rail Splitter". The originals usually have a brooch pin back and are usually made as a brass shell. These solid body examples are later remakes of the original. They probably started making them at the 1909 Centennial and were sold as recently as the 1964 World's Fair. One has a tie clip back (1964) and another a pin back. Value for original $450-$650, value of later models $15-$65.

RIBBON, ca. 1888. A political ribbon with hanging medal for the Original Wide Awakes of Hartford, Connecticut. This may be represented as a Lincoln item but was actually used in the William H. Harrison campaign of 1888. The Wide Awakes were active until the 1890s and many did not support Lincoln in the 1864 election since he was not a "pure" Republican but rather ran as a Unionist. 1.75 x 5 inches. *From the Frank & Virginia Williams Collection of Lincolniana.*

BOOKLET, 1864. The back cover of the Lincoln Campaign Songster has a great advertisement for CDVs and political badges, emblems, pins, and medals.

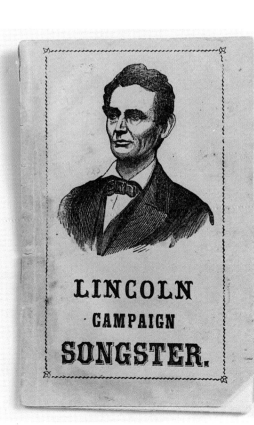

(11)

What by Mac could not be brought
By Lincoln has been wrought,
nd victory crowns our glorious arms;
Then for Lincoln we will strive,
And McClellan's friends we'll drive
uth, to join their traitorous friends.
s—Then up with the stripes and the stars, &c.

The Copperheads now fear
Their party's doom is near,
nd cry for a disgraceful peace;
But this we will not have,
So long as Lincoln live,
ho will ever be the Union's friend.
s—Then up with the stripes and the stars, &c.

URRAH! FOR LINCOLN AND JOHNSON!
Air: *"John Brown's Body."*
BY C. J. F., JR.

cted Abra'm Lincoln, and we've found him good
d true;
s labored long and hard for the red, white, and
ue;
untry he will save and our glorious Union too,
re go marching on.
s—Hurrah for the Union, hurrah for the flag,
Down with the traitors and the cursed rebel
rag;
With Lincoln and with Johnson we'll gain the
victory,
As we go marching on.

ith the Southerners who would the Union rend;
with McClellan, who is their boasted friend;
with the Copperheads, who him their influence
d,
re go marching on.
CHORUS—Hurrah, &c.

LINCOLN CAMPAIGN SONGSTER.

MASON & CO.,
No. 58 NORTH SIXTH STREET,
PHILADELPHIA.
DEALERS IN
ARTES DE VISITE, MEDALS,
POLITICAL EMBLEMS,
ngs, Campaign Song Books, etc. etc.

JUST OUT,

w and Beautiful Lincoln Badges,   25
   "   "   Emblems,   25
   "   "   Medals,   25
w Style Lincoln Pin,   25
e Photographs of Lincoln,   15
   "   "   Johnson,   15
el Engravings of A. Lincoln,
                         50 cts. to $1.
lies' Lincoln Emblems, 10 cts.
holesale Dealers supplied at half price.
☞ All orders by mail or express, promptly
filled.
MASON & CO.,
No. 58 North Sixth Street, Philadelphia, Pa.
☞ Six different Lincoln Campaign Songs
led for 50 cents per 100 or $3 per 1000.

5. Prints & Paintings

Possibly the most common item that Lincoln's image can be found upon is the paper print. (Do not let the word "common" mislead you—there are rare prints that sell for thousands of dollars.) There are lithographs (well known are the Currier & Ives prints which are hand colored), wood engravings, steel or copper engravings, etchings, wood block prints, chromoliths (introduced in 1851, popularized in the 1870s by Prang and others), oil painted lithographs (often printed on canvas to simulate an oil painting), aquatints (replaced by lithographs in the 1850s), mezzotints, etc.

There are books that can be studied to distinguish between the different types of prints, but probably more important, the collector must be able to distinguish between printing processes that were in existence before or during Lincoln's life and those that came about after he was dead. The most common post death process is the halftone introduced about 1883. Halftones use dots to make up the image. Only a few dots create a white area and lots of dots create a black area. Color halftone use colored dots in a pattern. Use a magnifying glass to look at midtone areas when buying prints. If it is made with halftones, it was printed well after Lincoln died. During Lincoln's life, photographs could only be reproduced in newspapers by having an engraver or woodcutter translate the photo to something that could be printed. Starting in the 1890s, newspapers began to use the halftone process to reproduce photos.

Wood engravings were the most popular process used in the 1800s, because the design on the wood was raised. The engraved wood block could be set in the same frame as metal or wood type. Many books and newspapers, such as *Harper's Weekly*, used this process almost exclusively.

Lithographs exhibit an irregular graining pattern which is actually the surface of the lithographic stone. A lithograph is made by drawing on a stone with a grease pencil and then applying acid to the surface of the stone to etch it. A separate stone is used for each color. The stone is wetted and coated with an ink that sticks only to the etched surface and is repelled by the glossy wet surface. Paper is laid on top and rolled. The ink transfers to the paper. There is no depressed plate mark on the paper. A good stone lithographer could produce twenty prints per hour from a stone. Chromolithography, a lithograph in printed colors, was in use as early as the 1850s, but was perfected at the end of the Civil War.

LITHOGRAPH, ca. 1860. A rare print by E.H. Brown of Chicago illustrating Lincoln. It says, "Abraham Lincoln, State Sovereignty, National Union" and was made for the Republican (Wigwam) convention where Lincoln was nominated for President. This was the first print of Lincoln ever published. 7 x 9 inches. *Courtesy of Rex Stark*. Value $1,100-$1,250 (in this condition).

Mezzotints are made from a copper plate. The face of the plate is roughened and inked. Some of the roughness is scraped and polished away until the design is completed. Only 200 or so prints can be made from the plate before it is worn away. It never became widely used and was used almost exclusively for portraits.

Paper damage is the greatest threat to a print collector. Water causes stains, wood backings cause deterioration and browning, mildew or other fungus cause brown lines called foxing, sunlight causes colors to fade, some insects eat paper, tears and rips get larger if the paper is handled, older "Scotch Tape" bleeds into the paper, dirt and dust may be impossible to remove without damaging the paper, and wood pulp paper deteriorates and becomes brown and brittle. Most are preventable or curable, while others may be a product of time. It is important to get wood surfaces away from print surfaces (remove old wood backings) and replace the old wood pulp mat board with acid free rag board.

Since prints are not unique items, condition counts when it comes to value. Restoration can cost hundreds of dollars, so a one hundred dollar print in thirty-five dollar condition may not be worth restoring. Most prints are not in pristine condition when found. "Fine" condition is defined as some minor browning or staining on the prints, but nothing that detracts greatly from the content. A mint condition print may be worth three to six times what a "fine" condition print is worth.

LITHOGRAPH, 1860. An E.B. & E.C. Kellog small folio, hand colored lithograph of candidate Stephen Douglas in a period frame. Currier & Ives and Kellog produced lithographs of the presidential candidates sitting in front of curtains. Douglas is very difficult to find. Value $200-$275.

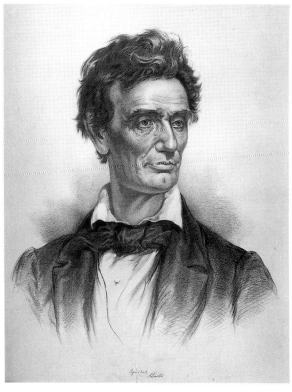

PHOTO OIL, 1860. A large sepia photograph taken by Joseph Hill of Springfield, Illinois, that has been colored with oil colors. These colored photos were used in the 1860 campaign to show the candidate. There are but two of these known to have survived. *Courtesy of Lloyd Ostendorf.*

LITHOGRAPH, 1860. A rare lithograph (one of five known) by Joseph Baker, lithographer, and published by J.H. Bufford of Boston. It is a young Lincoln from the life portrait by Charles Barry of Springfield. This was expected to be a popular print at the time but apparently the lithographic stone broke and few prints were actually produced. 21 x 26.5 inches. *Courtesy of the Old Print Shop, Inc., Kenneth M. Newman.* Value $9,000-$10,500.

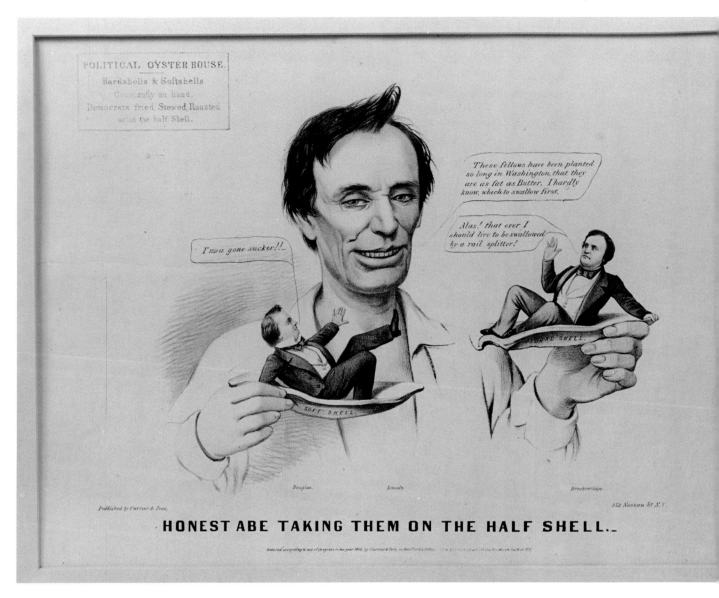

HONEST ABE TAKING THEM ON THE HALF SHELL.

LITHOGRAPH, 1860. *Honest Abe Taking Them On The Half Shell*, by Currier & Ives. A 16 x 20 inch political cartoon lithograph. Lincoln is shown about to eat Douglas and Breckenridge. Lincoln says, "These fellows have been planted in Washington so long that they are as fat as butter. I hardly know which one to swallow first". Value $500-$800.

POLITICAL "BLONDINS" CROSSING SALT RIVER.

LITHOGRAPH, 1860. *Political "Blondins" Crossing Salt River*, by Currier & Ives. A 16 x 20 inch political cartoon lithograph. Lincoln was the brunt of many political cartoons during his campaign and presidency. Blondin was a famous tightrope walker who crossed Niagara Falls. Value $500-$800.

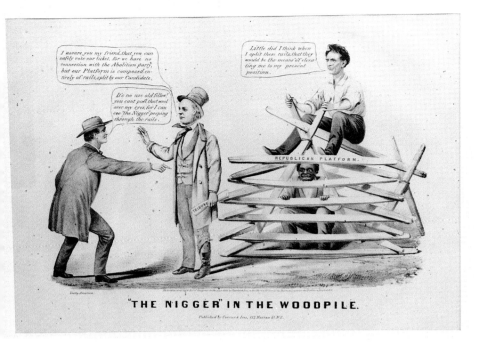

LITHOGRAPH, 1860. "The Nigger" In The Woodpile, by Currier & Ives. 16 x 20 inch political cartoon lithograph. Value $500-$800.

LITHOGRAPH, 1860. Storming The Castle, by Currier & Ives. 13.5 x 18 inch political cartoon lithograph. From the Frank & Virginia Williams Collection of Lincolniana. Value $500-$800.

LITHOGRAPH, 1860. The Great Exhibition of 1860, by Currier & Ives. 16 x 20 inch political cartoon lithograph. Value $500-$800.

ENGRAVING, ca. 1860. A steel engraving of Lincoln with facsimile signature. Engraver unknown. 7 x 10 inches. *From the Frank & Virginia Williams Collection of Lincolniana.* Value $50-$75.

LITHOGRAPH, 1860. Currier & Ives small folio of the new president. A short-lived print since Lincoln quickly grew a beard and the public wanted to see Lincoln with a beard. A highly sought after item. 11.5 x 15 inches. Value $500-$750.

MEZZOTINT, ca. 1861. Mezzotint or engraving of Lincoln from the Cooper Union pose. Engraved by D.J. Pound, London. 7 x 9 inches. *From the Frank & Virginia Williams Collection of Lincolniana.* Value $250-$350.

ENGRAVING, ca. 1861. Steel engraving of Lincoln based on the miniature from life by J. Henry Brown. The original was a clean shaven Lincoln. The beard was added to the engraving. Engraved and artist signed by Samuel Sartain. Sartain was one of three sons of engraver John Sartain. 5.5 x 8.5 inches. *From the Frank & Virginia Williams Collection of Lincolniana.* Value $125-$175.

LITHOGRAPH, ca. 1861. A Currier & Ives hand colored lithograph of the new president. 12 x 15 inches. *From the Frank & Virginia Williams Collection of Lincolniana.* Value $250-$350.

LITHOGRAPH, ca. 1861. A large beautiful hand colored lithograph, published by Bouclet, lithographed by A. Feusier, entitled, *"Presidents Of The United States".* 24 x 30 inches.

MEZZOTINT, 1862. Large mezzotint engraving showing Lincoln's head on John Fremont's body. The head is a reversed Cooper Union Brady image. The lamp on the table has replaced a globe that appeared in the Fremont image which was also engraved by J.C. Buttre. The print can also be found with a beardless Lincoln and Lincoln with George Washington. 25.75 x 32.25 inches. This is often found as a CDV. Value $250-$350.

ENGRAVING, 1863. A very popular engraving that hung in many homes across the northern portion of United States during the Lincoln presidency. It is based upon a Brady photograph of Lincoln and his son, Tad. It is 8.75 x 10.5 inches. It is marked "painted by F. Schnell, published by John Dainty, engraved by A.B. Walter." Value $75-$90.

LITHOGRAPH, ca. 1862. A Currier & Ives lithograph entitled, *The Lincoln Family*. 10 x 14 inches. Value $150-$200.

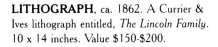

PAINTING ON IVORY, ca. 1864. This small wonderful oil painting
was done by the French artist, Dumont. It shows the painter's attempt to
make Lincoln more handsome. The painting is most likely based upon a
photograph taken by Brady on January 8, 1864. 5.125 x 5.75 inches in
an 18th or very early 19th century frame. Value $1,500-$2,500.

PAINTING ON IVORY, ca. 1864. A small painting on ivory, showing young Abe Lincoln, done by the American artist, Thomas Hicks (1823-1890). Hicks was a member of the National Academy of Design and in 1860 painted what is believed to be Lincoln's first portrait. That portrait is now in the Chicago Historical Society collection. 2.5 x 3.5 inches. Value $2,000-$2,500.

Above and right:
LITHOGRAPH, 1864. A rare Currier & Ives hand tinted lithograph. It is 10 x 14 inches and shows all of the presidents including Lincoln. Currier & Ives published it in the few months between Lincoln's re-election and his death using their popular beardless image of the president. The period of Lincoln's Presidency is listed on the print as 1861 to 1869. C & I must have expected to sell the print for the next four years that Lincoln was President. Value $700-$900.

CHROMOLITH, ca. 1864. This chromolithograph on canvas, done using oil paints, so closely resembles an oil painting, that it is often sold as such. The piece is copyrighted 1864 by E.C. Middleton. It is not hard to find, but is a very popular print. 13.75 x 17.5 inches. *From the Robert DeLorenzo collection*. Value $450-$600.

GEORGE WASHINGTON.
1789 to 1797.

JOHN ADAMS.
1797 to 1801.

THOMAS JEFFERSON.
1801 to 1809.

JAMES MADISON.
1809 to 1817.

JAMES MONROE.
1817 to 1825.

JOHN Q ADAMS.
1825 to 1829.

ANDREW JACKSON.
1829 to 1837.

MARTIN V. BUREN.
1837 to 1841.

Wm H. HARRISON.
4 March to 4 Apr. 1841.

JOHN TYLER.
Apl 4 1841 to 1845.

JAMES K. POLK.
1845 to 1849.

ZACHARY TAYLOR.
1849 to 1850.

MILLARD FILLMORE.
1850 to 1853.

FRANKLIN PIERCE.
1853 to 1857.

JAMES BUCHANAN.
1857 to 1861.

ABRAHAM LINCOLN.
1861 to 1869.

PUBLISHED BY CURRIER & IVES.   152 NASSAU ST NEW YORK.

THE PRESIDENTS.
OF THE UNITED STATES, FROM 1789 TO 1869.

ENGRAVING, ca. 1864. An engraving, 16 x 20 inches, from a painting by E.D. Marchant, engraved by John Sartain and published by Bradley & Co., Philadelphia. It has a facsimile signature. This is not difficult to find, but is a very popular print due to the high quality work of John Sartain. Value $250-$350.

ENGRAVING, 1864. A popular steel engraving of Lincoln, by H.B. Hall & Sons, New York. It is shown because of the good facsimile signature that inexperienced collectors could mistake as an original signature. Value $45-$60.

LINCOLN AT HOME.

LITHOGRAPH, 1864. A hand colored lithograph of the Lincoln family entitled *Lincoln At Home*, by Kellogg. It incorporates the Brady photo of Lincoln and Tad. 10 x 14 inches. Value $175-$250.

ENGRAVING, ca. 1864. An engraving by Virtue & Co. publishers and J.C. Mc Rae, engraver. 8 x 10 inches. Value $75-$100.

CHROMOLITH, ca. 1865. A chromolith done by Bingham & Dodd using oil colors on the print. It is a copy of the more popular 1864 Middleton print. 14 x 19 inches. *From the Robert DeLorenzo collection.* Value $85-$125.

LITHOGRAPH, 1865. *Grand Reception of the Notabilities of the Nation.* This approximately 18 x 23 inch illustration was probably the last print produced before Lincoln was assassinated. The lithography was by Henry Majors and Joseph Knapp. It was offered as a premium for new subscribers to Frank Leslie's *Chimney Corner* newspaper. Value $450-$550.

CHROMOLITH, ca. 1865. Another variation of a Bingham & Dodd print. 15 x 19 inches. Value $85-$125.

ENGRAVING, ca. 1865. An engraving with Lincoln's head, from the 1864 photo by Brady, grafted onto John C. Calhoun's body. Even the words on the papers on the table were changed from Calhoun slogans to Lincoln themes. This image was based upon a painting by Alonzo Chappel. 17 x 21 inches. *From the Frank & Virginia Williams Collection of Lincolniana.* Value $500-$800.

LAST MOMENTS OF PRESIDENT LINCOLN.
WASHINGTON, D.C. APRIL 15ᵗʰ 1865.

LITHOGRAPH, 1865. *Last Moments of President Lincoln*, by Bufford's Publishing, Boston. A 13 x 18 inch lithograph. *From the Frank & Virginia Williams Collection of Lincolniana.* Value $250-$350.

LITHOGRAPH, 1865. A Currier & Ives lithograph of the *Death of the Martyr President Abraham Lincoln*. Most of these death scenes show many people in the room where Lincoln lay dying. In reality, it was a small room and could not hold more than a few people at a time. Many dignitaries did come to visit the dying president. For a more realistic view of, and comment upon the size of the room, see the section on Lincoln postcards. 14 x 18 inches. Value $200-$300.

LITHOGRAPH, ca. 1865. A Currier & Ives print of the *Death of President Lincoln*. 11 x 15 inches. *From the Robert DeLorenzo collection.* Value $200-$300.

LITHOGRAPH, 1865. *Death of Abraham Lincoln*, by E.B. & E.C. Kellog. A 12 x 17 inch, hand colored lithograph. Value $250-$350.

WOODCUT, 1865. *Funeral Service In The East Room Of The White House*, from *Leslies Magazine*. A 16 x 20 inch, illustration drawn by C. Boswill. Value $100-$135.

LITHOGRAPH, 1865. A Kimmel & Forster lithograph of an allegorical scene called *The Outbreak Of The Rebellion in The United States, 1861*. There is a great deal of action in the print in which Lincoln stands ready to protect Liberty and Union. 21 x 28 inches. *From the Joseph Edward Garrera collection.* Value $600-$800.

LITHOGRAPH, ca. 1865. A lithograph, published by Kimmel & Forster "copyrighted" by Henry A. Wm. Vought, entitled *Columbia's Noblest Sons*. 19 x 22.5 inches. Value $550-$650.

ENGRAVING, 1866. *Lincoln and His Family*, from a painting by Samuel B. Waugh, steel engraving by William Sartain. 22 x 28.25 inches. Value $450-$550.

ENGRAVING, ca. 1865. Another example of the engraving by J.C. Buttre taken from the Brady photograph. More color makes it a more desirable print. 13 x 17 inches. *From the Frank & Virginia Williams Collection of Lincolniana.* Value $300-$450.

ENGRAVING, ca. 1866. An engraving by J.C. Buttre taken from the Brady photograph. The corner illustrations have been hand colored. This print was first issued in 1864. This print says at the bottom "Assassinated April 14, 1865". 12 x 16 inches. Value $200-$300 (colored), $125-$175 (not colored).

ENGRAVING, 1866. A signed engraving of Lincoln by William E. Marshall (1837-1906). Published by Ticknor & Fields, Boston. This is probably the most popular engraving of Lincoln sought by collectors. It is available in several styles: imprinted—not imprinted, signed—not signed. Size is 22 x 30 inches. *From the Robert DeLorenzo collection.* Value $750-$950 (signed).

ENGRAVING, 1866. Another example by William E. Marshall. What sets this apart from the standard framing usually found on this print is the use of South American iridescent butterfly wings in the border of the frame and under Lincoln's name. *From the Joseph Edward Garrera collection.* Value $600-$750 with frame.

ENGRAVING, ca. 1866. A steel engraving of Lincoln based on the profile photograph taken by the Brady Studio. Engraved and artist signed by John Sartain (1808-1897). Sartain had three sons, Henry, Samuel, and William, who also became printmakers. About 12 x 16 inches. Sartain's work is highly sought after. Value $300-$400.

ENGRAVING, 1866. *First Reading Of The Emancipation Proclamation Before The Cabinet.* This is one of the most popular prints made of Lincoln and his cabinet. Shown, from left to right are: Edwin M. Stanton, Secretary of War; Salmon P. Chase, Secretary of the Treasury; Lincoln; Gideon Wells, Secretary of the Navy; William H. Seward, Secretary of State (seated); Caleb B. Smith, Secretary of the Interior (standing); Montgomery Blair, Postmaster General; and Edward Bates, Attorney General. The original painting was made by Francis Bicknell Carpenter who spent six months at the White House and wrote a book about the experience. Every detail of the picture has meaning, from the placement of the Cabinet members to the things hanging on the wall or lying on the floor. It was engraved by Alexander Haye Richie. 28 x 36 inches. Value $600-$750.

LITHOGRAPH, 1867. A Lyon & Company lithograph entitled *President Lincoln And Family Circle.* 21 x 26 inches. This is a very strange print in that it is dated 1867, shows Mary Lincoln in what looks like her black mourning outfit (circa 1863) with an earlier flowered hair piece, Lincoln in an 1864 (photographic) pose and three children, allegedly, the three Lincoln children, one of which (Willie), had died in 1862. Value $250-$350.

CHROMOLITH, ca. 1890. A chromolith behind curved glass and framed in a period frame. 6 x 8 inches. *From the Robert DeLorenzo collection.* Value $75-$125.

ETCHING, ca. 1869. A 14 x 18.5 inch unsigned etching of Lincoln. The artist has captured Lincoln's spirit in the face. Value $250-$350.

LITHOGRAPH, 1876. A Currier & Ives lithograph of *The Lincoln Statue*. The statue was erected in Washington, D.C., dedicated to Lincoln's emancipation of the slaves. 12 x 16.5 inches. Value $150-$200.

SILHOUETTES, ca. 1890. A interesting pair of silhouettes of Abraham Lincoln with a cane and Mary Lincoln. 5 x 6 inches. Value $75-$125.

LITHOGRAPH, ca. 1900. This lithograph is signed "T. Johnson" in the margin (not T.M. Johnson, 1834-1869, who painted Lincoln in 1860). 10 x 18 inches. *From the Robert DeLorenzo collection.* Value $200-$300.

ENGRAVING, ca. 1899. A print signed by T. Johnson. 12 x 15 inches. Published by Dodd, Mead & Co., engravers. *From the Frank & Virginia Williams Collection of Lincolniana.* Value $200-$300.

PRINT, ca. 1909. A print, 10.5 x 13.5 inches, by Henry Taylor Jr. *From the Robert DeLorenzo collection*. Value $100-$125.

LITHOGRAPH, ca. 1905. This lithograph (remarked proof) is signed "Jacque Reich" in the margin. 13.5 x 17.5 inches. *From the Robert DeLorenzo collection*. Value $100-$125.

PRINT, ca. 1907. A print, 9 x 13 inches, taken from a book about the presidents. *From the Robert DeLorenzo collection*. Value $20-$30.

LITHOGRAPH, ca. 1909. This lithograph on a textured paper from a photograph of a sculpture called "Marble Head of Lincoln" is signed "Gutzon Borglum" in the margin. Borglum did the sculpture and was the man that conceived and developed the carving of the four presidents on Mount Rushmore. 12 x 14 inches. *From the Robert DeLorenzo collection.* Value $300-$400 with signature.

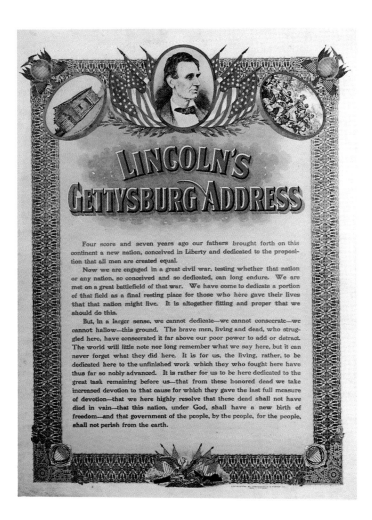

PRINT, ca. 1909. A print of the Gettysburg Address 14.5 x 19.5 inches by Umbdenstock & Porter, Chicago. *From the Robert DeLorenzo collection.* Value $100-$150.

ENGRAVING, ca. 1909. A steel engraving of Lincoln based upon the 1860 photo by William Marsh. Signed in the print by J.P. Murphy Co. 6.75 x 8.75 inches. *From the Frank & Virginia Williams Collection of Lincolniana.* Value $50-$100.

PRINT, ca. 1909. A very warm and unusual, unmarked illustration which was probably done for a magazine or book. 7.5 x 10.5 inches. *From the Robert DeLorenzo collection.* Value $45-$75.

CHROMOLITH, ca. 1909. A chromolith on canvas, done using oil paints, closely resembling an oil painting. 12 x 14.5 inches, also found in a 12 x 18 inch size. Value $125-$175.

PRINT, 1909. Lincoln's birthplace by J. Fagen. 12 x 16 inches. *From the Robert DeLorenzo collection.* Value $75-$95.

CHROMOLITH, ca. 1918. This advertising chromolith on canvas so closely resembles an oil painting that it is often sold as such. The original was an oil painting by R. Bohunak done in 1913. The Illinois Watch Company used the piece to advertise its Lincoln Watch. 7 x 10 inches. Value $350-$450.

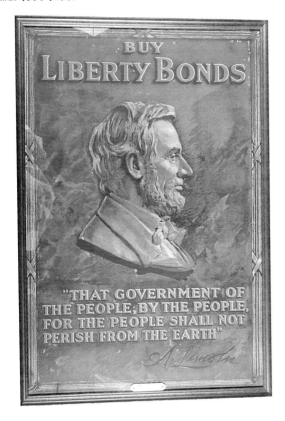

PAINTING, ca. 1920. An incredibly fine miniature oil painting by William Patterson (1865-1939) based upon an 1860 Hesler photograph. It is only 4.5 inches high. Patterson painted miniatures of many presidents and his work is actively collected by museums. There are a few stray reflections in this photo, not on the painting, due to the curved glass cover over the painting. *From the Frank & Virginia Williams Collection of Lincolniana.* Value $7,500-$8,500.

LITHOGRAPH, 1918. A World War I poster using Lincoln's image and words to sell Liberty Bonds. About 15 x 24 inches. Value $175-$250.

SILHOUETTE, ca. 1920. A profile of Lincoln. 4.5 x 5.25 inches including frame. Value $40-$60.

ENGRAVING, ca. 1920. A signed engraving of Lincoln by Schneider. The print is based upon the Alexander Gardner photograph taken in 1863. Size is about 14 x 22 inches. Value $200-$300.

PRINT, ca. 1925. A large image of Lincoln's face on this advertising piece for the Great American Insurance Company of New York. It is made to look like an oil painting. Competition from advertising collectors drives up the price of advertising pieces showing Lincoln. Size is 24 x 30 inches. Value $250-$350.

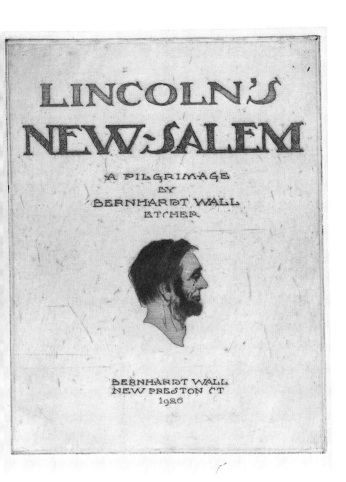

Hill-McNamer Store, New Salem, Ill., next door to Lincoln & Berry Store. Here Lincoln often helped out in 1834.

ETCHING, 1926. Bernhardt Wall produced a book of etchings of Lincoln and scenes from his life in New Salem. These were followed in the 1930s with a multi-volume set covering Lincoln's later life. Wall is well known among postcard collectors for his fabulous images which appeared, about 1910, on Halloween postcards. *From the Frank & Virginia Williams Collection of Lincolniana.*

PAINTING, ca. 1928. A James Montgomery Flagg painting of Lincoln awaiting news of the battle. Flagg is best known as the illustrator of the World War I poster of Uncle Sam saying "We Want You". 27 x 48 inches. *From the Frank & Virginia Williams Collection of Lincolniana.*

LITHOGRAPH, ca. 1928. A lithograph signed "Timothy Cole" in the print and on the margin. 13.5 x 17 inches. *From the Robert DeLorenzo collection.* Value $150-$200.

SILHOUETTE, ca. 1928. A small silhouette of Lincoln by J.J. Cuin. 3.75 x 4.75 inches. Value $30-$40.

PAINTING, ca. 1928. A James Montgomery Flagg painting of Lincoln praying for the Lord's guidance before issuing his proclamation to emancipate the slaves. 27 x 31 inches. *From the Frank & Virginia Williams Collection of Lincolniana.*

SILHOUETTE, ca. 1930. A profile of Lincoln. 3.25 x 5.25 inches. *From the Robert DeLorenzo collection.* Value $30-$40.

WOOD BLOCK PRINT, ca. 1930. A wood block print by Othmar Hoffler. 7.5 x 9.5 inches. *From the Robert DeLorenzo collection.* Value $20-$30.

PRINT, ca. 1930. A print 14 x 18 inches by Moses Hyman. *From the Robert DeLorenzo collection.* Value $100-$125.

PAINTING, ca. 1930. A painting showing a scene from the Lincoln-Douglas debates. J.H. Whiting has captured, with an illustrator's touch, the look and feel of the debates. The scene shows the protagonists in a town square setting, suggesting the debates in Ottawa, Quincy, or Alton, all which took place in such a setting. Oil on board, 16.5 x 24 inches. *From the Frank & Virginia Williams Collection of Lincolniana.*

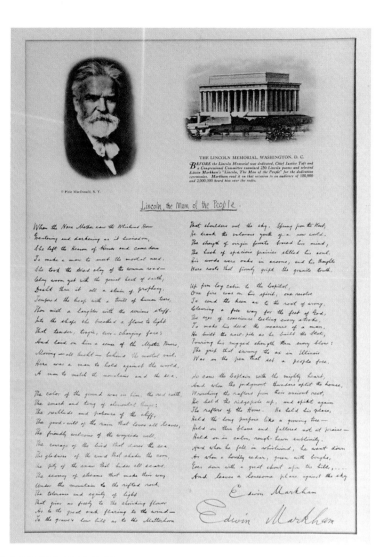

PRINT, 1932. An engraving of a poem written and read by Edwin Markham at the dedication of the Lincoln memorial. Markham has signed this copy below his printed signature. Apparently, Markham signed many of these copies and they are available. Value $75-$100.

ETCHING, 1933. Bernhardt Wall was an admirer of Lincoln history. He created a series of etchings of Lincoln and scenes from Lincoln's life. *From the Frank & Virginia Williams Collection of Lincolniana.*

DRAWING, 1995. The photo shows Chuck Levitan, a New York artist with three of his 6 x 10 foot tall drawings of Abraham Lincoln. The drawings are based upon period photographs of Lincoln.

6. Statues, Busts, & Plaques

There are numerous statues, busts, and plaques of Lincoln. Lincoln has been cast in bronze, brass, steel, iron, and plaster and carved in wood and stone. One might think that the bronzes are the most desirable, but there are plaster statues that sell for as much as many fine bronzes. The first pieces probably began to appear right after Lincoln died, others were made for events such as the 1876 centennial, the 1893 World's fair, the 1909 Lincoln centennial, the 1922 opening of the Lincoln monument and the 1939 World's fair. They are still being made today and there are high quality reproductions also made today.

Almost every sculptor who made Lincoln in a large statue for a public place also made or authorized smaller pieces. Sometimes these were used to raise money for the large piece or sold by the organization who paid for the large statue or just pirated. Three of the best known Lincoln artists are Leonard W. Volk, Gutzon Borglum, and Daniel C. French. For every statue that you find with an artist's name on it, you will find ten with no markings as to artist, foundry, or maker.

Dating a bust or statue is difficult when it contains no maker's name or mark. Many were made between 1890 and 1930, and some were made in countries other than the United States (Austrian bronze casters were among the best). Castings were made in inexpensive white metal to cast iron to expensive bronze. A magnet will help you to tell a ferrous (iron bearing) metal from a bronze. Statues and sculptures were also made in ceramic, plaster, and glass.

Alva Museum Reproductions, a current maker of nice quality Volk and French designed Lincoln bronzed busts, makes them from "Alva Stone", a sort of toned cast marble effect. When their copyright date on the side of the bust is not clear or has been removed, the bust can be confused with a much older piece. The Volk Lincoln hand casts and face casts are being reproduced today, usually with no markings or perhaps the Volk name. If you are paying a great deal for a bust, get a guarantee of authenticity and look for signs of age.

Most plaques are unmarked and many are based upon the photographs of Lincoln. The Victor D. Brenner plaque is a choice item, but there are numerous copies and variations of it. Plaques can be found in cast iron, brass, bronze, or copper, or stamped copper or brass backed with lead.

LIFE CAST, ca. 1860. A 6.5 inch long plaster life cast of Lincoln's right hand by Leonard W. Volk. A label on the reverse side states it was made in Springfield, Illinois, in 1860 by Volk and given to Mr. Whitehead by Douglas Volk, the artist's son, in 1931. *From the Joseph Edward Garrera collection.* Value $700-$800.

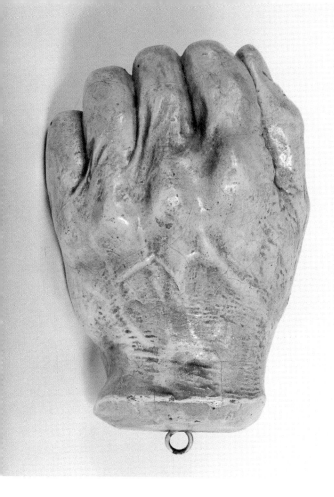

LIFE CAST, ca. 1860. A 7 inch long plaster life cast of Lincoln's left hand by Volk. *From the Joseph Edward Garrera collection.* Value $325-$400.

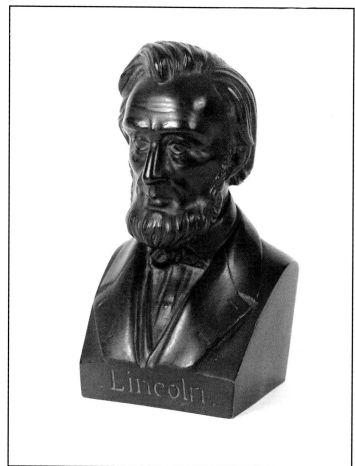

BUST, ca. 1861. A cast bronze bust of Lincoln marked on the back, "Chardigny, 1861". 5.25 inches tall. *From the Frank & Virginia Williams Collection of Lincolniana.* Value $450-$600.

STATUE, 1864. A Staffordshire statue of Lincoln on horseback. The English firm of Staffordshire had made the same statue facing right of Wellington. When there was a demand for Lincoln, Wellington was retooled to become Lincoln. *From the Frank & Virginia Williams Collection of Lincolniana.* Value $2,800-$3,200.

STATUE, 1868. This is the first variation (type "A") of the John Rogers group showing Lincoln with Grant and Secretary of War, Stanton, called *The Council of War*. The three variations can be distinguished by the hands of Stanton. Stanton was at one time implicated in the assassination of Lincoln (It was determined he was not involved). In this first variation, his hands, which are behind Lincoln's head, appear to be ready to threaten Lincoln. In the second variation, his hands are moved to the side of Lincoln's head. *From the Frank & Virginia Williams Collection of Lincolniana.* Value $2,000-$3,000.

STATUE, ca. 1868. A painted plaster or ceramic Lincoln statue, marked, "J. Nicoly Jr. 1865". 22 inches tall. This was probably made in England. *From the Frank & Virginia Williams Collection of Lincolniana.* Value $900-$1,000.

STATUE, 1868. This is the third variation of the John Rogers group showing Lincoln with Grant and Secretary of War, Stanton, called *The Council of War*. The three variations can be distinguished by the location of the hands of Stanton. This third variation shows the hands down and away from Lincoln. *From the Frank & Virginia Williams Collection of Lincolniana.* Value $2,000-$3,000.

BUST, ca. 1870. A bronze Lincoln bust by Joseph A. Bailly (1825-1883) marked, "Patent Bailly, May 1865, Warner Miskey Merrill, Phila." 10 inches tall. *From the Frank & Virginia Williams Collection of Lincolniana.* Value $2,800-$3,200.

STATUE, ca. 1890. A plaster bust of Lincoln in the "Classical Mode". It was popular to sculpt famous people wearing togas similar to the classic Greek and Roman statues. 30.5 inches tall. *From the Joseph Edward Garrera collection.*

PLAQUE, ca. 1880. A profile of Lincoln made of zinc mounted on velvet. The reverse tells that this is an example of the fine metal work Kreb Bros. can do on zinc and granite statues. They specialized in funeral and cemetery work. 5.5 inches tall. *From the Robert DeLorenzo collection.*

PLAQUE, ca. 1900. A brass profile piece mounted on a velvet background. Marked on back, "Cast by Fred Schobel, Jan. 1900 Pittsburgh Valve & Foundry for F.M. Busch." The profile is 4 x 5.5 inches. Value $40-$70.

STATUE, ca. 1891. A very rare, large (41 inches tall) plaster statue of Lincoln holding the Emancipation Proclamation. Sculpted by Leonard Volk. *From the Garrera Family Collection*. Value $5,000-$6,000.

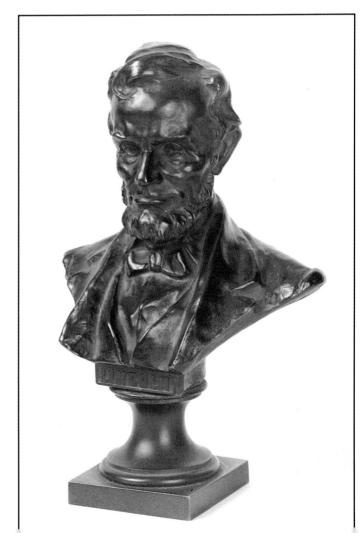

BUST, ca. 1900. Bearded Lincoln cast bronze bust on a pedestal, made in Austria. The sculptor is Hans Muller (1872-1931). Overall 11 inches tall. Value $1,500-$2,000.

BUST, ca. 1900. A gilded wooden bust on a marble base. 7.5 inches tall. Value $125-$200.

BUST, ca. 1904. A Lincoln bust made by George Bissell and cast in bronze by the Gorham Foundry, Providence, Rhode Island. Bissell's name is signed in the casting and foundry's name is stamped into the rear. These were very popular and may have originally sat in court houses or in college halls. 18 inches tall. *From the Frank & Virginia Williams Collection of Lincolniana.* Value $6,500-$12,000.

BUST, ca. 1904. A bronze bust marked on the back, "George Bissell, Gorham Foundry". 16.5 inches tall. It is believed that Bissell or someone with control of the molds recast Bissell's work in the mid-1920s and possibly again in the 1950s. There are several variations. The newest castings usually do not have the Gorham Foundry mark stamped (not cast) into the back and are worth less than the earlier castings. Value $6,000-$9,000.

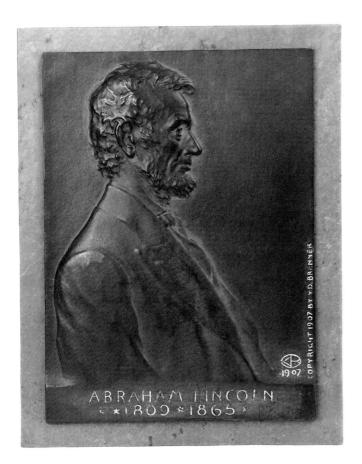

PLAQUE, ca. 1909. A bronze profile plaque marked, "Copyright 1908—M. Wolfson". 3.5 x 4.5 inches.

PLAQUE, 1907. A high relief plaque (7.125 x 9.375 inches) mounted on a green marble backing (8.5 x 10.75 inches) with a stand, by Victor D. Brenner (1871-1924). This image replaced the Indian head on the Lincoln penny introduced in 1909. The original image was from a photograph taken by Anthony Berger at Brady's studio in February 1864. This plaque is found in several configurations. This one with the green marble with stand was allegedly created as a limited edition of twelve (unlikely, since at least seven have been sold during the past few years). It sometimes appears without the marble back and is also found in a smaller size (2.5 x 3.5 inches) which has less artist information on the right front side. Value $1,250-$1,500 with marble back & stand, $450-$550 without marble & stand, $50-$75 in the smaller size.

PLAQUE, ca. 1909. A very nice bronze plaque mounted on wood made for the Lincoln Birth Centennial. 4 x 7.5 inches on a 6 x 9.5 inch mount. *From the Robert DeLorenzo collection.*

PLAQUE, ca. 1909. An 8 inch tall nickel plated metal profile plaque mounted on velvet. *From the Robert DeLorenzo collection.*

PLAQUE, ca. 1909. A 10 inch wide cast brass plaque with Lincoln in profile is unsigned. Value $175-$250.

PLAQUE, ca. 1909. A small brass plaque, 2.5 x 3.5 inches, maker unknown. Value $40-$60.

PLAQUE, ca. 1909. A young Lincoln's face appears on this self-framed plaster plaque created or designed by the J.S. Hartley Co. 7.75 x 7.75 inches. Value $70-$90.

STATUE, ca. 1909. A cast iron statue of Lincoln. It stands 7.25 inches tall. Value $45-$75.

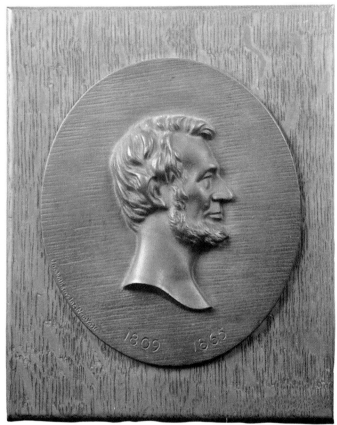

PLAQUE, ca. 1909. A bronze profile plaque marked, "Jno. Williams, Inc., NY" mounted on oak. 6 x 7.25 inches.

PLAQUE, ca. 1909. Heavy cast iron profile bust of Lincoln mounted to a frame. The inner gold bordered section is 12 inches across. Value $100-$150.

BUST, ca. 1909. A nicely executed bust of Lincoln done in bronze. No maker's name, 8.5 inches tall. Value $450-$650.

BUST, ca. 1909. A cast metal bust of Lincoln, unmarked. 7 inches tall. *From the Frank & Virginia Williams Collection of Lincolniana.* Value $300-$400.

BUST, ca. 1909. A ceramic bust of Lincoln, unmarked. 6.5 inches tall. *From the Frank & Virginia Williams Collection of Lincolniana.* Value $125-$225.

PLAQUE, ca. 1909. A superb bronze allegorical Lincoln plaque, 4 inches tall, with great detail and imagery. *From the Frank & Virginia Williams Collection of Lincolniana.* Value $700-$750.

PLAQUE, ca. 1909. A lead backed copper Lincoln plaque, 5 inches tall, marked "J. Kratina copyright" *From the Frank & Virginia Williams Collection of Lincolniana*. Value $100-$125.

PLAQUE, ca. 1909. A bronze profile Lincoln plaque, 7.25 x 10 inches. *From the Frank & Virginia Williams Collection of Lincolniana*. Value $350-$425.

PLAQUE, ca. 1909. A bronze profile Lincoln plaque, 10.25 x 13.75 inches, marked "KVE". *From the Frank & Virginia Williams Collection of Lincolniana*. Value $350-$425.

PLAQUE, ca. 1909. A cast iron profile Lincoln grill, 9 x 10.5 inches. *From the Frank & Virginia Williams Collection of Lincolniana.* Value $250-$350.

BUST, ca. 1909. A bronzed and toned metal Lincoln nude bust, unmarked. 11.5 inches tall. Similar to a bust done in 1864 by Thomas Dow Jones (1811-1881) *From the Frank & Virginia Williams Collection of Lincolniana.* Value $500-$700.

STATUE, ca. 1909. A metal Lincoln statue, unmarked. The word "Emancipation" is on the scroll in Lincoln's hand. 11 inches tall and originally part of a mantle clock. *From the Frank & Virginia Williams Collection of Lincolniana.* Value $600-$750.

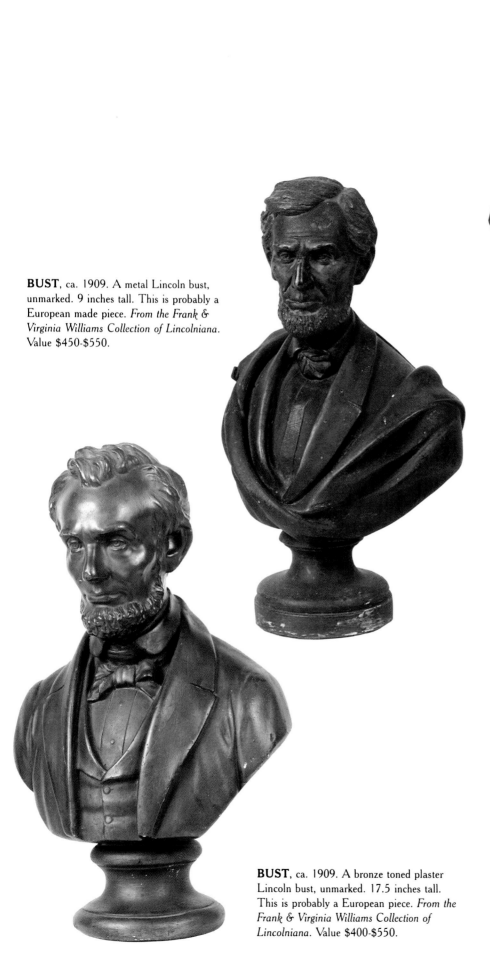

BUST, ca. 1909. A metal Lincoln bust, unmarked. 9 inches tall. This is probably a European made piece. *From the Frank & Virginia Williams Collection of Lincolniana.* Value $450-$550.

STATUE, ca. 1910. A white metal, probably zinc, bust of Lincoln marked "Warner Miskey Merrill, Phila., Artist J. A. Bailly, May, 1865". This is a particularly difficult bust to date. The earlier date leads one to believe it is from 1865, but the material and execution seems to place it after the turn of the century. It is 10.5 inches tall. *From the Robert DeLorenzo collection.* Value $100-$150.

BUST, ca. 1909. A bronze toned plaster Lincoln bust, unmarked. 17.5 inches tall. This is probably a European piece. *From the Frank & Virginia Williams Collection of Lincolniana.* Value $400-$550.

PLAQUE, ca. 1912. Plaster plaque of a young Abe Lincoln reading a book by firelight, entitled "The Boyhood of Abraham Lincoln" and marked "Copyright 1912 Republican Club of City of New York, Lincoln Dinner Committee". Made by Petrax Co., New York. 8.75 x 10 inches.

BUST, ca. 1916. A 13.5 inch tall bronze bust of Lincoln by Louis Mayer signed in the mold. *From the Joseph Edward Garrera collection.* Value $2,500-$3,000.

BUST, ca. 1918. A 7.5 inch tall plaster bust of Lincoln by Gutzon Borglum, signed in the mold. *From the Joseph Edward Garrera collection.* Value $400-$500.

BUST, ca. 1918. A 11.5 inch tall plaster bust of Lincoln, unsigned. Value $200-$300.

BUST, ca. 1920. A 12 inch tall copper finished metal bust of Lincoln, unsigned. Value $300-$400.

BUST, ca. 1918. A 10 inch tall plaster bust of Lincoln, unsigned. Value $300-$400.

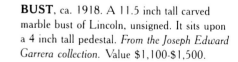

BUST, ca. 1918. A 11.5 inch tall carved marble bust of Lincoln, unsigned. It sits upon a 4 inch tall pedestal. *From the Joseph Edward Garrera collection.* Value $1,100-$1,500.

BUST, ca. 1928. This 8.5 inch tall plaster bust of Lincoln was made by Mazzolini Sculpturers in Cleveland, Ohio. Value $250-$350.

STATUE, ca. 1920. A bronze manquette entitled *Abraham Lincoln—The Hoosier Youth*. The artist is Manship and the piece stands 18 inches tall. The original is in front of the Lincoln National Life Insurance building in Ft. Wayne, Indiana. They commissioned the piece. *From the Frank & Virginia Williams Collection of Lincolniana.* Value $17,000-$19,000.

STATUE & NOTE, 1926. A short note to Valentine Bjorkman from a friend showing the sculpture George Waters with his 10 foot high statue of Lincoln erected in Portland (Maine?).

Dear Mr. B —
    I found this photo in my desk — I knew the sculptor in France. — The "model" lived in our hotel.
    Waters came to America to see his statue put up in Portland.
    I doubt if you have this picture in your collection —
        Sincerely
        Chas. Grant Sheffer

LIFE MASK, ca. 1928. A 12 inch tall plaster life mask of Lincoln with full face and hair, unsigned. *From the Joseph Edward Garrera collection.* Value $600-$800.

BUST, ca. 1930. A 17 inch tall plaster bust of Lincoln. There are no identifying markings, but the bust shows the skill of a talented artist. Value $400-$500.

STATUE, ca. 1930. A small, fairly accurate version of the seated Lincoln statue that stands in front of the Essex County courthouse in Newark, New Jersey. There are no makers markings. The original was sculpted in 1910 by Gutzon Borglum who also designed the Mount Rushmore sculpture. 4.5 inches tall.

STATUE, ca. 1930. A plaster statue of Lincoln without markings. It is 22.5 inches tall. *From the Robert DeLorenzo collection.* Value $150-$175.

BUST, ca. 1930. A plaster head painted white. 14.5 inches tall. Value $90-$140.

BUST, ca. 1930. A 14 inch tall plaster bust of Lincoln, signed by David Griesbach and dated in the mold. *From the Joseph Edward Garrera collection.* Value $800-$1,200.

STATUE, ca. 1930. A bronzed white metal, probably zinc, bust of Lincoln without markings. It is 18 inches tall. *From the Robert DeLorenzo collection.* Value $550-$700.

STATUES, ca. 1930 & 1961. Bronze toned white metal busts of Lincoln. The one on the left is marked "souvenir of Gettysburg" and the older one on the right is a souvenir of the Lincoln rug and Carpet Cleaning Co. of Newark, New Jersey. Both are 4.5 inches tall. *From the Robert DeLorenzo collection.*

PLAQUE, ca. 1930. This cast iron plaque was made as a flue cover. Many older homes had wood stoves. As the stoves were replaced with more modern fixtures, a hole would be left where the stove pipe entered the wall of the chimney. The hole was plugged and a decorative flue cover could be hung over the plugged area. 11.5 inches and made by the Foster Merrian Company. Value $100-$140.

BUST, ca. 1932. A cast glass bust of Lincoln, 6.5 inches tall. No maker markings. *From the Frank & Virginia Williams Collection of Lincolniana.* Value $75-$100.

STATUES, ca. 1957. Two small statues of Lincoln. The left one is metal and the other is a composition material. The metal one is marked "L.A. Fleck 1957". 6.5 inches and 6 inches tall. *From the Robert DeLorenzo collection.* Value $15-$20.

BUST, ca. 1943. A plaster bust marked "Jo Davidson 1943". Davidson lived from 1883 to 1952 and his work appears in the National Portrait Gallery in Washington. 10 inches tall. Value $450-$600.

STATUES, ca. 1957. Two small statues of Lincoln made of metal. 3.5 inches tall. *From the Robert DeLorenzo collection.* Value $15-$20.

BUST, ca. 1958. A bronze Lincoln bust by Berke. 17 inches tall with base. Berke is well known for his presidential series of busts. *From the Frank & Virginia Williams Collection of Lincolniana.* Value $4,800-$5,000.

STATUE, ca. 1960. A ceramic rendition of the 1915 Daniel C. French Lincoln Memorial statue 11 inches tall. Unusual in that the artist has given Lincoln blue eyes. Designed by B. Merer and produced by Capo Dimonti of Italy. *From the Frank & Virginia Williams Collection of Lincolniana.* Value $900-$1,200.

STATUE, ca. 1964. A bronze toned plaster bust of Lincoln marked "Austin, 1964". It is 13 inches tall. *From the Robert DeLorenzo collection.*

BUST, ca. 1970. A cast bronze Lincoln bust made by Mayer. 14 inches tall. *From the Frank & Virginia Williams Collection of Lincolniana.* Value $3,500-$4,000.

BUST, ca. 1979. A bronze bust by William Perry. One of ten cast. *From the Frank & Virginia Williams Collection of Lincolniana.*

STATUETTE, ca. 1970. A very nice reproduction of the 1915 Daniel C. French Lincoln Memorial statue. This is an Alva Museum reproduction cast in "Alva Stone". 11.5 inches tall. *From the Frank & Virginia Williams Collection of Lincolniana.* Value $175-$200.

BUST, ca. 1976. Ben contemplating the bust of Lincoln. A bronzed plaster bust of a beardless Lincoln, by Volk. Verso base reads, "A. Lincoln, modeled from life by Leonard W. Volk, Chicago, 1860, c. Alva Studios" with a marble base, 13 inches tall. This bust is of recent vintage, very nicely made and currently available in this and a larger size, albeit with a different finish to the base. Value: these have sold for $200-$400 at auction, but if you can live with a more recent one, they cost about $90 from museum shops.

SCULPTURE, 1988. *Lincoln at Brady's Gallery*, by Daniel P. Gray. Unlimited edition, cold cast in bronze. 5 inches tall. Daniel Gray is a talented Ohio sculptor who has concentrated on Lincoln. His work is highly valued among Lincoln collectors. Value $900-$1,200.

SCULPTURE, 1990. *Abraham Lincoln and his son, William,* by Daniel P. Gray. Cold cast in bronze. 10 inches tall. Value $1,700-$1,900.

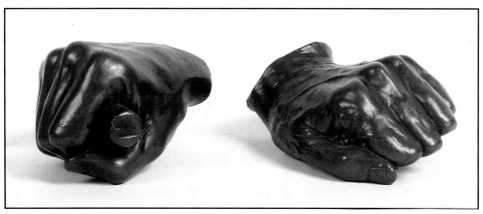

LIFE CAST, ca. 1990. A 6.5 inch long plaster life cast of Lincoln's right and left hand by Volk. Bronze toned plaster with no markings at all. These are current reproductions that are sometimes available at museum shops.

SCULPTURE, 1991. *The 1862 Council Of War*, by Daniel P. Gray. Number nine of a limited edition of fifteen, cold cast in bronze. Lincoln is 10.75 inches tall. Value $4,400-$4,600.

SCULPTURE, 1993. *Abraham and Mary*, by Daniel P. Gray. Number two of a limited edition of fifteen, cold cast in bronze. Lincoln is 10.75 inches tall. Value $2,200-$2,600.

BUST, 1992. A 24.5 inch tall bronze bust of Lincoln by Louis Mayer, signed and dated 1916 in the mold. This is a limited edition of five that were recast in bronze in 1992. Cost $4,500.

7. BOOKS, PAMPHLETS, & NEWSPAPERS

By Date

Collecting books about Lincoln is one of the major fields of Lincolniana. There were bibliographies created that listed almost every book ever written about Lincoln. If you like reading about Lincoln, this field is for you. There are books that give details of every aspect of Lincoln's life. Read about his youth, his romance, his businesses, his senate campaign, his presidential campaign, his presidency, his day to day activities and all the events surrounding his death. In looking through the titles of the books illustrated here, you will see that no field seems to be left out. One book was even written about how the weather affected the Lincoln-Douglas debates. In figuring how to show the books, it was decided to show the cover if it had some personality, or the frontispiece if it was informative, autographed, or inscribed. Books and pamphlets have been listed by author.

Pamphlets are another interesting field of Lincolniana. Especially sought after are the pre-Presidential biographies introducing the new Presidential candidate to the public. Also sought are the pamphlets about the assassination. Like today, big news sells. When Lincoln died, there was a rush to produce and sell pamphlets telling all the details of the assassination and trial (sound familiar?) or eulogizing Lincoln.

Books can be found everywhere. Public libraries often have a summer book sale where they sell duplicates or books that they do not consider to be worth the shelf space. Check out small book stores, garage sales, antique shows, and mail order book dealers and be sure to ask friends if they have any old Lincoln books. Keep in mind that Lincoln's signature may be found in books. It can be a printed signature or a true autograph. Remember though, that at least two forgers specialized in signing Lincoln's name in books.

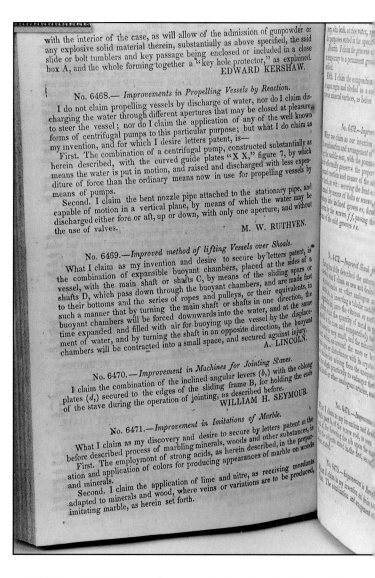

BOOK, ca. 1850. An entry for a patent by Lincoln in the *Report of The Commissioner of Patents for The Year 1849*, published in 1850. Lincoln had patented a method of floating a ship over a shoal. *From the Frank & Virginia Williams Collection of Lincolniana.*

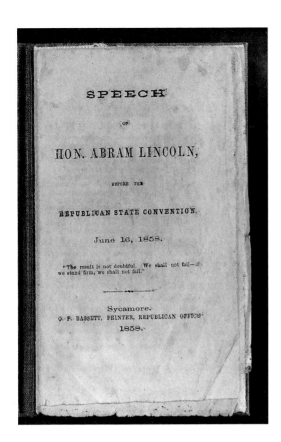

PAMPHLET, 1858. The first printing of Lincoln's "House Divided" speech. *Courtesy of Christies, New York.* Value $10,000-$15,000.

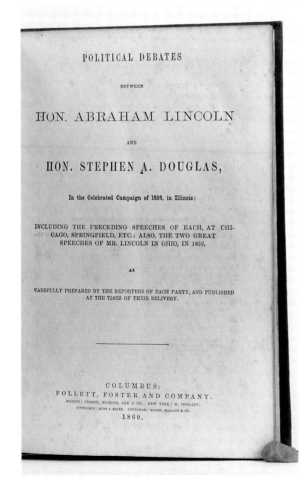

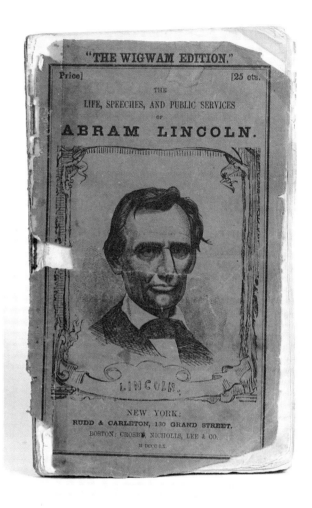

PAMPHLET, 1860. *The Wigwam Edition. The Life, Speeches and Public Services of Abram Lincoln.* The most popular campaign biography pamphlet giving details of his life and public service. Note the misspelling of Lincoln's first name in the rush to get the pamphlet printed and into circulation. 7.5 x 4.5 inches and 110 pages. *From the Joseph Edward Garrera collection.* Value $350-$450.

BOOK, 1860. *Political Debates Between Lincoln & Douglas.* 268 pages, 6.5 x 9 inches, 3rd edition. This edition notes over 16,000 copies have been sold. The 2nd edition states 8,000 copies sold. The 1st edition says nothing about copies sold. Value $125-$150.

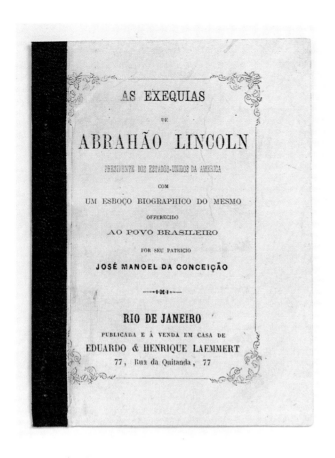

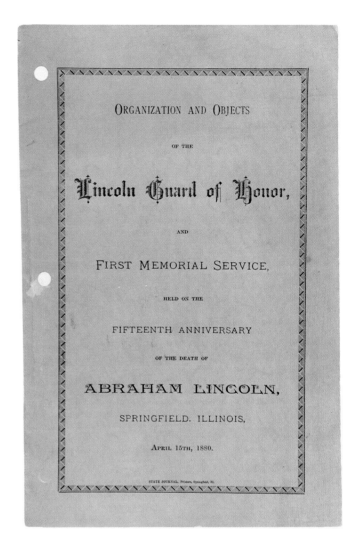

PAMPHLET, ca. 1865. *As Exequias de Abrahao Lincoln.* A very unusual eulogy pamphlet after the Lincoln assassination from Brazil. 4.5 x 5.75 inches and 40 pages. Value $100-$200.

PAMPHLET, 1880. A fifteen-year anniversary of a Lincoln Guard of Honor memorial service after Lincoln was assassinated. 5.75 x 8.75 inches and 14 pages. Value $35-$45.

TEMPERANCE PAMPHLET, 1894. Lincoln was constantly used by the temperance and prohibitionist groups to support their crusade against drinking. This is the reprint of an 1842 Lincoln speech. 8.75 x 6 inches and 14 pages. Value $60-$80.

BOOKS. A nice grouping of books about Lincoln and the assassination held up by a pair of plaster bookends showing Lincoln reading.

BOOKS, 1950-1970. Three miniature (2.75 inches to 3.25 inches tall) books about Abraham Lincoln. *A Song In His Heart*, published in 1970; *The Address of Carl Sandburg*, published in 1959; and *Abraham Lincoln*, published in 1950. Value $30-$50 each.

By Author

BAKER, LAFAYETTE C., 1897. *The United States Secret Service In The Late War*, by LaFayette C. Baker (1826-1868). The original issue came out in 1867 and sports a plain cover. This later edition has a great cover. Baker was chief of the Secret Service and in charge of the manhunt for Booth. Size 7 x 10 inches. Value $30-$40.

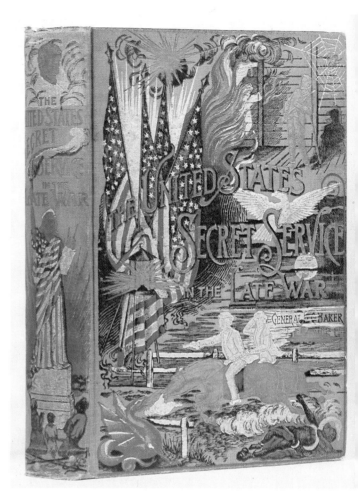

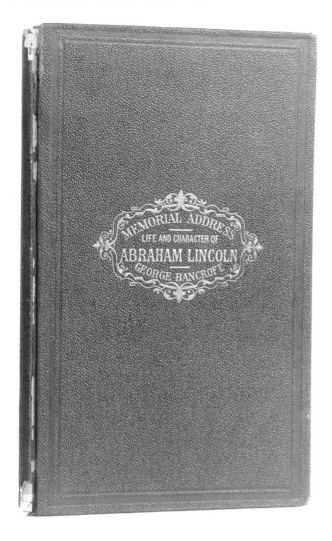

BANCROFT, GEORGE, 1866. *Memorial Address Life and Character of Abraham Lincoln*, by George Bancroft. 69 pages, 6 x 9.125 inches. Value $25-$35.

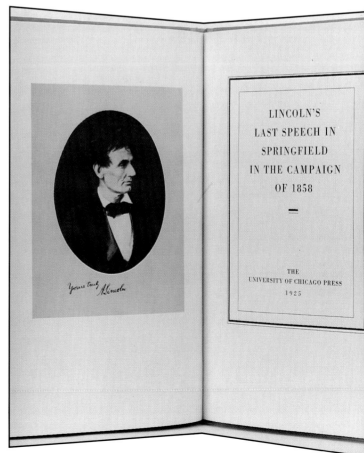

BARRETT, OLIVER R., 1925. *Lincoln's Last Speech In Springfield In The Campaign Of 1858*, created by Oliver R. Barrett and published by The University Of Chicago Press. 22 pages, 9.25 x 11.75 inches. Value $55-$85.

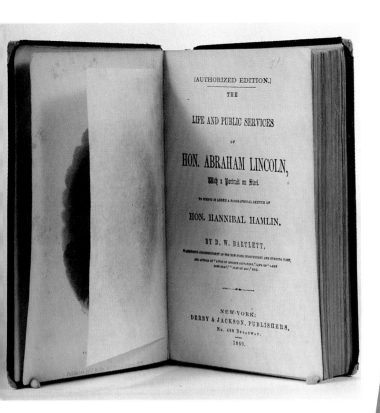

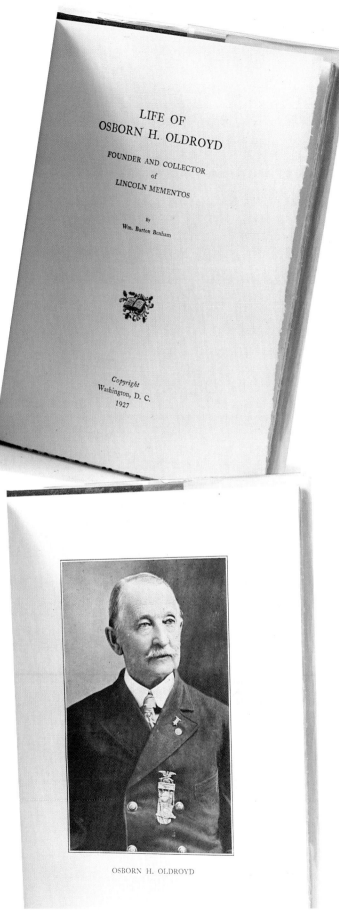

BARTLETT, D.W., 1860. *The Life and Public Service of Honorable Abraham Lincoln with a Sketch of Hannibal Hamlin*, by D.W. Bartlett. 354 pages, size 5 x 7.25 inches. An early biography of the Presidential and Vice Presidential candidates. This is a second edition. The first edition does not say "(Authorized Edition)" at the top. Value $75-$100.

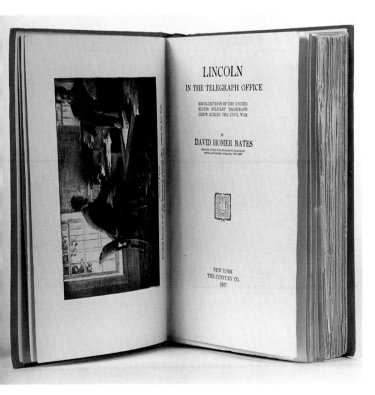

BATES, DAVID, 1907. *Lincoln In The Telegraph Office*, by David Homer Bates, manager of the War Department Telegraph Office during the Civil War. 432 pages, size 6 x 8.5 inches. Included with this copy is a tipped-in note from the author. Value $75-$100.

BENHAM, WM. B., ca. 1927. The early Lincoln collector, Osborn Oldroyd, who wrote numerous books about Lincoln, is the subject of this book. He is also pictured here. Value $40-$50.

BEVERIDGE, ALBERT J., 1928. A book collector's dream. The original four volume "Manuscript Edition" of Albert J. Beveridge's *Abraham Lincoln—1809-1858*. Beveridge completed the work but died before the set was printed. His widow wanted to create something special for those who supported her husband's work and had a special set made that incorporated tipped in pages of Beveridge's original handwritten manuscript. *From the Joseph Edward Garrera collection.* Value $450-$550.

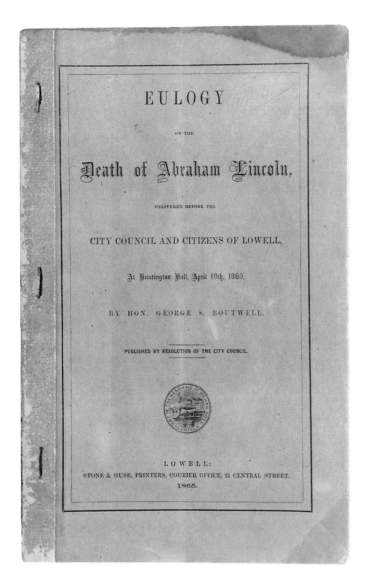

BOUTWELL, GEORGE, 1865. *Eulogy On The Death of Abraham Lincoln*, by George Boutwell. A pamphlet of the eulogy given in Lowell, Massachusetts, on April 19, 1865. 6 x 9.25 inches and 17 pages. Value $50-$75.

BUCKINGHAM, J.E., 1894. A rare copy of *Reminiscences And Souvenirs of The Assassination of Abraham Lincoln*, by J.E. Buckingham, Sr. 89 pages, size 6 x 9 inches. This was written by the man who was the ticket taker at Ford's Theater the night Lincoln was shot. Value $150-$200.

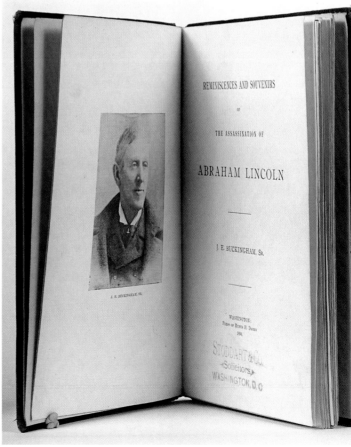

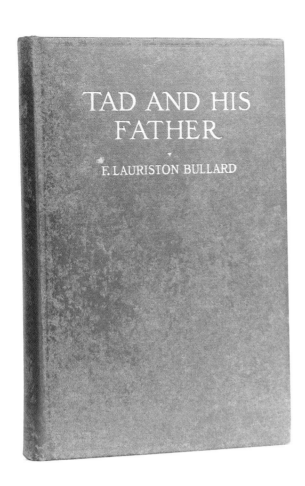

BULLARD, F.L., 1917. *Tad And His Father*, by F. Lauriston Bullard. 102 pages, 5.25 x 7.75 inches. Value $30-$45.

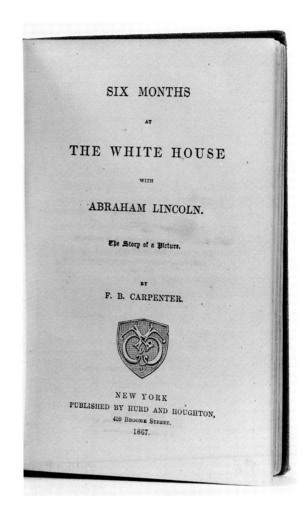

CARPENTER, F.B., 1867. *Six Months at The White House With Abraham Lincoln*, by Francis Bicknell Carpenter. Carpenter painted the painting entitled *First Reading Of The Emancipation Proclamation Before The Cabinet*. 359 pages, 5 x 7 inches, 1st Edition. Value $65-$85.

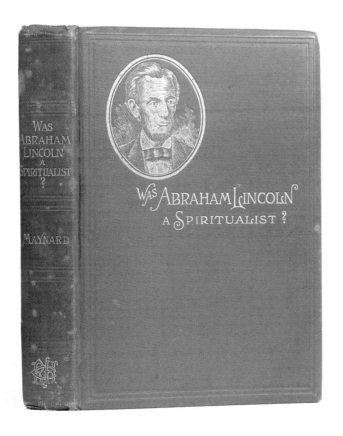

COLBURN, NETTIE, 1891. *Was Abraham Lincoln a Spiritualist?*, by Nettie Colburn Maynard. 262 pages, 5.5 x 7.5 inches. Value $50-$80.

CROSBY, FRANK, 1865. *The Life of Abraham Lincoln*, by Frank Crosby. 476 pages, 5.5 x 7.5 inches. Value $40-$55.

HILL, F.T., 1913. *Lincoln The Lawyer*, by Frederick Trevor Hill, 334 pages, 6 x 8.5 inches. The book was produced for the Lincoln Centennial Association and is number 787 out of an edition of 800. It was presented at their banquet on February 12, 1914. Value $50-$65.

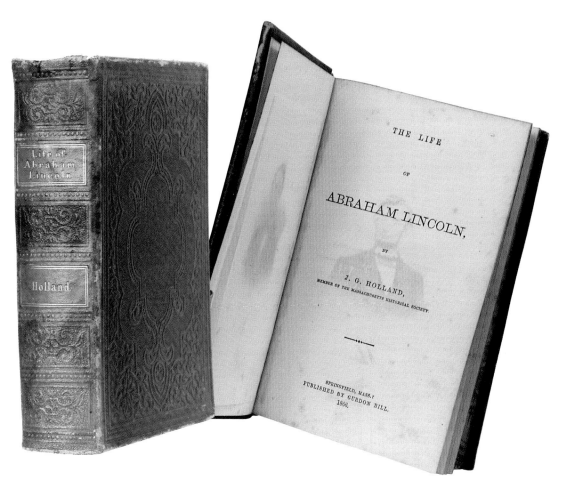

HOLLAND, J.G., 1866. *The Life of Abraham Lincoln*, by J.G. Holland, 544 pages, 6 x 8.75 inches. Value $50-$75.

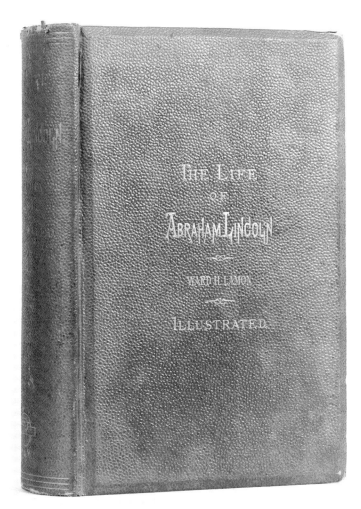

LAMON, WARD HILL, 1872. *The Life of Abraham Lincoln*, by Ward Hill Lamon. Lamon was Lincoln's friend and personal bodyguard for better than half of his presidency. 547 pages, 7 x 9.5 inches, 1st edition. Value $150-$200.

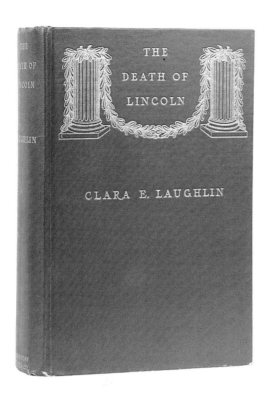

LAUGHLIN, CLARA, 1909. *The Death of Lincoln*, by Clara Laughlin. 336 pages, size 5 x 7.5 inches. Value $55-$80.

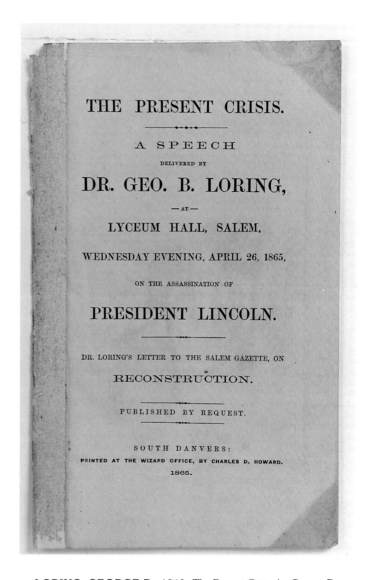

LORING, GEORGE B., 1865. *The Present Crisis*, by George B. Loring. After Lincoln was assassinated, speakers and books and pamphlets began to appear on the subject (is it any different today?). Value $45-$65.

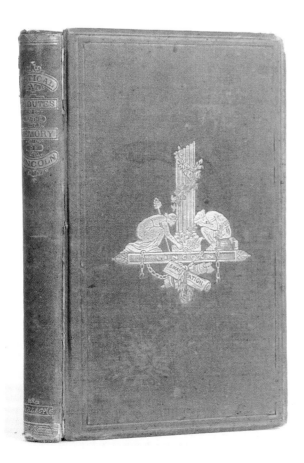

LIPPENCOTT & CO., 1865. *Poetical Tributes to the Memory of Lincoln*, by J.B. Lippencott & Co. 306 pages, 5.5 x 8 inches. Value $30-$40.

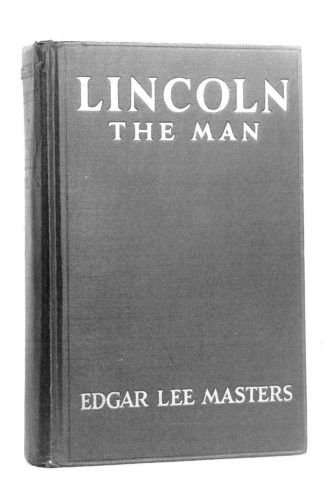

MASTERS, E.L., 1931. *Lincoln The Man*, by Edgar Lee Masters. An anti-Lincoln book. 520 pages, 6.5 x 9.5 inches. Value $40-$50.

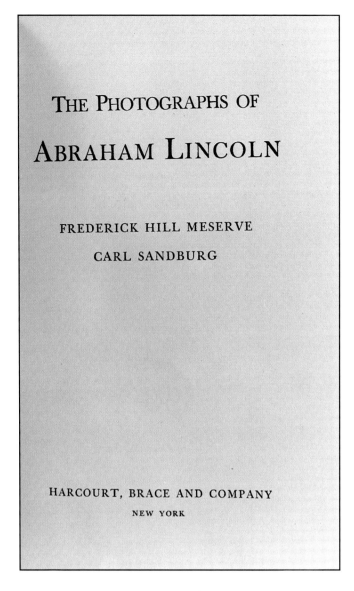

THE PHOTOGRAPHS OF
ABRAHAM LINCOLN

FREDERICK HILL MESERVE
CARL SANDBURG

HARCOURT, BRACE AND COMPANY
NEW YORK

MESERVE & SANDBURG, 1944. *The Photographs of Abraham Lincoln*, by Frederick Hill Meserve and Carl Sandburg. 100 photographs of Lincoln and more of the people around him, 6.5 x 9.5 inches. Value $50-$65.

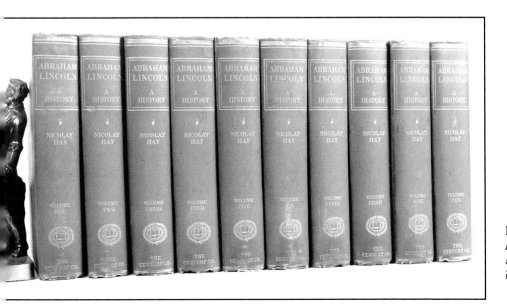

NICOLAY & HAY, 1890. *Abraham Lincoln—A History*, ten volumes by Nicolay and Hay, Lincoln's secretaries. 6.75 x 9.5 inches, 1st edition. Value $400-$500.

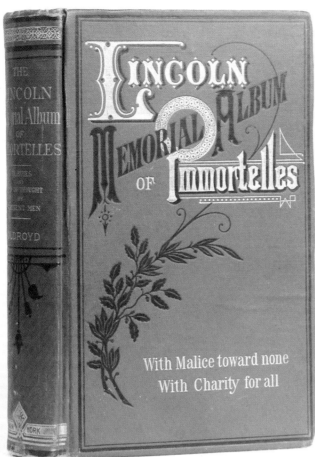

OLDROYD, O.H., 1883. *Lincoln Memorial Album of Immortelles*, by O.H. Oldroyd, the early Lincoln collector. 571 pages, 6.5 x 9.5 inches. Value $40-$50.

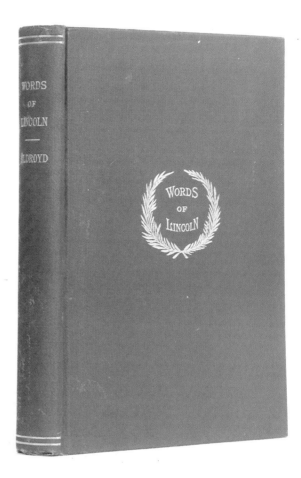

OLDROYD, O.H., 1895. *Words of Lincoln*, by O.H. Oldroyd, the early Lincoln collector. 221 pages, 5.75 x 8 inches. Value $30-$50.

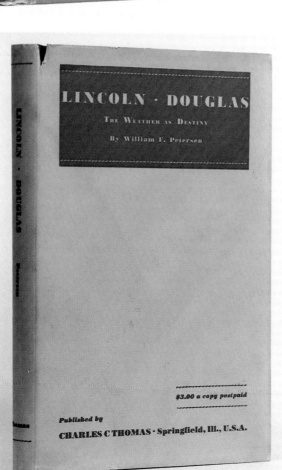

PETERSON, WILLIAM, 1943. *Lincoln-Douglas, The Weather of Destiny*, by William Peterson. How the weather affected the outcome of the Lincoln-Douglas debates. 211 pages, 6 x 9 inches. Value $40-$50.

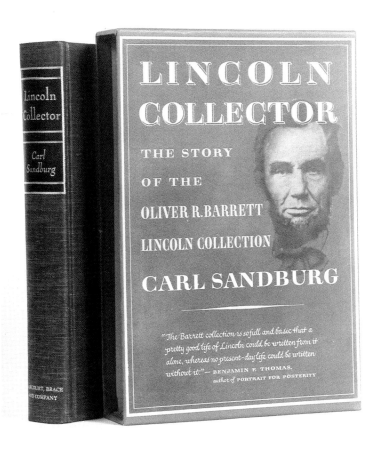

THE FIRST EDITION OF *Lincoln Collector* IS LIMITED TO 2425 COPIES, ON ALL RAG PAPER, NUMBERED AND SIGNED BY THE AUTHOR, OF WHICH ALL BUT ONE HUNDRED COPIES ARE FOR SALE. THIS IS COPY NUMBER 1154

Carl Sandburg

SANDBURG, CARL, 1949. *Lincoln Collector—The Story of Oliver R. Barrett's Great Private Collection*, by Carl Sandburg. 344 pages, 6.75 x 9.75 inches, signed and limited boxed edition. Value $100-$125.

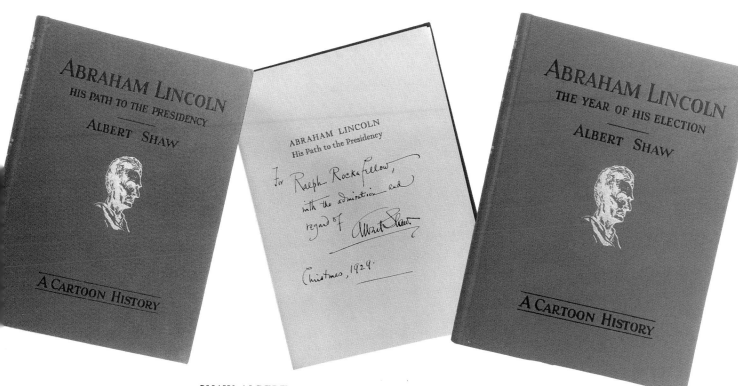

SHAW, ALBERT, 1929. *Abraham Lincoln, A Cartoon History*, two volumes by Albert Shaw. 263 pages (*Path to Presidency*) 277 pages (*The Year of His Election*), 8.5 x 11 inches, Inscribed 1st edition (the 2nd edition has a blue cover). Value $200-$250 (inscribed).

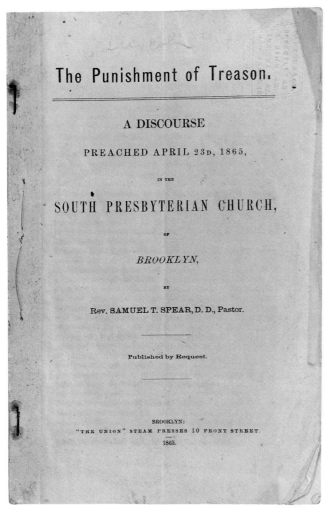

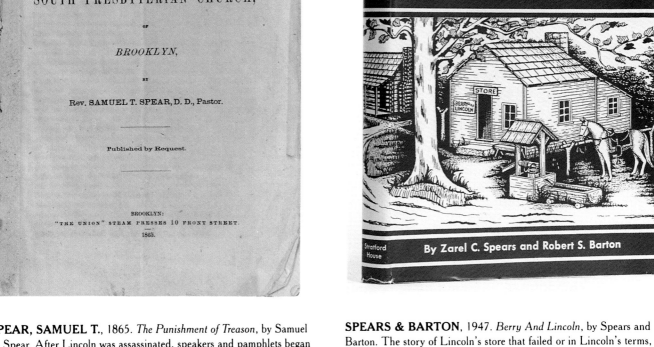

SPEAR, SAMUEL T., 1865. *The Punishment of Treason*, by Samuel T. Spear. After Lincoln was assassinated, speakers and pamphlets began to appear on the subject. 5.75 x 8.5 inches and 38 pages. Value $65-$80.

SPEARS & BARTON, 1947. *Berry And Lincoln*, by Spears and Barton. The story of Lincoln's store that failed or in Lincoln's terms, "winked out". 139 pages, 6.25 x 9.5 inches. Value $25-$35.

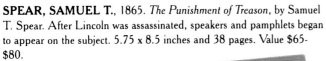

TARBELL, IDA, 1909. *The Life of Abraham Lincoln*, two volumes by Ida Tarbell. 426 pages (vol. 1) , 5.25 x 9 inches, Inscribed 1st edition. Value $140-$160.

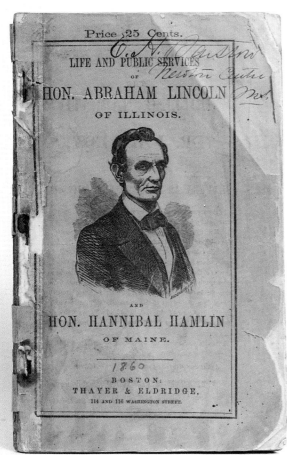

THAYER & ELDRIDGE, 1860. *Life and Public Services of Hon. Abraham Lincoln of Illinois and Hon. Hanibal Hamlin of Maine*, printed by Thayer & Eldridge. After Lincoln was nominated, books and pamphlets began to appear giving details of his life and public service. Not many have survived. 7.5 x 4.5 inches and 117 pages of which 110 are devoted to Lincoln and 7 to Hamlin. *From the Joseph Edward Garrera collection*. Value $300-$400.

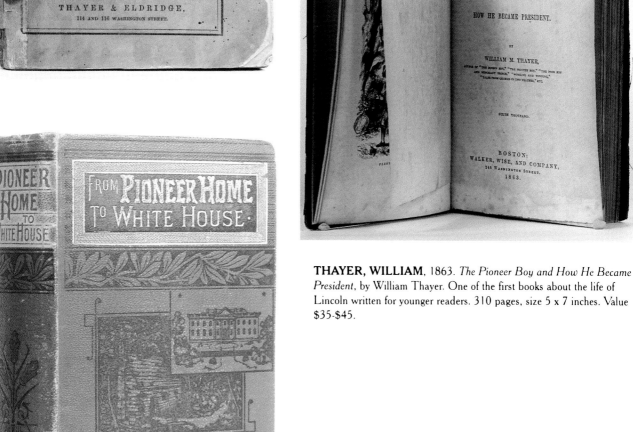

THAYER, WILLIAM, 1863. *The Pioneer Boy and How He Became President*, by William Thayer. One of the first books about the life of Lincoln written for younger readers. 310 pages, size 5 x 7 inches. Value $35-$45.

THAYER, WILLIAM M., 1883. *From Pioneer Home to White House*, by William M. Thayer. 469 pages, 5.5 x 7.75 inches. Value $30-$40.

THOMAS, BENJAMIN, 1952. *Abraham Lincoln*, by Benjamin Thomas. Thomas is acknowledged to be one of the finest authors on Lincoln's life. 561 pages, 6.5 x 9.5 inches, Signed and limited 1st edition. Value $250-$300 (signed), $40-$50 (regular ed.).

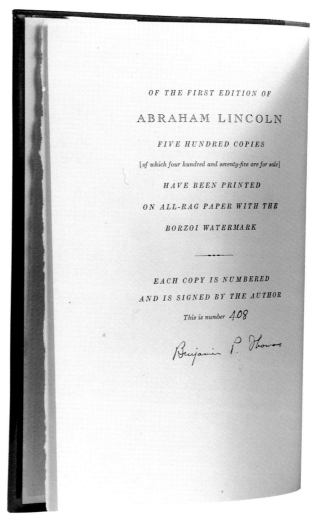

OF THE FIRST EDITION OF

ABRAHAM LINCOLN

FIVE HUNDRED COPIES

[*of which four hundred and seventy-five are for sale*]

HAVE BEEN PRINTED

ON ALL-RAG PAPER WITH THE

BORZOI WATERMARK

EACH COPY IS NUMBERED

AND IS SIGNED BY THE AUTHOR

This is number 408

Benjamin P. Thomas

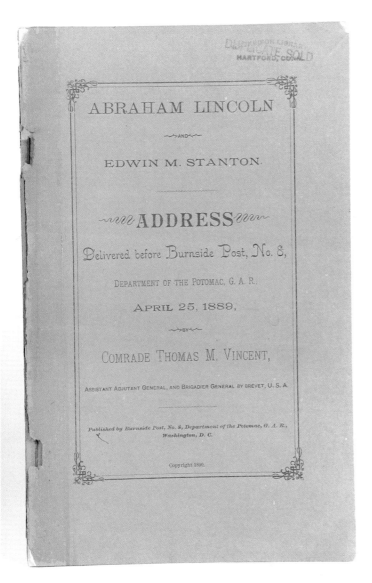

VINCENT, THOMAS M., 1890. *Address*, by Thomas M. Vincent Pamphlet of the text of a speech about Lincoln and Stanton given in 1889. 5.75 x 9 inches and 26 pages. Value $25-$35.

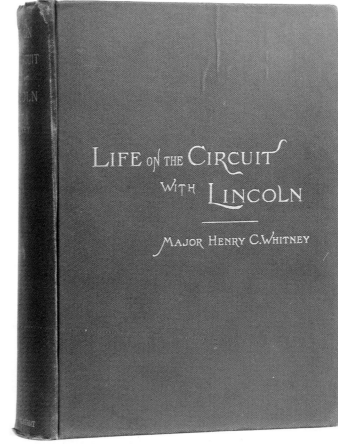

WHITNEY, H.C., 1892. *Life on The Circuit With Lincoln*, by Henry Clay Whitney who rode the circuit with Lincoln. 601 pages, 7 x 9.25 inches, 1st edition. Value $220-$280.

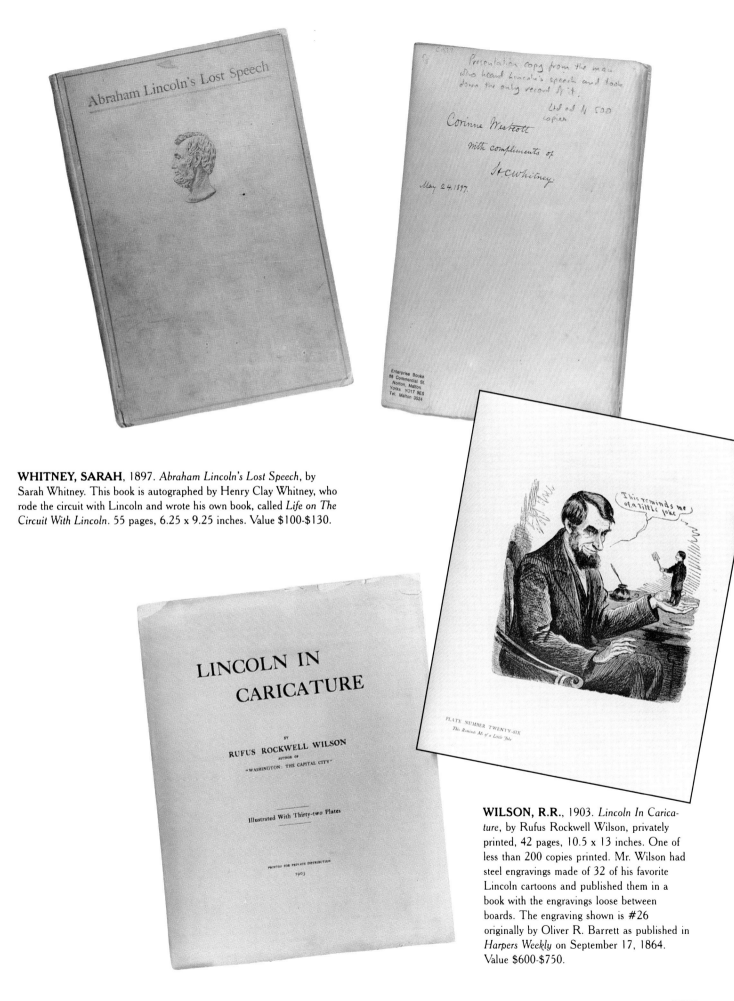

WHITNEY, SARAH, 1897. *Abraham Lincoln's Lost Speech*, by Sarah Whitney. This book is autographed by Henry Clay Whitney, who rode the circuit with Lincoln and wrote his own book, called *Life on The Circuit With Lincoln*. 55 pages, 6.25 x 9.25 inches. Value $100-$130.

WILSON, R.R., 1903. *Lincoln In Caricature*, by Rufus Rockwell Wilson, privately printed, 42 pages, 10.5 x 13 inches. One of less than 200 copies printed. Mr. Wilson had steel engravings made of 32 of his favorite Lincoln cartoons and published them in a book with the engravings loose between boards. The engraving shown is #26 originally by Oliver R. Barrett as published in *Harpers Weekly* on September 17, 1864. Value $600-$750.

NEWSPAPERS

NEWSPAPER, 1865. The *New York Times* of April 15, 1865, announcing the President has been shot at Ford's Theater. It states that he is believed to still be alive. *From the Joseph Edward Garrera collection.* Value $600-$800.

NEWSPAPER, 1860. *Harper's Weekly* of November 10, 1860, announcing the election of Lincoln and showing what he looks like. *From the Robert DeLorenzo collection.* Value $300-$400.

NEWSPAPER, 1865. The *New York Herald* of April 15, 1865, announcing the assassination of Lincoln. *From the Robert DeLorenzo collection.* Value $600-$800.

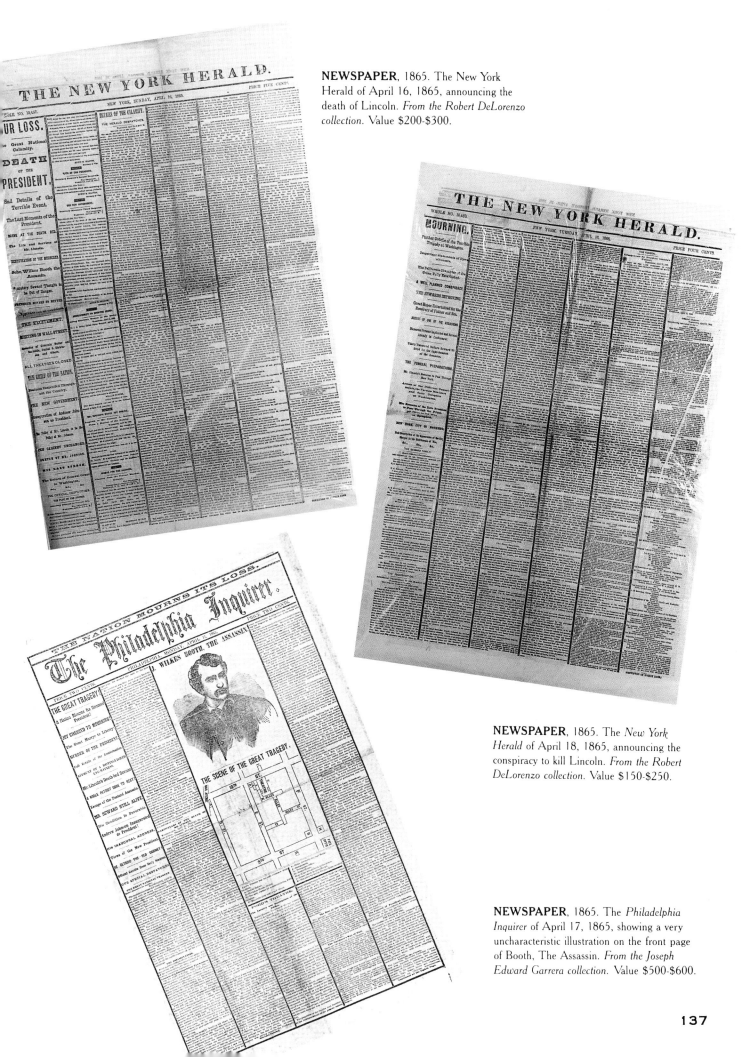

NEWSPAPER, 1865. The New York Herald of April 16, 1865, announcing the death of Lincoln. *From the Robert DeLorenzo collection.* Value $200-$300.

NEWSPAPER, 1865. The *New York Herald* of April 18, 1865, announcing the conspiracy to kill Lincoln. *From the Robert DeLorenzo collection.* Value $150-$250.

NEWSPAPER, 1865. The *Philadelphia Inquirer* of April 17, 1865, showing a very uncharacteristic illustration on the front page of Booth, The Assassin. *From the Joseph Edward Garrera collection.* Value $500-$600.

NEWSPAPER, 1865. The *New York Herald* of April 19, 1865, announcing the preparation for the funeral. *From the Robert DeLorenzo collection.* Value $150-$225.

NEWSPAPER, 1865. The *Washington Chronicle* of April 22, 1865, showing an uncharacteristic illustration on the front page of Lincoln and telling about the funeral service at the Capitol and the remains lying in state. Value $250-$350.

NEWSPAPER, 1865. The *New York Tribune* of April 25, 1865, reporting on the funeral procession in the city on April 24th. Value $125-$200.

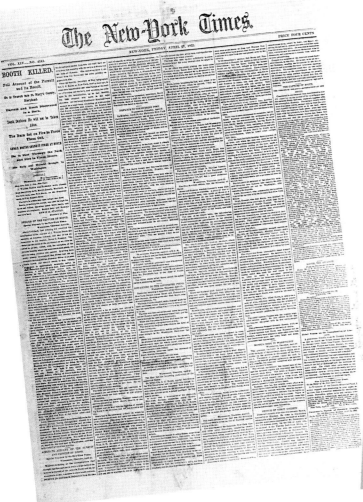

NEWSPAPER, 1865. The *New York Times* of April 28, 1865, announcing Booth was shot in the neck by Boston Corbett and died three hours later. Value $200-$350.

NEWSPAPER, 1865. An illustration from *Harper's Weekly* of April 29, 1865, showing the assassination of Lincoln. *From the Robert DeLorenzo collection.* Value $75-$120.

NEWSPAPER, 1934. A February 11 issue of a New Jersey paper showing some of the items from the Valentine Bjorkman collection.

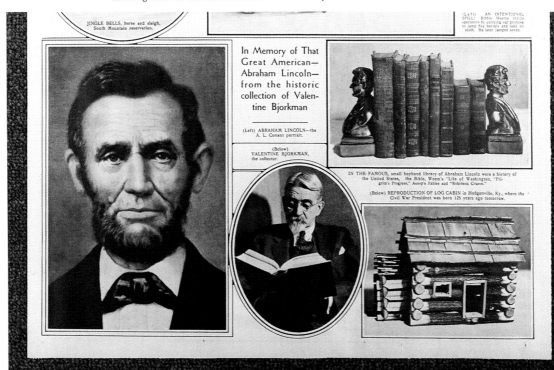

8. Coins, Currency, Tokens, & Medals

Lincoln was the first U.S. president to be depicted on regular U.S. coins. An unusual distinction that Lincoln has is that he is the only president to be facing right on a coin. All other presidents face left (Ben Franklin and Susan B. Anthony face right). Lincoln cents are among the most popular coins to collect. A good coin book or a subscription to a good coin magazine or newspaper will start the collector off in the right direction. Lincoln's image appeared on the penny in 1909, the centennial year. The image was created by Victor D. Brenner, who placed his initials on the reverse side of the penny until public outcry demanded that they be removed. The initials were removed part way through the year and stayed off the coin until 1918 when they were relocated to the underside of Lincoln's shoulder on the front side. Brenner's design was taken from the Brady photograph of Lincoln's profile.

Lincoln's image is easily recognized on the five dollar bill, but he also appeared on other bills. During Lincoln's presidency, there was a shortage of coins, which was the medium with which most people did business. Private banks printed their own currency (now called "Obsolete Currency") and to help further combat the shortage of coins, fractional currency (less than a dollar) was printed by the government. Lincoln appeared on the fractional currency. For dating purposes, obsolete currency showing Lincoln's image was printed during his presidency. The "Greenback" (currency with a green back) made its appearance during the Civil War when the government could not produce enough coins. Due to the shortage of gold, it decided to print paper money. $432,000,000 in greenbacks were issued between 1861 and 1865. In March 1862, Congress passed the Legal Tender Act requiring the acceptance of greenbacks as legal tender. The government took total control of printing money and private banks were stopped from printing their own. This created a money shortage. As the North was losing the War, or so it seemed, people lost faith in the government and began to hoard gold and silver coins. A coin shortage ensued, which led to merchants issuing tokens.

Tokens bearing Lincoln's face were minted before, during, and after the Civil War. They are known as Political Tokens, Civil War Tokens (CWTs), Store Cards, and Memorial Tokens. There are fifteen known different CWT varieties, showing Lincoln's face, available in several different metals. Politi-

MEDALET, 1861. 28mm medalet. Marked "Abraham Lincoln President—War Of 1861". Engraved by F.B. Smith who worked at 122 Fulton Street in New York City. The reverse side is blank. This has been called a dog tag or soldier's identification tag. Worth more with a traceable soldier's name. Value $140-$175.

cal Tokens were used to promote the candidate while the Civil War tokens were issued by private banks, merchants, and mints to use as regular coinage. Most CWTs did not have Lincoln's portrait and were either used as advertisements for a particular business (Store Cards) or contained patriotic themes such as "Preserve the Union". It is estimated that over 25 million tokens were produced during the war. In 1864, the government stopped all private production of tokens which were to be used as money and took over and increased production of all coins. Memorial tokens were produced after Lincoln's death and often had a hole in them to be worn as jewelry or just cherished as a keepsake.

When Lincoln ran for president, there were political medalets and tokens struck with his image, a log cabin, or some other popular campaign slogan. These were often made to be pinned or attached to the outside of a coat, just like today's political buttons. The 1864 election pieces are a bit tougher to find than the 1860 pieces. Medalets are currently very reasonably priced, but as with all Lincoln items, they are on the rise. Numismatic dealers treat them like coins rather than political items over 130 years old. The same medalet with a hole or in used condition is valued much lower than one in uncirculated condition. It is possible to put together a wonderful collection of these political medalets for very little money if you are willing to accept them in less than uncirculated condition. Most Lincoln collectors appreciate pieces that show wear or use. They like to know that someone wore the medalet or carried it in their pocket during the campaign. It is expected that within ten years, these medalets will be hard to find and expensive, regardless of condition.

To define some terms, the word "token" is used to describe a coin, usually about the size of a penny that could have been used as money. The word "medalet" is used to describe a Lincoln "coin" not used as money, with a diameter up to about 1.75 inches. The word "medal" is used to describe a Lincoln "coin" not used as money with a diameter from about 1.75 inches to about 3 inches. It also describes metal convention badges attached or usually attached to a ribbon. The word "medallion" is used to describe a Lincoln "coin" not used as money, with a diameter 2.5 inches to over 3 inches. A "badge" is usually worn as a means of identifying a participant in an event. A "fob" was usually attached to a watch or a set of keys to make them easy to locate or pull out of a pocket.

Medalets for the political races were produced during Lincoln's presidency (there are about fifty different Lincoln for President types and about eleven for Douglas), with many more produced after he died. There are reproductions of some of these medalets. Once Lincoln died, there were memorial medalets, Centennial medals, medals for the Lincoln monument in 1922, the opening of the Lincoln Tunnel in 1937, etc. Lincoln medals are still being made today to celebrate any Lincoln connected event.

TOKEN, 1864. A patriotic Lincoln Civil War token with a portrait on one side and a chain of thirteen links (for the original thirteen states) and the letters "OK". This is one of the more common Civil War Tokens showing Lincoln. 22 mm. Value $30-$50 (bronze), $100-$150 (white metal or nickel).

MEDAL, ca. 1862. This is a beautiful high relief Indian Peace medal created by the US Mint that would have been given to Indian leaders making treaties with the United States in 1862. It was made in silver, white metal, or bronze. 76 mm. It was also sold to the public Salathiel Ellis engraved the front, Joseph Willson engraved the back. Value $5,000-$6,000 (silver), $1,800-$2,200 (white metal), $300-$350 (bronze). There is a 62 mm size also available.

MEDALET 1864. The Lincoln/Washington 14kt Gold proof medalet was privately struck at the U.S. Mint. It was struck between September 1864 and October 1866. Records show 169 were struck in gold and 5,677 were struck in silver. The engraver was Anthony C. Paquet. Value $650-$800 (gold), $50-$65 (silver), $12-$15 (bronze).

MOURNING TOKEN, 1865. A memorial piece with an 1864 date on the front and memorial inscription on the reverse. The front side had been used on a political token in 1864. 22 mm. Value $70-$90.

TOKEN, 1864. A Lincoln Civil War token with a portrait facing right. 22 mm. Value $35-$45 (bronze), $100-$150 (white metal or nickel).

MOURNING TOKEN, 1865. A Lincoln memorial token with a portrait on one side and a sentiment on the reverse. 22 mm. Value $45-$55.

MOURNING TOKEN, 1865. A memorial token saying "Assassinated by the Plotters of Treason April 14, 1865". The reverse shows an obelisk and says, "Martyr for Liberty". White metal, 22 mm. Value $75-$100.

MOURNING MEDALET, 1865. A rare gilded brass medalet 32 mm. One side says, "Ab'm Lincoln, Died April 15, 1865 by the Hands of a Rebel Assassin, President of the U.S.". The other side says, "A Sigh, The Absent Claim, The Dead, A Tear." *From the Frank & Virginia Williams Collection of Lincolniana.* Value $250-$325.

MOURNING MEDALET, 1865. A memorial item made to look like a twenty-five cent piece. The 1864 date indicates it originally may have been a political medalet. White metal, 24 mm. Value $75-$100.

MOURNING MEDALET, 1865. Gilded brass medal meant to be worn as a pendant or hung from a pin. 25 mm long. The reverse says, "Abraham Lincoln, Martyr to Liberty, April 15, 1865". The dies were probably cut by Hugues Bovy of Geneva, Switzerland. Found in several metal finishes. Value $50-$75.

MEDALLION, ca. 1886. Bronze medallion honoring Lincoln. The first presidential medallion with a raised wreath pattern on the reverse. This item was reproduced. The later edition is a cheaper copy that lacks the fine detail and relief. 76 mm. *From the Robert DeLorenzo collection.* Value $200-$300 ($450-$600 in aluminum).

MOURNING MEDAL, 1866. Bronze medalet 3.25 inches (82 mm) in its presentation box. One side says, "Salvator Patriae". The other side says, "In Memory of the Life Acts and Death of Abraham Lincoln." The dies were cut by Emil Sigel. This medal can be found in different metals and in a 1.25 inch size (32 mm). *From the Frank & Virginia Williams Collection of Lincolniana*. Value $275-$325.

MEDALETS, MEDALLIONS & FOBS, A collection of medalets, medallions, and watch fobs showing Lincoln. (Top row) The left piece was issued for the opening of the Lincoln Tunnel in 1937, the center medallion is from the Lincoln Hotel in Paris, the right is dated 1909. (Middle row) top left is a silver 1909 Guardian Savings & Loan Ass'n. award, the large right piece is a GAR 1909 reunion item, top right is allegedly a Civil War badge. (Bottom row) left to right—H & D Suits advertising piece, Illinois Watch Co. advertising piece, Unknown, 1912 Republican National Convention piece, a school medalet for an essay, 1929 Jackson Michigan 75th anniversary of Republican party, Compeer fob. *From the Robert DeLorenzo collection.*

LINCOLN PENNY, 1909 S VDB. This is the first and most famous Lincoln penny. Victor D. Brenner's initials appear at the bottom of the reverse side. Critics complained the initials were too prominent. They were removed, and in 1918 replaced on the front side below Lincoln's shoulder. Uncirculated Value $800-$900.

MEDALET, 1906. A 1.5 inch (38 mm) brass medalet produced for the 1906 Republican convention in Philadelphia. A very high quality piece. Value $35-$50.

MEDAL, ca. 1909. A Lincoln medal, 3 inches in diameter (76 mm), by the son of life mask maker Leonard Wells Volk, marked "copyright Douglas Volk, Del., Charles Hinton, Sc." *From the Frank & Virginia Williams Collection of Lincolniana.* Value $100-$125.

MEDALLION, ca. 1909. A 2.5 inch medallion celebrating the Emancipation Proclamation on the centennial of Lincoln's birth. Brass, sculpted by J.E. Roine. Value $75-$90.

WATCH MEDALET, 1909. A 1.25 inch (32 mm) medal advertising the Lincoln watch made by the Illinois Watch Company. The medal was made by Whitehead & Hoag. Value $35-$45.

MEDALET, 1926. This medal, showing Lincoln and Washington, was given or sold at the International Philatelic Exhibition in New York. 1.25 inches (32 mm). Value $35-$45.

COIN, 1918. A silver commemorative fifty cent piece honoring the Centennial of the State of Illinois. Value $60-$80.

MEDALLION, ca. 1928. A 4 inch medallion from the Lincoln Highway. In 1927, the Lincoln Highway Association was granted the right to install markers along the 3,000 mile highway. These medallions were set into concrete markers. On September 1, 1928, the Boy Scouts set up the markers at one mile intervals the length of the highway. Additional markers were made available to the public. Value $100-$150.

MEDALET, 1934. A "medalet" made of wood with Lincoln's image made for the Lincoln exhibit at the Century of Progress World's Fair. 1.375 inches (36 mm) in diameter. Value $20-$35.

MEDALLION, ca. 1937. Bronze medallion honoring the opening of the Lincoln Tunnel between New York and New Jersey. 3 inches (76 mm). *From the Robert DeLorenzo collection.* Value $50-$65.

LINCOLN PENNY, 1955. A 1955 double die. This is the most famous double die coin. Doubling is most visible on all the words and date. The doubling occurred when the original die was made. Somehow it moved and upon a second impressing, the die was doubled. Value $700-$900.

CENTENNIAL MEDALET, 1961. A brass medalet made to celebrate the centennial of Lincoln's inauguration. The front image of Lincoln and Hamlin was originally produced on a 1860 campaign medalet. 34 mm. Value $15-$20.

MEDAL, ca. 1963. Bronze medal for the 100th anniversary of the Emancipation Proclamation. 2.5 inches (63 mm). *From the Robert DeLorenzo collection.* Value $35-$45.

MEDAL, ca. 1972. Silver medal issued by the Lincoln Memorial University. It is unusual in that the reverse shows the back of Lincoln's head. 1.5 inches (38 mm). *From the Robert DeLorenzo collection.* Value $20-$30.

LINCOLN PENNY, 1972. A 1972 double die. Doubling is most visible on the words, "Liberty" and "In God We Trust". Value $175.

LINCOLN PENNY, 1983. A 1983 double die. The reverse side is doubled. Doubling is most visible on the words, "One Cent". Value $175.

MEDALLION, ca. 1993. A handsome medal created by the Ford's Theater Society. 3 inches (76 mm). Value $15-$20.

LINCOLN PENNY, 1995. A 1995 double die. Doubling is most visible on the word, "Liberty". Value $45.

9. PHILATELIC ITEMS

ENVELOPE, 1860. This envelope was found in an old desk that contained Lincoln's household effects. It was addressed to the President in Springfield and Lincoln's secretary, John Nicolay, has written "Needs no answer" on the side of the envelope. Value $250-$350.

This cover addressed to the Hon. Abraham Lincoln was found in an old desk. The desk had been sold at an auction of Lincoln household effect's. John Nicolay, Lincoln's secretary, wrote "needs no anser" on the left side.

STAR OF THE NORTH, OR THE COMET OF 1861.

PATRIOTIC ENVELOPE, 1861. The[re] was a great comet in the skies in 1861 and Lincoln is pictured as "the Star of the Nor[th]" Comets have been considered portents of important historical events. Value $80-$11[0]

ENVELOPE, ca. 1861. A wonderful hand colored patriotic envelope from Rhode Island. Most patriotic envelopes are somewhat dull, but not this one. It has great visual appeal. *From the Frank & Virginia Williams Collection of Lincolniana.* Value $60-$75.

ENVELOPE, ca. 1861. A patriotic Col. Ellsworth cover. Ellsworth was shot while removing a confederate flag from a hotel in Alexandria, Virginia. *From the Frank & Virginia Williams Collection of Lincolniana.* Value $25-$35.

ENVELOPE, ca. 1861. A patriotic Col. Ellsworth "event" cover. Here, Ellsworth lays dying while his men kill his attacker. *From the Frank & Virginia Williams Collection of Lincolniana.* Value $45-$55.

ENVELOPE, ca. 1862. A patriotic envelope showing Major General McClellan. *From the Frank & Virginia Williams Collection of Lincolniana.* Value $85-$100.

PATRIOTIC ENVELOPE, ca. 1863. A war period envelope stating "They can afford to do a wrong, I cannot". Value $65-$100.

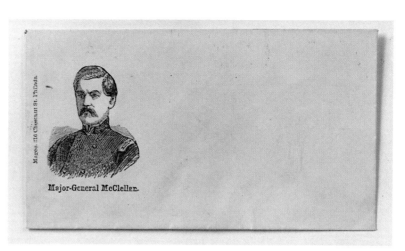

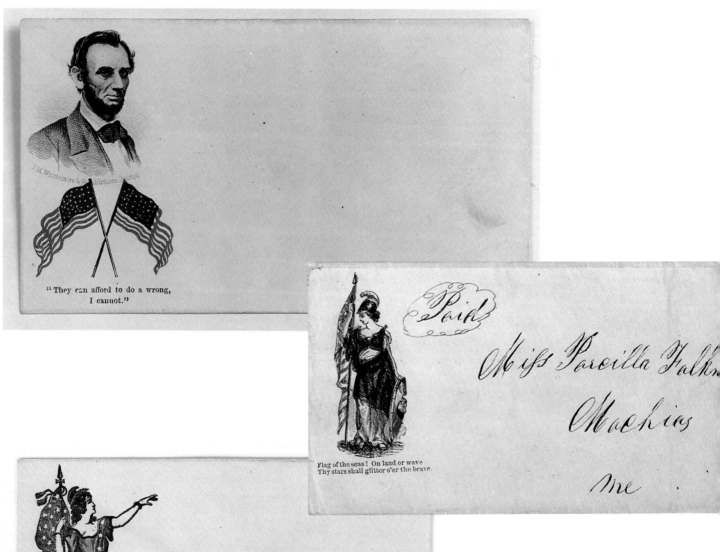

PATRIOTIC ENVELOPES, 1864. Patriotic envelopes showing Lady Liberty. Value $30-$40.

LINCOLN

ISSUE OF 1869 NINETY CENT LINCOLN

Carmine and Black - produced by the National Bank Note company
perforated 12 - grill 9 1/2 x 9 mm. photograph by C.S.German.
designed by E.Pitcher- vignette engraved by Joseph Ourdan -
frame by Douglas S. Ronaldson.

Plate Proof on India - Plate Proof on Card

Essay Proofs - These are colors and designs not
approved-

STAMPS, ca. 1869. The Lincoln 90 cent stamp from the issue of 1869 is one of the more difficult stamps to find. This sheet shows the stamp and some plate proofs that were tried in different colors that were never used. Value of the 90 cent Lincoln alone in canceled condition $1,500-$1,600.

STAMPS & COVER, 1923. Lincoln 3 cent stamps in a rare block of six with a Lincoln's birthday cancel. Value $375-$425.

FIRST DAY COVER, ca. 1934. Stamps attached to envelopes (usually cached or decorated) and postmarked on the first day of issue of that stamp are called first day covers. This is for a Lincoln event rather than the first day of issue of the stamp and is better called a commemorative cover. *From the Robert DeLorenzo collection.* Value $4-$6.

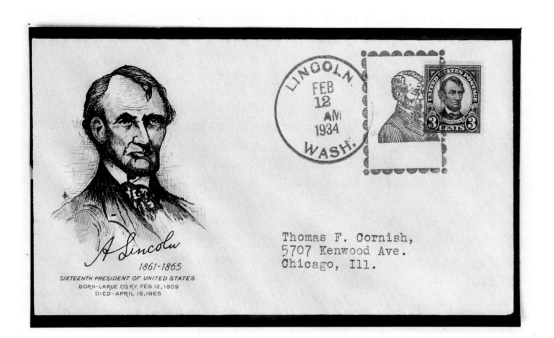

ENVELOPE, 1934. This envelope is known as a "five way cancel". It has a Lincoln stamp, a Lincoln cancel, a Lincoln post office, Lincoln's birthdate, and a Lincoln cachet. Value $90-$100.

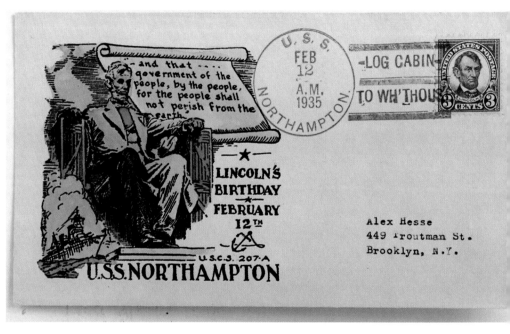

FIRST DAY COVER, ca. 1935. This is for a Lincoln event rather than the first day of issue of the stamp and is better called a commemorative cover. *From the Robert DeLorenzo collection.* Value $2-$4.

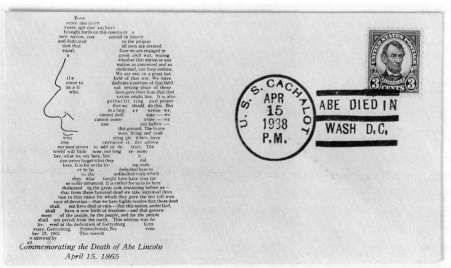

NAVAL COVER, 1938. Some philatelic collectors collect stamped envelopes postmarked on navy ships. There is a series of Lincoln covers from different ships.

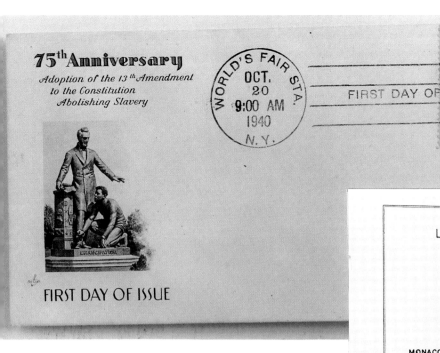

FIRST DAY COVER, ca. 1940. For the 75th anniversary of the abolition of slavery 3 cent stamp. *From the Robert DeLorenzo collection.* Value $2-$3.

STAMPS, 1956. Lincoln stamps from Monaco.

FIRST DAY COVER, ca. 1954. For the Lincoln 4 cent stamp. *From the Robert DeLorenzo collection.* Value $1.

57

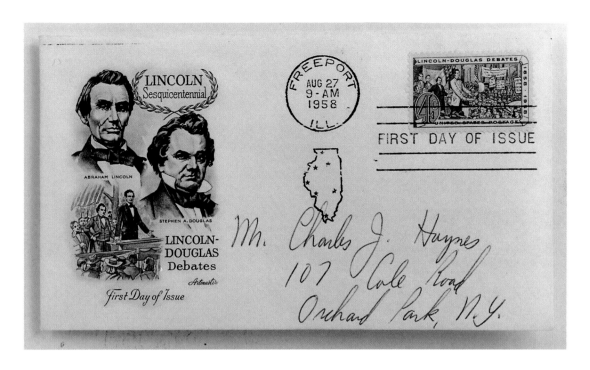

FIRST DAY COVER, ca. 1958. For the Lincoln-Douglas Debates
Sesquicentennial 4 cent stamp. *From the Robert DeLorenzo collection.*
Value $1.

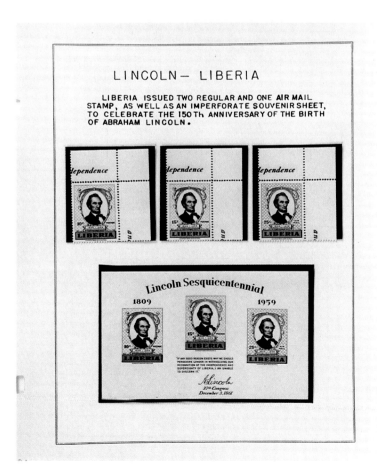

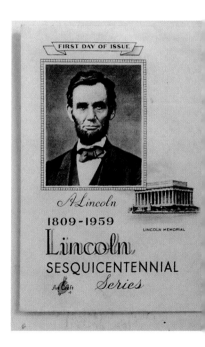

STAMPS, 1959. Lincoln stamps from Liberia.

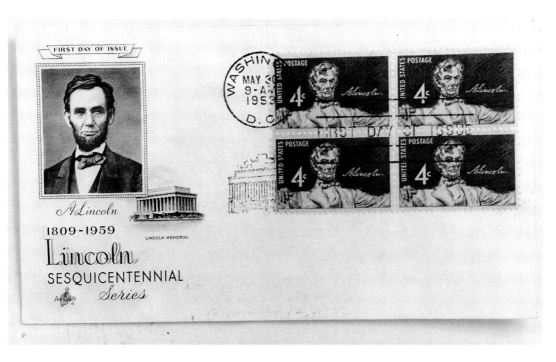

FIRST DAY COVER, ca. 1959. For the Lincoln Sesquicentennial. *From the Robert DeLorenzo collection*. Value $1.

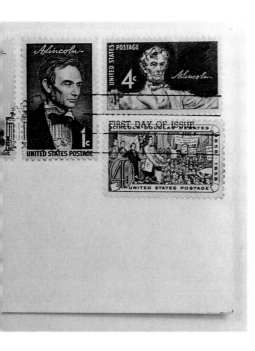

FIRST DAY COVER, ca. 1959. For the Lincoln Sesquicentennial. *From the Robert DeLorenzo collection*. Value $1.

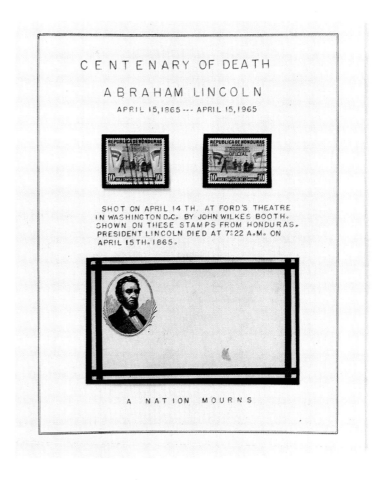

STAMPS & ENVELOPE, 1965 & 1865. Stamps honoring the 100 year anniversary of Lincoln's death along with an 1865 mourning envelope. Value, envelope $50-$80.

10. THE LINCOLN CENTENNIAL OF 1909

The year 1909 marked the 100th anniversary of Lincoln's birth. It was a big year for Lincoln items and the beginning of a greatly increased interest in the slain President and all items associated with his deeds. There were hundreds of Lincoln souvenirs including buttons, postcards, calendars, plates, busts, plaques, prints, etc. The Lincoln penny was introduced in 1909. While this book has a section that is identified as Centennial items, there are many more Centennial items distributed throughout the other sections as well.

BUTTONS, ca. 1909. This group of celluloid covered buttons were issued at the time of Lincoln's birth centennial. From left to right, top to bottom, they are a merchant advertising button (1.25 inches), Whitehead & Hoag—celluloid button makers advertisement (.875 inches), Indiana League (political group?) (.75 inches), and a shirt maker's advertisement (.875 inches). Value $15-$30 ea.

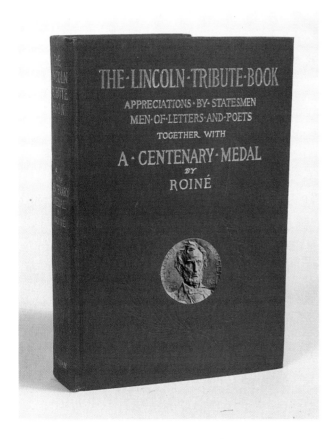

BOOK, 1909. This small (6.5 x 4.5 inches) book of 146 pages—*The Lincoln Tribute Book*—contains a centennial medal bound into its center. *From the Robert DeLorenzo collection.* Value $100-$150.

BUTTON, ca. 1909. A great button issued for the centennial. It is 1.5 inches in diameter. Value $20-$30.

BUTTON, ca. 1909. A celluloid covered button issued for the centennial. It is 1.25 inches in diameter. Value $20-$30.

BADGE, ca. 1909. A souvenir badge issued at the time of the centennial. It is 2.5 inches long. *From the Robert DeLorenzo collection.* Value $30-$50.

BUTTON, ca. 1909. A great button issued by Ward's Bread for the centennial. The artist gave him a good mouth and good eyes but lost it on the transition from one to the other. It is 1.25 inches in diameter. *From the Robert DeLorenzo collection.* Value $20-$30.

BUTTON, ca. 1909. A button and ribbon issued by a hotel for the centennial (black ribbon is added later). It is 3.5 inches tall. *From the Robert DeLorenzo collection.* Value $20-$25.

BUTTONS, ca. 1909. Two celluloid covered buttons made about the time of the 1909 centennial. From left to right, 1.25 inches and .875 inches. Value $15-$25.

CALENDAR, 1909. A Lincoln centennial calendar given out by the *Philadelphia Inquirer*. About 15 inches long. *From the Robert DeLorenzo collection*. Value $30-$40.

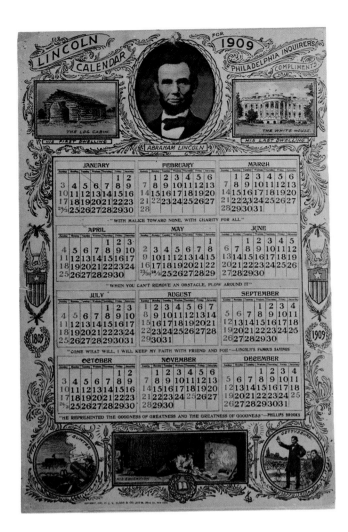

BUTTON, 1909. A button and ribbon issued for a reunion of the 19th Connecticut Volunteers. It is 3 inches tall. *From the Robert DeLorenzo collection*. Value $35-$45.

CALENDAR, 1909. A Lincoln centennial calendar published by the Westchester Women's Club. About 15 inches long. *From the Robert DeLorenzo collection*.

SHEET MUSIC, 1909. The Lincoln Centennial Grand March by E.T. Paull. Paull published sheet music is very collectible due to the great graphics they put on most of their covers. About 12 inches long. *From the Robert DeLorenzo collection*. Value $35-$45.

CENTENNIAL MEDALET, 1909. A 1.375 inch medalet made in honor of the Lincoln centennial. Value $35-$45.

CENTENNIAL MEDALET, 1909. This brass medalet was given out by the *Sunday American* newspaper. It probably was a prize for an essay on Lincoln at a school. 32 mm. Value $30-$40.

11. Lincoln's Birthday as a Holiday

Following Lincoln's death, there were calls from prominent politician and civic groups to celebrate Lincoln's birthday as a holiday. Little was done. It was believed that the southern states would fight against it. However, some states began to celebrate Lincoln's birthday as a state holiday, and by 1896 New York, New Jersey, Illinois, Minnesota, and Washington had declared Lincoln's birthday a state holiday. In 1900, Hanibal Hamlin joined the voices calling out for a Lincoln holiday. After the turn of the century and approaching the Centennial of Lincoln's birth, the concept of a Lincoln's birthday holiday became well established throughout the country. Its popularity can be measured by the hundreds of Lincoln's birthday postcards created and available to collectors. After the 1930s, the holiday celebrations began to fade. February became President's month and the nation began to find the fourth of July a better holiday for parades and celebrations. As we approached the Bicentennial of 1976, the leaders of our country began to look for holidays (where government employees were paid not to work) that could be phased out, since new Federal holidays had been officially declared. In 1971, Lincoln's birthday and George Washington's birthday were lumped together as "President's Day".

12. LINCOLN RELICS

The ultimate items for a collector to possess may be the relics from Lincoln's life or death. Examples can be the chair from his law office, a lock of his hair, a piece of his bloodstained collar worn the night that he was shot, items used during his funeral, and bits of wood, cloth, and stone from places he visited, lived, etc. These were the things that Lincoln used, touched, or that were directly associated with his life or death.

There has been a robust business of selling Lincoln relics that began right after he was shot. One bizarre story says that as Lincoln lay dying, the attending doctors would take the blood soaked bandages, sheets, and pillowcases, replace them with fresh linens and throw the soiled ones away. One enterprising individual took all the blood soaked items that he could find and began selling them the very next day. The doctors and others attending Lincoln were aware of the historical importance of the assassination and also saved bits and pieces of that dark day. Relic collectors went to Lincoln's home in Springfield and collected or bought up every item that was a part of Lincoln's life.

In collecting relics, the most important aspect is its provenance. A lock of Lincoln's hair is only a lock of hair until it can be proven to be cut from Lincoln's head. Without reliable provenance, a piece is only as authentic as the owner's word and worth what another collector will pay with that type of authentication. Some of the pieces shown may not carry a paper trail of their provenance, but it is believed that each is what it is claimed to be.

Wooden items are popular relics. The tree that Lincoln planted in front of his home, the wood from the Edward's house where Lincoln was married, a piece of the log cabin in which he was born and the rails that Lincoln allegedly split may be available to the collector. They are only as authentic as someone can prove or as a handwritten notation may claim.

Other interesting aspects of provenance are conflicting claims about who did the act that created the relic. The best example is the coins put over Lincoln's eyes when he died. Illustrated in this book is one of the coins placed over Lincoln's eyes by Dr. Leale, his attending doctor. There are at least two other people who were present at the time of Lincoln's death and who claimed to have placed the coins on Lincoln's eyes (coins were placed on a dead persons eyes to keep the eyelids closed until rigor mortis set in). It is actually possible that all of

them did so and that some souvenir seeker took the first and second set of coins, allowing time and opportunity for the next coin placer to lay down his coins. When offered relics of Lincoln's life or death, it is prudent to be skeptical and ask a few questions about provenance.

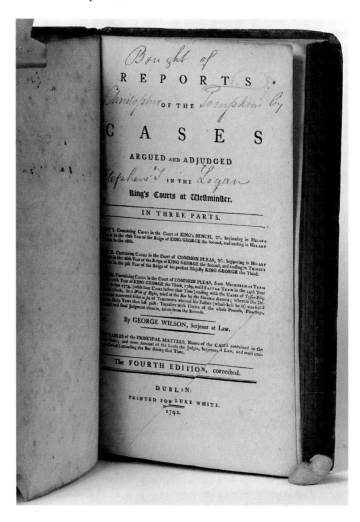

BOOK, ca. 1841. In 1840 Lincoln became partners with Stephen Logan, a partnership that lasted four years. This is Logan's copy of the 1792 *Reports of the Cases Argued and Adjudged in the King's Court At Westminster*. The early English law books were used in the United States, since there were not many American law books. Logan's name is written several times inside the book. It was typical for a lawyer to write his name numerous times in a book to prevent it from "walking off" with another lawyer. *From the Frank & Virginia Williams Collection of Lincolniana.*

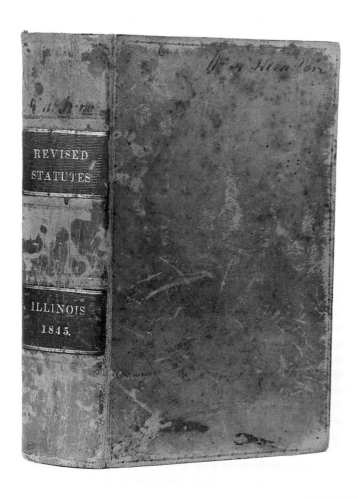

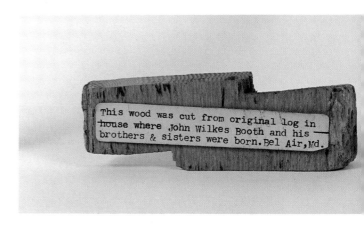

RELICS. A piece of wood cut from the log house in Maryland where John Wilkes Booth was born and a piece of the chimney from the farm house in Virginia where he died. These were personally collected at the two sites by Lincoln collectors.

BOOK, ca. 1845. In 1844 Lincoln became partners with William Herndon. This is Herndon's copy of the *Revised Statutes of 1845*. His name is written at the top on the cover and at least six more times inside the book. *From the Frank & Virginia Williams Collection of Lincolniana.*

GAVEL. The gavel is from a tree that Lincoln planted in front of his house in Springfield and the handle is from wood taken from the Edwards' house door frame under which Abe and Mary were married. A 1925 affidavit of H.E. Barker attests to these facts. Barker's Art Store sold these items in 1925. An interesting relic that can be found with or without its affidavit. *From the Joseph Edward Garrera collection.* Value $800-$1,200.

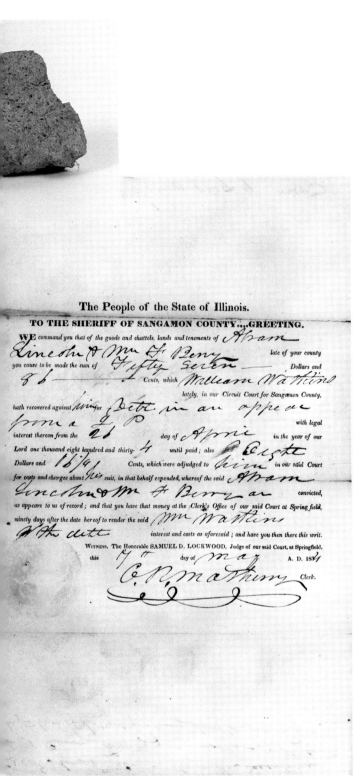

CHAIR FROM LINCOLN'S LAW OFFICE, ca. 1858. This chair was used by Lincoln in his law office in Springfield, Illinois. Bits of the splint seat are missing as one of the owners, many years ago, would give his friends a piece of the seat as a relic from the Lincoln Law office. *From the Gary Lattimer Family collection.*

WILLIE LINCOLN'S PICTURE AND HAIR, ca. 1860. A lock of Willie Lincoln's hair along with his photograph. Willie Lincoln died during Lincoln's presidency. *From the Gary Lattimer Family collection.*

LEGAL WRIT, 1834. A legal writ ordering the sheriff to seize and sell Lincoln's and his partner William F. Berry's property to satisfy the debts of their creditors. Their business failed and they could not pay creditors. Folio. *Courtesy of Christies, New York.* Value $5,000-$7,500.

TRUNK FROM LINCOLN'S HOME, ca. 1860. This trunk covered with undressed cowhide and original lock and key was left by Lincoln in Springfield, Illinois, when he moved to Washington. It was left at Elizabeth Todd Brown's (Cousin Lizzie—Mrs. Grimsley) house with things Lincoln wanted to save but did not want to take to Washington. He expected to get it on his return to Springfield. Cousin Lizzie would, after Lincoln's death, give friends and relic hunters items from the trunk. The trunk was in the Grimsley family for fifty years when it was given to H.E. Barker in 1919, who sold it to William H. Townsend in 1929. It is 33 x 17 x 14 inches. *From the Gary Lattimer Family collection.*

I send as you request, the pen with which President Lincoln signed the bill, emancipating the slaves in the District of Columbia.

April 16 1862   B. F. Wade

LINCOLN'S PEN, 1862. The pen reportedly used by Lincoln to sign the Act of Emancipation of the District of Columbia slaves on April 16, 1862. The outside of the box has "The Pen Of Liberty" written on it. *Courtesy of Christies, New York.* Value $8,000-$10,000.

LINCOLN'S INK WELL, ca. 1862. A 3.5 inch tall ink well that Lincoln brought with him from Springfield. You can make out the remains of the painted gold eagle on the front. Lincoln used this as his everyday inkwell and penned the Emancipation Proclamation's draft with it. When the Proclamation was formally signed, a fancier inkwell was used. *From the Gary Lattimer Family collection*

LINCOLN'S PENS, PENCILS & LETTER ACCESSORIES, ca. 1862. A leather case holding two dip pens, a pencil, a letter opener and a scraper/eraser that belonged to President Lincoln. All have wooden handles. They are appropriate to the period and there is a note attached indicating provenance. *From the Gary Lattimer Family collection.*

SPECTACLES, ca. 1864. These are the spectacles Lincoln owned and wore during his presidency, with the original case from C.R. Smith & Sons, Opticians, in Philadelphia. *From the Gary Lattimer Family collection.*

LINCOLN'S DIVIDERS, 1865. A metal divider, 5 inches tall, that belonged to Lincoln along with its provenance. The provenance is a letter on mourning paper from Robert Todd Lincoln dated May 21, 1865, along with its envelope to Major F.F. Eckert. Robert writes that Major Hay has told me that you would like a relic of my father and I would like to comply as I know how high you stood in his esteem. I am sending you these dividers which you have seen him use countless times on (battle) maps. *From the Gary Lattimer Family collection.*

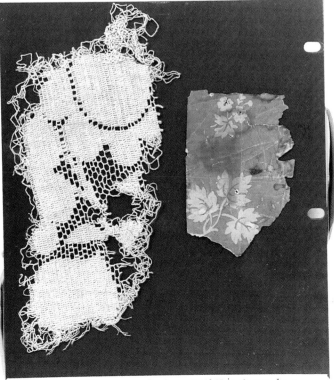

Section of wall paper, and piece of Nottingham lace from box No. 7 Ford's theater occupied by President and Mrs. Lincoln the night of April 14, 1865.

THEATRE RELICS, 1865. "Seat Taken" card, "Seat Reserved" card, and a Ford's Theatre ticket used in the theater on the night of the assassination. Accompanying them is a blood stained piece of paper that is marked as noting that the blood is that of Lincoln. The blood is more likely from Major Rathbone who was slashed by Booth as he made his escape from the box. *From the Gary Lattimer Family collection.*

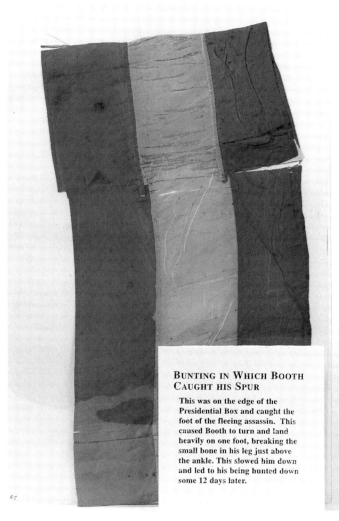

BUNTING IN WHICH BOOTH CAUGHT HIS SPUR

This was on the edge of the Presidential Box and caught the foot of the fleeing assassin. This caused Booth to turn and land heavily on one foot, breaking the small bone in his leg just above the ankle. This slowed him down and led to his being hunted down some 12 days later.

THEATRE RELIC, 1865. A portion of the bunting used on the President's box at Ford's Theatre in which Booth caught his spur when he jumped to the stage on the night of the assassination. *From the Gary Lattimer Family collection.*

THEATRE RELICS, 1865. A portion of the wallpaper and a piece of the Nottingham lace used in the President's box (Number 7) at Ford's Theatre on the night of the assassination. *From the Gary Lattimer Family collection.*

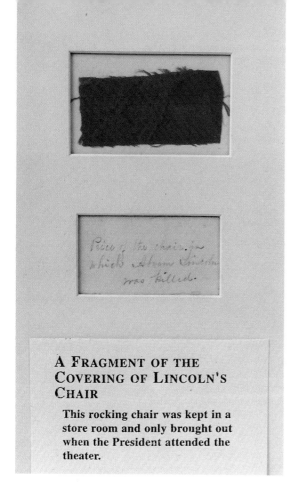

A Fragment of the Covering of Lincoln's Chair

This rocking chair was kept in a store room and only brought out when the President attended the theater.

THEATRE RELIC, 1865. A portion of the chair covering upon which Lincoln sat on the night of the assassination. It was taken from the bottom of the rocker. *From the Gary Lattimer Family collection.*

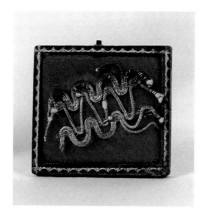

RELIC, ca. 1865. A piece of the fringe from one of the Lincoln funeral procession catafalques. This came with only a collector's assurance of authenticity. Value $40-$375 (depending upon accompanying provenance).

HANDKERCHIEF USED TO HOLD LINCOLN'S MOUTH CLOSED, 1865. This handkerchief was tied around Lincoln's chin after he died by Doctor Leale to hold his jaw from dropping and until rigor mortis had set in. The jaw has a tendency to drop open after death. It still shows Lincoln's blood upon it. The person who saved this relic put it into a book for safekeeping. *From the Gary Lattimer Family collection.*

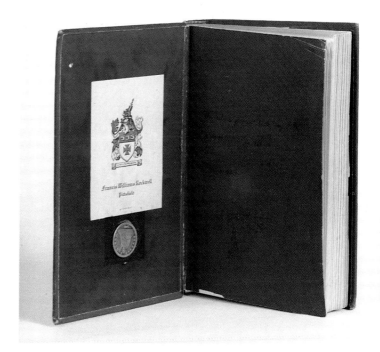

COIN PLACED OVER LINCOLN'S EYES, 1865. This coin is one of the two coins placed over Lincoln's eyes after he died. Coins were placed over the eyes to keep the eyelids down. The person who saved this relic put it into a book for safekeeping and noted when it was given to the recipient along with the above piece. *From the Gary Lattimer Family collection.*

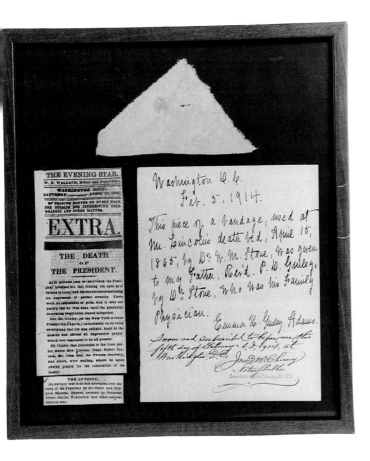

BANDAGE USED TO COVER LINCOLN'S WOUND, 1865.
This piece of cloth (4.5 inches along the bottom) was a portion of the bandage used by Doctor Stone to try to stop the bleeding. As the bandages became bloody, they were taken off and thrown away. At the time, an enterprising person gathered up the pieces and sold them as mementos. It still shows Lincoln's blood upon it. *From the Gary Lattimer Family collection.*
Pieces of the bloody bandage show up from time to time at auction and in sections, about the size of a postage stamp. With reasonable provenance, they sell for $700-$950.

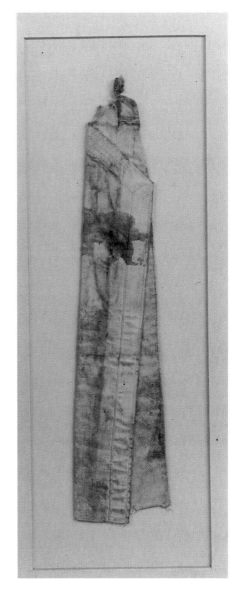

A PIECE OF LINCOLN'S SHIRT COLLAR, 1865. This piece of collar (8 inches long) was cut from the shirt Lincoln was wearing the evening he was shot. It shows Lincoln's blood upon it. *From the Gary Lattimer Family collection.*

PROVENANCE, ca. 1865. A wonderful piece of provenance that is about all one can expect to find to validate a lock of hair or other relic of Lincoln. The inscription says, "Touch not these locks of the hair of Abraham Lincoln and John Brown. They belong to and are held sacred by Frank J. Garrison". Years ago, some idiot ripped open the envelope and removed the locks of hair.

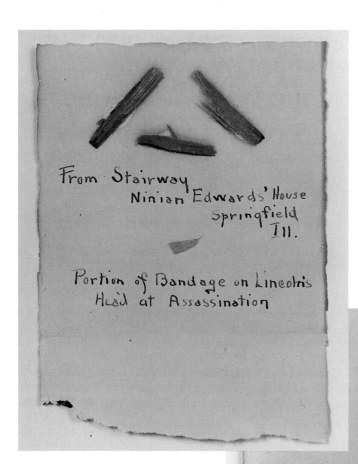

RELICS ca. 1865. A piece of wood taken from Governor Ninian Edwards house where Lincoln was married on November 4, 1842; a tiny piece of the bloody bandage from Lincoln's head; and a few specks of wood from rails Lincoln split. While these pieces have no provenance, other than the notations, they are probably authentic. The paper and writing are from the right period and the pieces are very small (if they were fakes, they would probably be bigger). The more common fakes would probably not include wood from the house where Lincoln was married. The linens used to stop the bleeding from Lincoln's wound are known to have been gathered up and sold to the public. Value $400-$600 for all.

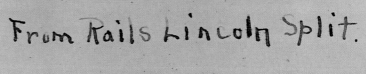

PASS, 1865. A print of the funeral catafalque showing Lincoln's coffin along with a pass (2.25 x 3.5 inches) permitting the bearer into the State House in Springfield to view Lincoln's remains. *From the Gary Lattimer Family collection.*

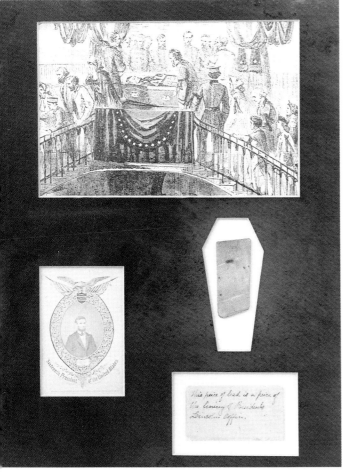

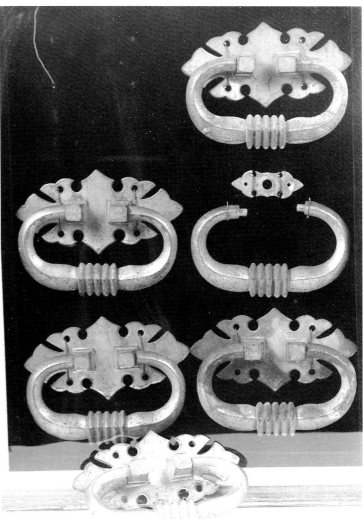

MOURNING RELICS, 1865. A grouping of leaves, fringe, and a star taken from one of the catafalques that bore Lincoln's body, mounted with a mourning card. *From the Gary Lattimer Family collection.*

LINCOLN'S COFFIN'S HANDLES, 1865. In 1901 Lincoln's coffin was disinterred to make sure that the body had not been stolen by Southern sympathizers and to rebury it in a new tomb. After removal and confirmation that the body was Lincoln's, the handles were removed and the coffin resealed in a lead sheath. The custodian of the Lincoln tomb, a Mr. Fay, accepted the handles and other items for display in a sort of museum he created at the tomb. When he died, his family claimed that the items in the museum were theirs, as heirs of Mr. Fay and the Government also claimed the items. A legal battle was about to begin when the Government dropped the claim. The family sold the relics that it had obtained from Fay's museum. Handles are about 6 inches wide. *From the Gary Lattimer Family collection.*

LINCOLN'S COFFIN SHEATHING, 1865-1901. A fragment of the lead sheathing which was cut away from Lincoln's coffin on September 26, 1901, so that Lincoln's face could be viewed before it was reburied in the new tomb. A plumber's helper, John F. Willey, cut away the lead, then soldered back a larger piece. Present at the time were Fleetwood Lindley, Mrs. Ed Johnson, F.K. Whittemore, J.C. Thompson, and John Whitney. *From the Gary Lattimer Family collection.*

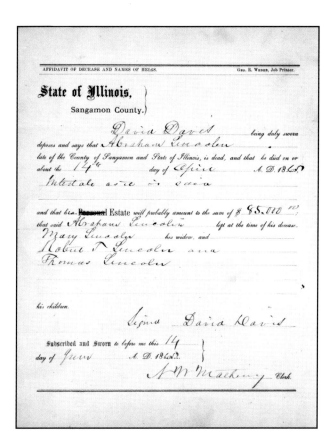

AFFIDAVIT OF DECEASE, 1865. The affidavit of decease for Abraham Lincoln filed by his friend David Davis. It notes his estate to be worth about $85,000. 4to. *Courtesy of Christies, New York.* Value $8,000-$10,000.

ROBERT TODD, 1922. Abraham Lincoln's surviving son as an older man wearing his spectacles.

SPECTACLES, ca. 1880. These are bifocal spectacles which belonged to Robert Todd Lincoln with the original case from Charles Waldin, Opticians, in Burlington, Iowa. The magnifying portion of the lens is glued into a cut out in the general viewing portion. *From the Gary Lattimer Family collection.*

PHOTO, ca. 1902. A photograph of
Lincoln's hat box. The information on the
back says Mrs. Lincoln gave the hat box to
Hugh Gallager who kept it for many years. He
sold it to H.E. Barker in 1900 and then it
was sold to Sam Hinkle who owned it when
the photo was taken. The card is from Ross
Photo Studio in Springfield. *From the Frank
& Virginia Williams Collection of Lincolniana.*
Value $300-$450.

REPLICA OF LINCOLN'S ROCKING
CHAIR. One dedicated Lincoln collector
wanted his Lincoln den to have the ambiance
of the Presidential box in the restored Ford's
Theater which shows how the scene appeared
the night of the assassination. He purchased a
modern copy of the famous rocker Lincoln was
sitting in when he was shot. The furniture
company agreed to make alterations to his
specifications to recapture historic accuracy.
The fabric of the chair had to be made
specially by the famous house of Scalamandre
and an upholsterer was instructed in reproduc-
ing the exact look and feel of the original. The
wallpaper is an exact facsimile of that in the
box at Ford's Theater. A glass model of
Booth's derringer is on the desk. A statue of
Lincoln stands guard near the chair.

13. MARY LINCOLN

MARY TODD, ca. 1843. This oil painting on canvas is believed to be a young Mary Todd. The reverse side of the canvas is marked, "J.H. Simpson", but the name appears to be the maker of the canvas and frame. This was acquired by noted Lincoln collector, Valentine Bjorkman, in 1932 at a cost of $125.00. This was at a time when autographed Lincoln letters were available for $100.00. 17 x 21 inches. *From the Joseph Edward Garrera collection.*

CDV, 1861. Mary Lincoln second generation or later (copy) photograph printed when Lincoln was President. This is identifiable as a second generation or later photograph as there are no back markings on this Brady photo and Mrs. Lincoln's features, such as the flowers in her hair, are washed out and contrasted. Value $70-$90.

MARY LINCOLN'S FATHER'S PICTURE AND HAIR, ca. 1860. A lock of Mary Todd Lincoln's father's hair is on the reverse side of this photograph of her father. *From the Gary Lattimer Family collection.*

Mrs. Lincoln. No 1.
Entered according to the act of Congress, in the year 1861, by M. B. BRADY, in the Clerk's office of the District Court of the District of Columbia.

Mrs. Lincoln. No 6.
Entered according to the act of Congress, in the year 1861, by M. B. BRADY, in the Clerk's office of the District Court of the District of Columbia.

CDV, 1861. Three poses of Mary Lincoln during her first year in the White House. The squarish photo is a portion of an unmounted CDV. The photos were taken by Brady's studio. Value $275-$350 each.

CDV, 1861. Two variations of Mary Lincoln in her inaugural ball gown.
The photos were taken by Brady's studio. Value $275-$350 each.

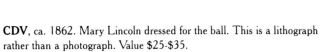

MRS. LINCOLN

CDV, ca. 1862. Mary Lincoln dressed for the ball. This is a lithograph
rather than a photograph. Value $25-$35.

MARY LINCOLN'S HAIR, ca. 1862. A lock of Mary Todd
Lincoln's hair along with her photograph. *From the Gary Lattimer Family
collection.*

CDV, 1861. Mary Lincoln during her first year in the White House. The photo was taken by Brady's studio. Value $275-$350.

CDV, 1861. Mary Lincoln while on a visit to Springfield. The photo was taken by Preston Butler and printed by Anthony's studio. *From the Frank & Virginia Williams Collection of Lincolniana.* Value $275-$350.

CDV, 1861. Mary Lincoln during her first year in the White House. The photo was taken by Brady's studio. *From the Frank & Virginia Williams Collection of Lincolniana.* Value $275-$350.

CDV, 1863 & 1861. Mary Lincoln second generation or later (copy) photograph printed when Lincoln was President. The right photo is the earlier of the two while the left photo is Mrs. Lincoln in a mourning (Willie's death in 1862) dress. Value $75-$100.

CDV, 1862. Mary Lincoln dressed in her mourning clothes after the death of Willie Lincoln. *From the Frank & Virginia Williams Collection of Lincolniana.* Value $275-$350.

PRINT, 1864. A Rice & Allen engraving of Mary Lincoln, engraved by Samuel Sartain. Mary is wearing the mourning clothing she had taken to wearing since her son, Willie, died in 1862. 15 x 18.5 inches. Value $250-$350.

MARY LINCOLN'S EARRINGS, ca. 1865. Hand painted earrings that Mrs. Lincoln wore. It is believed that she wore these on the night that the President was shot. *From the Gary Lattimer Family collection.*

MARY LINCOLN'S VEIL, 1865. Mary Todd Lincoln's veil, worn on the night that the President was shot, along with a note from Elizabeth Keckly, Mrs. Lincoln's dressmaker identifying the piece. *From the Gary Lattimer Family collection.*

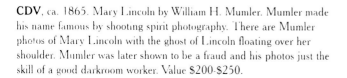

CDV, ca. 1865. Mary Lincoln by William H. Mumler. Mumler made his name famous by shooting spirit photography. There are Mumler photos of Mary Lincoln with the ghost of Lincoln floating over her shoulder. Mumler was later shown to be a fraud and his photos just the skill of a good darkroom worker. Value $200-$250.

COMMODE BELONGING TO MARY LINCOLN, ca. 1868. This commode was used by Mary Lincoln when she traveled after Lincoln's death. She probably used it on her travels in Europe where one could not always rely upon the quality of the hotel accommodations. It has a drawer in front, probably for holding paper and such. It stands 19 inches tall when closed. *From the Gary Lattimer Family collection.*

181

14. BOOTH, THE CONSPIRATORS, & THE ASSASINATION

CDV, ca. 1863. John Wilkes Booth. *From the Frank & Virginia Williams Collection of Lincolniana.* Value $150-$200.

CDV, ca. 1862. John Wilkes Booth. This is probably a second generation copy. It has no back markings. Value $75-$100.

CDV, ca. 1863. John Wilkes Booth by C.D. Fredericks & Co. of New York. Fredericks was a well known photographer of theatrical people. Value $125-$175.

J. WILKES BOOTH.

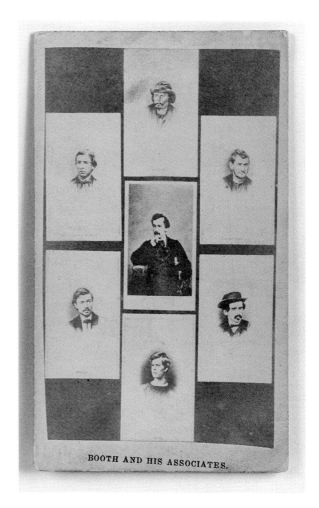

CDV, 1865. John Wilkes Booth and his associates. A composite of several photos on one CDV. Value $200-$275.

BROADSIDE, 1863. A J. Wilkes Booth theater bill from his January 28, 1863, performance in Othello. Booth theater bills turn up from time to time. *From the Frank & Virginia Williams Collection of Lincolniana.* Value $950-$1,500.

CDV, 1865. A view of the rocking chair Lincoln was sitting in when he was assassinated. Value $100-$125.

PRINT, 1865. A Currier & Ives uncolored lithograph *The Assassination of President Lincoln*. The portraits were based upon readily available photos and assembled to produce this print for the public. About 10.5 x 16 inches. Value $225-$325.

PRINT, 1865. A Currier & Ives hand colored lithograph, *The Assassination of President Lincoln*. 11 x 15 inches. *From the Frank & Virginia Williams Collection of Lincolniana.* Value $275-$375.

WOOD ENGRAVING, 1865. An H. H. Lloyd & Co. wood engraving *The Assassination of President Lincoln*. 12 x 16 inches. *From the Frank & Virginia Williams Collection of Lincolniana.* Value $250-$350.

MICHAEL O'LAUGHLIN.

Entered according to Act of Congress, in the year 1865, by A. GARDNER, in the Clerk's Office of the District Court for the District of Columbia.

EDWARD SPANGLER.

Entered according to Act of Congress, in the year 1865, by A. GARDNER, in the Clerk's Office of the District Court for the District of Columbia.

SAMUEL ARNOLD.

Entered according to Act of Congress, in the year 1865, by A. GARDNER, in the Clerk's Office of the District Court for the District of Columbia.

CDV, 1865. Michael O'Laughlin by Gardner. O'Laughlin was one of the Booth conspirators who was to take part in the abduction of Lincoln in 1864. When that attempt failed, Booth decided to kill Lincoln and O'Laughlin refused to take part in the murder. *From the Frank & Virginia Williams Collection of Lincolniana.* Value $250-$350.

CDV, 1865. Edman Spangler by Gardner (erroneously called Edward). Spangler was implicated as one of the Booth conspirators in the assassination of Lincoln. Spangler was a stage hand at Ford's Theater and probably took care of Booth's horse during the assassination. *From the Frank & Virginia Williams Collection of Lincolniana.* Value $200-$250.

CDV, 1865. Samuel Arnold by Gardner. Arnold was another of the Booth conspirators who was to take part in the abduction of Lincoln in 1864. When that attempt failed, Booth decided to kill Lincoln and Arnold would not take part in the murder. *From the Frank & Virginia Williams Collection of Lincolniana.* Value $250-$350.

CDV, 1865. Mary Surratt was implicated as one of the Booth conspirators. Her son, John Surratt was also involved. Mrs. Surratt owned a boarding house in Surrattsville, Maryland, and one in Washington, D.C., where the conspirators met. She was the first woman executed by the Federal government. This is probably a second or later generation photo and there are those that believe that this is not actually Mrs. Surratt. *From the Frank & Virginia Williams Collection of Lincolniana.* Value $100-$150.

MRS. SURAT.

DAVID E. HEROLD.

Entered according to Act of Congress, in the year 1865, by A. GARDNER, in
the Clerk's Office of the District Court for the District of Columbia.

CDV, 1865. David Herold by Gardner. Herold was one of the Booth conspirators. Herold accompanied Thomas Paine to Seward's house where Paine was to kill Seward. Then he was to help in the escape from Washington. *From the Frank & Virginia Williams Collection of Lincolniana.* Value $250-$350.

CDV, 1865. Thomas P. "Boston" Corbett, probably by Brady's studio. Corbett shot Booth when he resisted capture. The men were told to capture Booth alive, but Corbett claims the Lord's angel told him to shoot Booth. *From the Frank & Virginia Williams Collection of Lincolniana.* Value $100-$125.

PHOTO, ca. 1865. A photo of the congressional committee that accompanied Lincoln's body on the train as it toured parts of the country. Here the committee stands before Lincoln's home in Springfield. 7.5 x 9.5 inches. *From the Frank & Virginia Williams Collection of Lincolniana.* Value $300-$400.

LITHOGRAPH, 1865. *The Capture of Harrold and Shooting of Booth,* by Kimmel & Forster. A 12 x 18 inch hand colored lithograph. *From the Frank & Virginia Williams Collection of Lincolniana.* Value $450-$650.

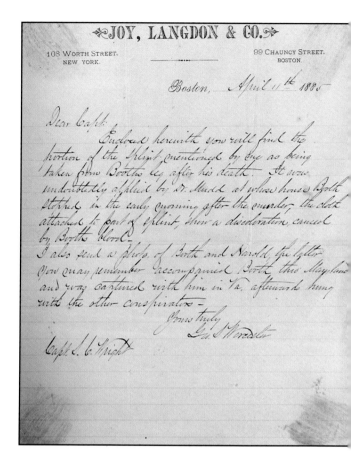

BOOTH'S BLOOD ON A PIECE OF SPLINT, ca. 1865. A photograph of John Wilkes Booth, a piece of the splint taken from his leg after his death and the written provenance. The 1885 letter signed by George Winston and addressed to Capt. S.C. Wright says that this is a piece of the splint with Booth's blood that was applied to Booth's leg by Dr. Mudd. *From the Gary Lattimer Family collection.*

PHOTO, 1865. Alexander Gardner's photograph entitled *The Execution of Mrs. Surratt and the Lincoln Conspirators.* There are at least seven different photos. They can be found in several sizes from a CDV to a large format such as this one (7 x 9 inches) and as reprints, made in the 1870s, by Taylor and Huntington. *From the Frank & Virginia Williams Collection of Lincolniana.* Value $3,500-$4,000 (large format with Taylor & Huntington or no markings); $4,500-$5,250 (large format with Gardner markings).

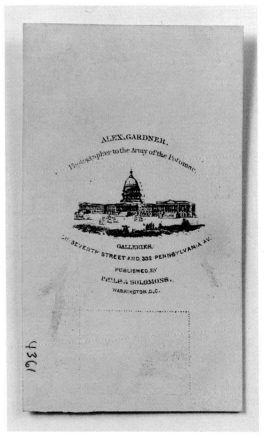

PHOTO, 1865. Alexander Gardner's photograph entitled (short version) *The Execution of the Conspirators, Photo 4.* This shows the completed hanging. It can be found in several sizes from a CDV to 7 x 9 inches. *From the Frank & Virginia Williams Collection of Lincolniana.* Value $750-$1,000 (CDV format with Gardner back marking).

PAMPHLET, 1865. *The Life, Crime and Capture of John Wilkes Booth*, by George A. Townsend. A booklet of 80 pages containing the story of the life, crime, and capture of Booth. 6 x 9.75 inches. Value $250-$350.

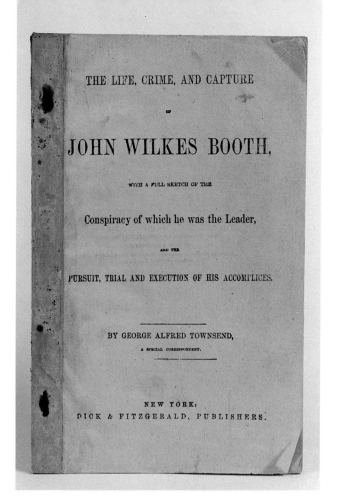

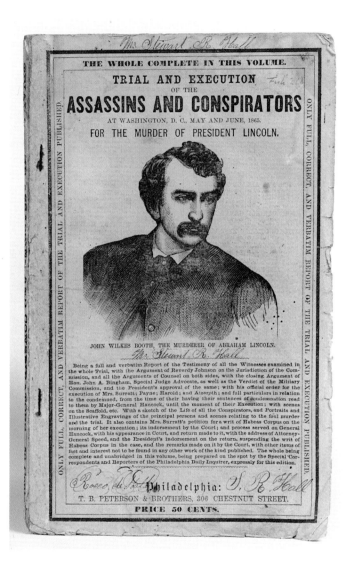

PAMPHLET, 1865. *Trial and Execution of the Assassins and Conspirators*, by T.B. Peterson & Bros. A wonderful illustrated booklet of 210 pages containing woodcuts of the assassins, maps of the escape, a transcript of the trial, the hanging, and other scenes and details of the event. 9.75 x 6.25 inches. *From the Joseph Edward Garrera collection.* Value $450-$550.

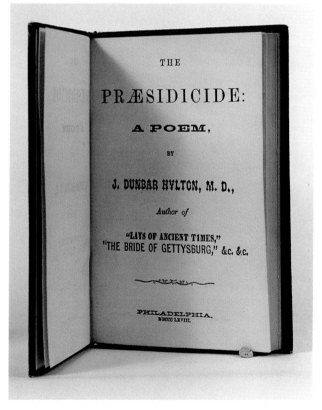

BOOK, 1868. A rare copy of *The Praesidicide: A Poem*, by J. Dunbar Hylton. This was a sympathetic poem about J.W. Booth, his feelings, and emotions. 194 pages, size 4.25 x 6 inches in bright blue covers. Value $100-$135.

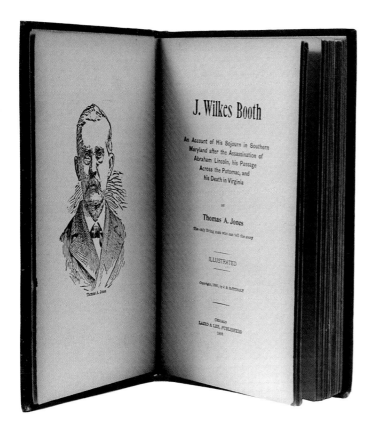

BOOK, 1893. A rare copy of *J. Wilkes Booth*, by Thomas Jones, the man who helped the assassin cross the Potomac. 126 pages, size 5 x 8 inches. Value $475-$500.

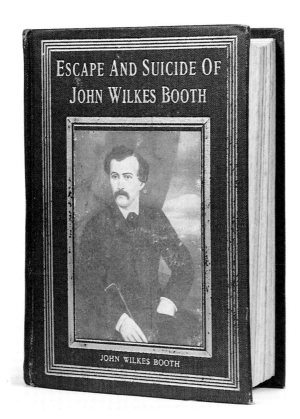

MEDALLION, 1871. This medal was awarded to George Robinson on March 1, 1871. George Robinson was credited with fighting off Lewis Paine and saving the life of Lincoln's Secretary of State, William Seward, on the night of the assassination plot to kill Lincoln, Seward and others. Engraved by Anthony C. Paquet, 3 inches (77 mm). Value $400-$500 (bronze); $4,000-$4,500 (silver).

BOOK, 1907. The *Escape and Suicide of John Wilkes Booth* by Finis Bates. 309 pages, size 5.25 x 7.25 inches. Value $225-$300.

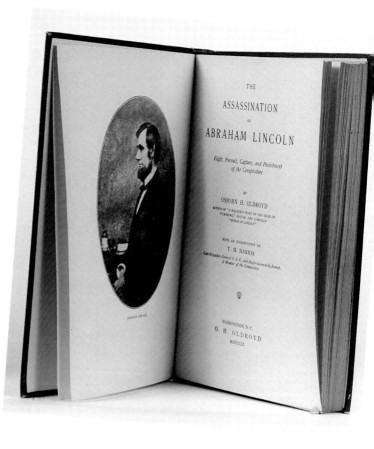

BOOK, 1901. *The Assassination of Abraham Lincoln* by the Lincoln collector, O.H. Oldroyd,. 305 pages, size 5.5 x 8 inches. Value $50-$80.

BOOK, 1928. A rare reprint of the even rarer copy of *The Unwritten History of the Assassination of Abraham Lincoln* by Richard Smoot. Twenty-four pages, size 5.5 x 7.75 inches. This is a signed limited edition (#74 of 100) reprinted by Orra Stone. There are currently three known copies of the original. Value $125-$175.

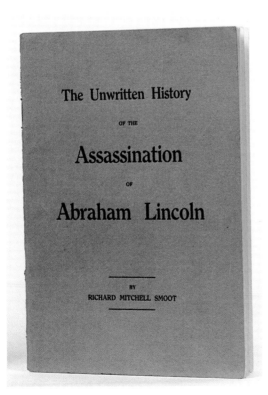

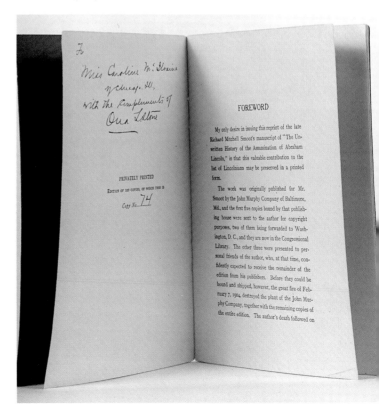

15. Autographs & Written or Printed Documents

One of the most popular Lincoln items a collector can own are letters and documents that he actually wrote or signed. Autographs are a field unto themselves. It is difficult to be an expert in numerous fields and to be an expert with Lincoln autographs. One must study hundreds of examples, including the best forgeries, to be right about a signature 95% of the time. If you are going to spend one thousand dollars or more on a Lincoln autograph, buy from an reliable dealer and get your guarantee in writing that the piece is what it is offered to be. The best dealers in this material will give you a lifetime guarantee on authenticity.

As you will see in these pages, Lincoln's signature varies in size and style. He signed thousands of documents and wrote thousands of notes and letters. The value of his signature varies. The least expensive item is the "cut" or "clipped signature". A cut signature is where someone, for whatever purpose, cut off Lincoln's signature from a document and saved just the signature. A step up from that is the "Document signed" (DS) or "Letter Signed" (LS) piece where someone else printed or wrote the document and Lincoln signed it. Next is the "autograph letter, signed" or "ALS" where Lincoln wrote the letter and signed it. Along with this category, you may find unsigned autograph letters where Lincoln, for example, wrote out a court document and did not sign it. Autograph dealers sometimes use the following notations: "folio" for an 11 x 14 inch or larger item, "4to" for an approximately 8 x 10 inch item and "8vo" for an approximately 5 x 7 inch item.

The most important criteria of value in an ALS is content. Letters discussing his emotions or the War (his grief over a military defeat or a dead soldier) or his dealing with top military leaders (questions to McClellan asking him when he will engage the enemy) or legislation (a reference to the Emancipation Proclamation) or a famous speech (the Gettysburg Address) are among the most sought after documents and will sell for tens or hundreds of thousands of dollars with some reaching over a million dollars. This is often the field for the collectors with the deepest of pockets. If you are offered an original Lincoln document of this caliber for only a portion of its value, be skeptical. Often it is not what it is offered to be.

Facsimiles and Forgeries

To make a complex matter more complex, there are older facsimiles of Lincoln's letters and autograph. There are documents, prints, and books containing what on first inspection appears to be an original autograph. Usually it is one printed by mechanical means. Lincoln's signature was printed on many prints and in many books about Lincoln. An amusing example: One woman with a machine printed "autograph" was sure hers was real because, in her naive reasoning, "Lincoln was an honest man and he never would have made a forgery." These printed autographs are not difficult to recognize. Carry an 8 to 10 power magnifying glass with you. A look with the loupe will greatly aid your quest for the authentic signature. Printed signatures lack many characteristics of the real signature. When writing, the hand presses up, down and across and varies its pressure on the paper. Signatures should show some of these variations. Printed signatures do not.

With the increasing value of and interest in Lincoln items, after his death, forgeries of Lincoln signed letters and documents began to appear. Two lesser known forgers were Eugene Field II and Harry D. Sickles. They often wrote Lincoln's name in old books, passing the book off as having been Lincoln's. Two better known Lincoln forgers were Charles Weisburg, who forged short autographed endorsements, that were appended to the bottom of authentic period letters, and Joseph Cosey, who forged legal briefs and letters (whose Lincoln signatures do not pass the Hamilton test below). For the collector of autographs, forgeries will always be a problem. For a good overview of Lincoln forgeries, read Charles Hamilton's book, *Great Forgers and Famous Fakes*. Hamilton gives the following tips for spotting a real Lincoln signature. The base of the "A" should be lower than the rest of the signature and the "A" is usually shorter than the "L". The "Lin" is written, the pen is then lifted from the paper, and the "coln" is attached to the "n". The "ln" is a bit higher than the other parts of the signature. There are obviously many more things to look for but if the signature fails several of the above tests, there is a good chance that it is a forgery. Also note that Lincoln liked to write with a very dark ink.

Collectors always want to believe that the piece that they have is rare and real. Forgers prey upon these beliefs. One collector purchased a framed "Lincoln" letter at a large flea market for several thousand dollars. He thought that he obtained a bargain that was worth five times what he paid, but learned that the signature was a forgery. In hindsight, he admitted that all he had paid attention to was the signature. It looked "good" and the overall letter, although written in a different handwriting, looked to be of the right period. He had not studied examples of Lincoln's handwriting but wanted to believe that he found an original. While it is not impossible to find an original Lincoln letter at a flea market, one should be skeptical and ask some questions of themselves and the dealer before spending a great deal of money.

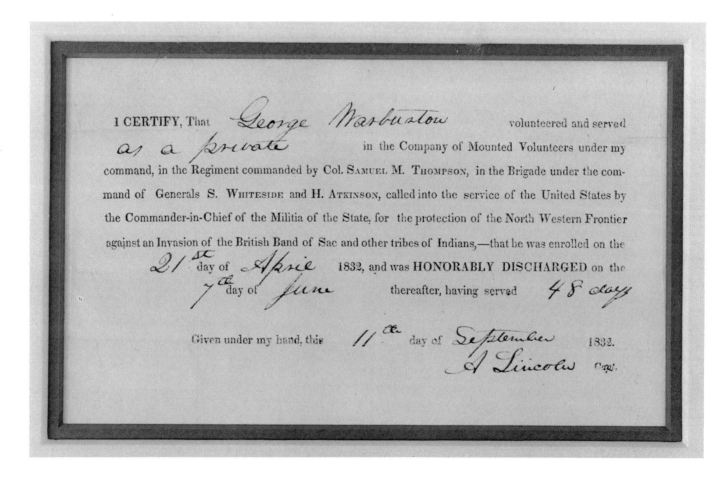

AUTOGRAPHED DISCHARGE, 1832. A very rare discharge from service for a soldier of the Blackhawk Wars, signed by Captain A. Lincoln. In 1832, an unemployed Lincoln joined the militia to make some money. His men elected him Captain. He served from April 21st to July 10th. *From the Frank & Virginia Williams Collection of Lincolniana.*

AUTOGRAPH LEGAL PAPER, 1839. A three page legal document prepared by Lincoln with three of his signatures and two of "Stuart & Lincoln". Lincoln was in partnership with Stuart from 1836 to 1841. Folio. *Courtesy of Christies, New York.* Value $18,000-$25,000.

AUTOGRAPH DOCUMENT, 1847. An autographed letter from Lincoln to his friend Andrew Johnston of Quincy, Springfield, Illinois, regarding some of Lincoln's poetry. 4to. *Courtesy of Christies, New York.* Value $20,000-$30,000.

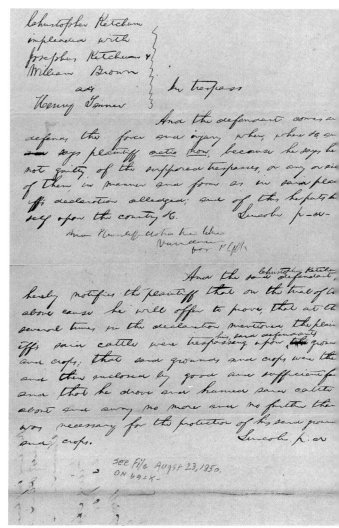

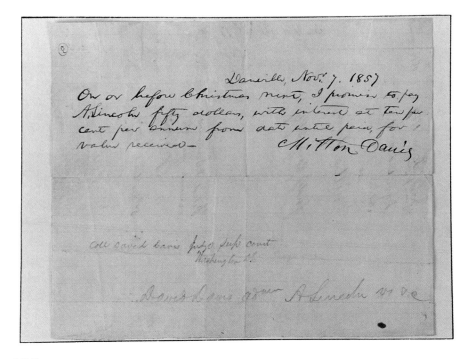

AUTOGRAPH LEGAL PAPER, 1850. A one page legal document prepared by Lincoln and signed "Lincoln & Herndon". 4to. *Courtesy of Christies, New York.* Value $15,000-$18,000.

AUTOGRAPHED PLEADING, 1850. An answer in a trespass case bringing in another person and saying his client is not guilty of the alleged trespass and that another person was the trespasser, written and signed twice by Lincoln. *From the Frank & Virginia Williams Collection of Lincolniana.*

AUTOGRAPHED NOTE, 1857. Apparently Milton Davis owed Lincoln fifty dollars and failed to repay it. Lincoln notes that he asks U.S. Supreme Court Justice David Davis, whom Lincoln had appointed, to collect the money. The note is entirely in Lincoln's hand, except for the signature of Milton Davis. *From the Frank & Virginia Williams Collection of Lincolniana.*

AUTOGRAPHED LETTER, 1858. A portion of a letter written by Hanibal Hamlin. Value $100-$125.

AUTOGRAPHED PLEADING, 1858. A pleading in assumpsit (an undertaking or promise to pay costs), signed by Lincoln and Herndon. *From the Frank & Virginia Williams Collection of Lincolniana.*

AUTOGRAPHED LETTER, ca. 1861. An ALS written and signed by Lincoln. It has particularly good content as it appoints George Thomas (the "Rock of Chicamaugua") and James Shields brigadier generals. Lincoln almost got into a duel with Shields in 1842, when Lincoln and Mary Todd, under assumed names ridiculed him in the newspaper. *From the Frank & Virginia Williams Collection of Lincolniana.*

Executive Mansion
June 13, 1861
Hon. Secretary of War
My dear Sir.

Owing to the pecu=
liar circumstances of Col. W.
H. Emory's case, and especially
because of the Commanding
General's written statement that
he is perfectly satisfied of
Col. Emory's loyalty to the Gov=
ernment, and that he deems
it important Col. Emory should
be restored to the service, especi=
ally if it can be done, to his
position of Colonel 1st Cavalry,
I direct that said Col. W. H.
Emory be allowed to withdraw
what purports to be his resignation,
and that he join his Regiment of 1st
Cavalry.—
Yours truly A. Lincoln

Executive Mansion,
Washington, Nov. 6, 1862.

Major General Butler:
My dear Sir

This morning the Secretary of the Treas-
ury read to me a letter of yours to him. He read to me, at
the same time, one from Mr. Denison (I think) at New
Orleans. I was much interested by the information in
one of them that some of the planters were making
arrangements with their negroes to pay them wages. Please
write me to what extent, so far as you know, this is
being done. Also what, if anything, is being done
by Mr. Bouligny, or others, about electing members
of Congress. I am anxious to hear on both these
points.

Yours truly
A. Lincoln

AUTOGRAPH DOCUMENT, 1862. A handwritten letter from
Lincoln to General Benjamin Franklin Butler on Executive Mansion
stationary wherein Lincoln asks for details on "Free Black Labor" in
occupied Louisiana. Some planters abandoned crops rather than pay
wages to former slaves to harvest them. 4to. *Courtesy of Christies, New
York.* Value $30,000-$40,000.

AUTOGRAPH DOCUMENT, 1861. A
handwritten letter from Lincoln to the
Secretary of War wherein Lincoln reinstates a
distinguished veteran of the Western Frontier
Wars. 8vo. *Courtesy of Christies, New York.*
Value $18,000-$22,000.

Sent from Washington

To Samuel T. Glover, Esq
St. Louis, Mo.
What news from up
river? — Lexington, Booneville,
or Jefferson City? Please answer.
A. Lincoln

AUTOGRAPH NOTE, ca. 1862. Lincoln
sends a telegram to a friend to find out the
news from the wild west of Missouri. *From the
Frank & Virginia Williams Collection of
Lincolniana.*

Executive Mansion,

Washington, January 8 . 1862.

...ajor General McClernand

My dear Sir

Your interesting communication by th...
...of Major Scates is received. I never did ask more,
...ever was willing to accept less, than for all the
...tes, and the people thereof, to take and hold their
...ces, and their rights, in the Union, under the Con-
...itution of the United States. For this alone have
...elt authorized to struggle; and I seek neither more
...less now. Still, to use a coarse, but an expressive
...us, broken eggs can not be mended. I have issued
...emancipation proclamation, and I can not retract it.
...fter the commencement of hostilities I struggled nearly
...year and a half to get along without touching the
...titution"; and when finally I conditionally determined
...touch it, I gave a hundred days fair notice of my
...pose, to all the States and people, within which time they
...la have turned it wholly aside, by simply again becom-
...good citizens of the United States. They chose to dis-

AUTOGRAPH DOCUMENT, 1862. Part of a handwritten two and a quarter page letter from Lincoln to General John Alexander McClernand on Executive Mansion stationary wherein Lincoln says "Broken eggs cannot be mended. I have issued the Emancipation Proclamation and I can not retract it". 4to. *Courtesy of Christies, New York.* Sold for $728,500 in 1991.

...im, according to the rules and discipline of
...re of the President of the United States, for
...this Twelfth day of June in the year
...d Sixty two, and in the Eighty sixth year

Abraham Lincoln

...ritten

AUTOGRAPH, 1862. A close-up of Lincoln's autograph on an engraved appointment document. *Courtesy of Christies, New York.* Document value $4,000-$6,000.

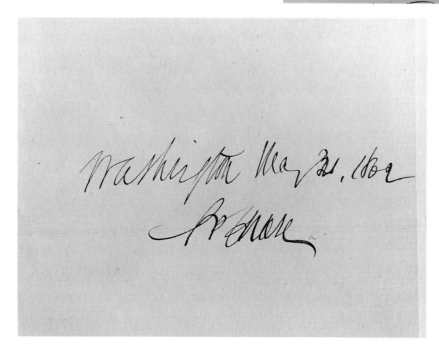

Executive Mansion
May 21. 1862.
Hon. Senator Simmons
  My dear Sir:
    This distressed
girl says she belongs to your
state; that she was here with
her father and brother, in
our Army, till they went
with it to the peninsula; that
her brother has been killed there, &
her father was prisoner—
and that she is here,
wanting employment to support herself. If you can be
satisfied that her story is
correct, please see if you
can not get Mr. Sec. Chase
or friend Newton to find her
a place. Yours truly A. Lincoln

To his Excellency,
  Abraham Lincoln,
    President of the United States.
  The undersigned memorialists, composing
the Board of Inspection of the Washington
Asylum, respectfully represent, that it is frequent-
ly the case, that we want the services of a
Magistrate, at the Asylum, which is attended
with inconvenience, and delay of business; to
obviate this we recommend Mr. Slater one of
the Commissioners, who is a reliable union
man, and is qualified for the position.
    W. G. H. Newman
    Wm McDuvitt

Mr. Slater was nomi-
nated as a Justice of the Peace
at my suggestion, unknown
to him, and was rejected by
the Senate, simply because no
one of the committee knew
him; nor did Mr Bowen,
then a clerk in the Senate, on
whom the committee much
relied for necessary information. Mr. S. was much mortified,
as I was also, & Mr Bowen ex-
pressed great regret when
learning who Mr S. was, &
at whose instance he was

AUTOGRAPHED LETTER, 1862. A
letter showing the human side of Lincoln,
written and signed by Lincoln to Rhode
Island U.S. Senator Simmons who was later
forced to resign in disgrace. It begins, "This
distressed girl says that she belongs to your
state…" *From the Frank & Virginia Williams
Collection of Lincolniana.*

LETTER, ca. 1862. An unusual item—a
letter to President Lincoln asking for the
appointment of a Magistrate—with a response
from someone other than the President,
written on the back of the letter. *From the
Robert DeLorenzo collection.* Value $300-
$400.

Washington May 21, 1862
  S P Chase

AUTOGRAPH, 1862. The autograph
signature of Salmon P. Chase—Secretary of
the Treasury. Value $100-$135.

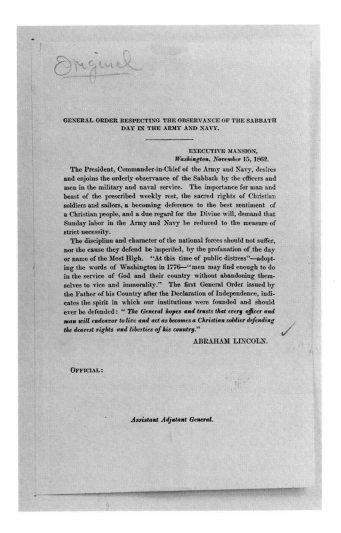

GENERAL ORDER RESPECTING THE OBSERVANCE OF THE SABBATH
DAY IN THE ARMY AND NAVY.

EXECUTIVE MANSION,
Washington, November 15, 1862.

The President, Commander-in-Chief of the Army and Navy, desires and enjoins the orderly observance of the Sabbath by the officers and men in the military and naval service. The importance for man and beast of the prescribed weekly rest, the sacred rights of Christian soldiers and sailors, a becoming deference to the best sentiment of a Christian people, and a due regard for the Divine will, demand that Sunday labor in the Army and Navy be reduced to the measure of strict necessity.

The discipline and character of the national forces should not suffer, nor the cause they defend be imperiled, by the profanation of the day or name of the Most High. "At this time of public distress"—adopting the words of Washington in 1776—"men may find enough to do in the service of God and their country without abandoning themselves to vice and immorality." The first General Order issued by the Father of his Country after the Declaration of Independence, indicates the spirit in which our institutions were founded and should ever be defended: "*The General hopes and trusts that every officer and man will endeavor to live and act as becomes a Christian soldier defending the dearest rights and liberties of his country.*"

ABRAHAM LINCOLN.

OFFICIAL:

Assistant Adjutant General.

GENERAL ORDER, 1862. Lincoln would issue a general order to his commanders during the war. The order would be printed and distributed. This one is about respecting the observance of the Sabbath day. It is about 4 x 6 inches. *From the Robert DeLorenzo collection.* Value $100-$135.

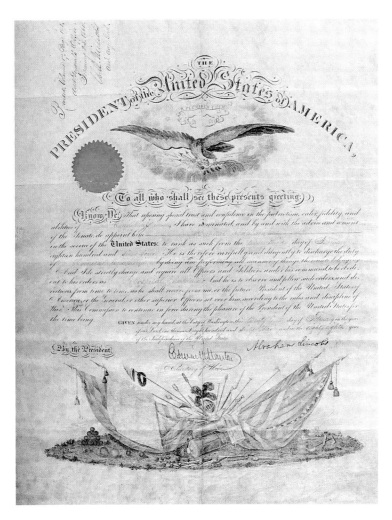

AUTOGRAPH DOCUMENT, 1863. An autographed appointment document appointing James B. McPherson a Major General. It also contains Edward Stanton's signature. 4to. *Courtesy of Christies, New York.* Value $9,000-$12,000.

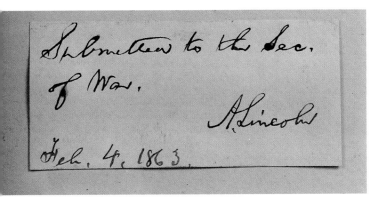

AUTOGRAPH, 1863. A cut signature from a note to the Secretary of War, signed "A. Lincoln". Value $2,200-$3,500.

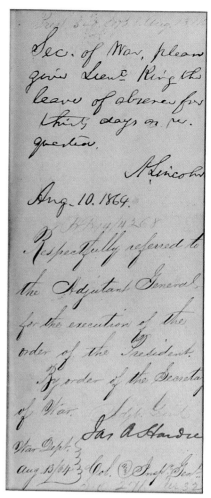

AUTOGRAPH LETTER, 1863. An autographed letter from Lincoln to Henry Wright of Boston, Massachusetts with a quote stating in part "I shall not attempt to retract or modify the emancipation proclamation, nor shall I return to slavery any person who is free by the terms of that proclamation". 4to. *Courtesy of Christies, New York.* Value $200,000-$300,000.

AUTOGRAPH NOTE, 1864. A short note to the Secretary of War asking him to give a lieutenant a thirty-day leave of absence, signed "A. Lincoln". *From the Joseph Edward Garrera collection.* Value $5,000-$6,000.

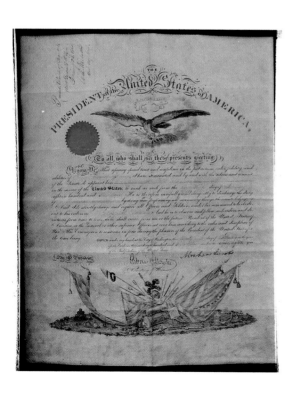

AUTOGRAPH DOCUMENT, 1864. An autographed appointment document from the President and Secretary of War, appointing a Chaplain. *From the Joseph Edward Garrera collection.* Value $9,000-$12,000.

AUTOGRAPH LETTER, 1864. Mary Lincoln writes to C.C. Moore agent for Colgate & Co. (toothpaste, soap, etc.) thanking him for the variety of soap he sent. The letter says in part, "please accept the thanks of the President & Myself. The former would be pleased to acknowledge the receipt himself if he had the leisure." Also shown is the envelope, addressed and franked by the President. *From the Colgate-Palmolive Collection.*

AUTOGRAPH LETTER, 1865. An autographed appointment letter from the Secretary of the Navy, signed "Gideon Welles". Value $300-$400.

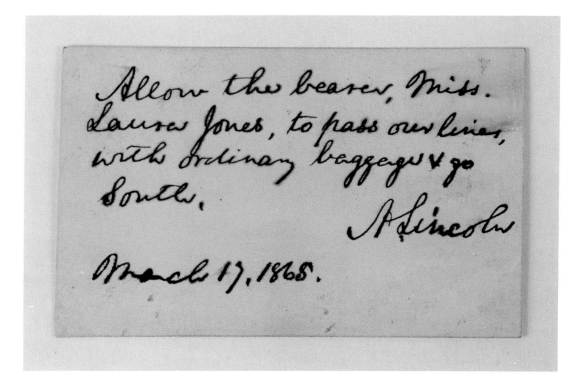

AUTOGRAPHED PASS, 1865. A pass to let the bearer go South, written and signed by Lincoln. *From the Frank & Virginia Williams Collection of Lincolniana.*

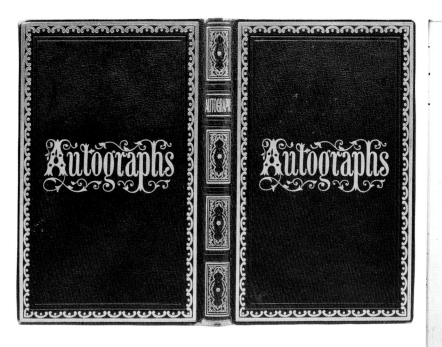

AUTOGRAPH MANUSCRIPT, 1865. An autographed manuscript of the concluding paragraph of his second inaugural address that was contained in an autograph album belonging to Caroline Wright, a friend of Mary Lincoln. 8vo. *Courtesy of Christies, New York.* Sold for 1.1 million dollars in 1992.

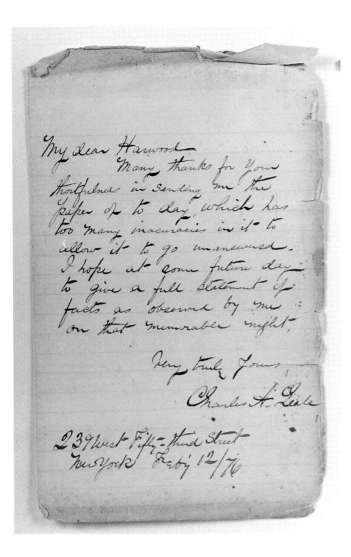

AUTOGRAPH LETTER, 1876. An autographed letter from Doctor Charles Leale, one of Lincoln's attending doctors after he was shot. Wonderful in content, it states Dr. Leale found inaccuracies in an newspaper article about the night of the assassination and indicated his desire "to one day, give a full statement of facts as observed by me on that memorable night." Value $400-$500.

AUTOGRAPH, 1871. George Robinson was credited with saving the life of Lincoln's Secretary of State, William Seward, on the night of the assassination, by fighting off the attack by Lewis Paine, Booth's co-conspirator. Value $500-$750.

AUTOGRAPH LETTER, 1894. Joseph Sessford was the ticket seller at Ford's Theater the night Lincoln was shot. He thereafter sold souvenirs and relics of the Lincoln assassination. This letter discusses some of the items he was offering to E. Rosenburger, who claimed he was writing a book. Value $75-$125.

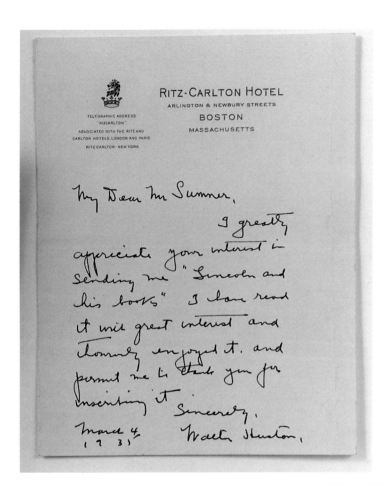

AUTOGRAPH LETTER, 1935. An autographed letter from Walter Huston thanking an author for sending him a copy of his book, *Lincoln and His Books*. Huston had starred in D.W. Griffith's film, *Abraham Lincoln*, in 1930. Value $90-$125.

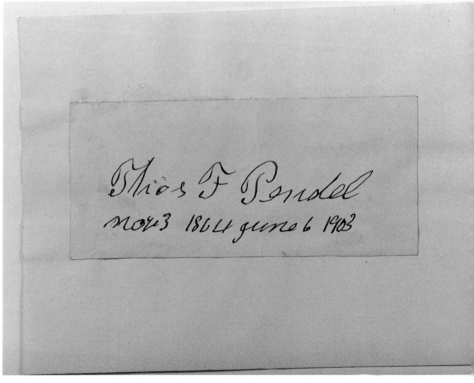

AUTOGRAPH, 1903. Cut signature of Thomas Pendell, the door keeper at the White House when Lincoln was President. Value $50-$65.

16. Miscellaneous

Lincoln's Death

Lincoln's death had a profound impact on the public. Lincoln was the first president to be assassinated in office. He had just presided over the country's bloodiest war and saw it to its conclusion. He was re-elected by a landslide and he was just about to guide America into a post war peace. News of his death was emotionally charged. Millions of people mourned and came out to see his funeral procession, held in multiple cities. Mourning badges, ribbons, posters, tokens, medalets, music, eulogies, and miscellaneous pieces appeared by the tens of thousands. No collection of Lincolniana would be complete without several mourning pieces. Entire collections exist devoted to Lincoln's death. Interesting pieces to look for are framed relics belonging to soldiers who marched in the funeral procession and took a piece of the catafalque or saved their armband. Look for photos of the processions, mourning cards, mourning badges with Lincoln's picture, and funeral march sheet music.

Lincoln's Good Name

Lincoln's image has been used since his death to promote products (see tradecards for example) and to represent the Republican Party. The name Lincoln denoted honesty, humble beginnings and fairness. His name began to be used by commercial ventures in 1905. One of the first was the Lincoln Life Insurance Company of Fort Wayne, Indiana. There was the Lincoln watch by the Illinois Watch Co. (Advertising pieces from around the turn of the century, featuring Lincoln, can fetch big money from advertising collectors.) Toy building logs became Lincoln Logs. An automobile was named the Lincoln (Why don't we drive Washingtons or Jeffersons?). Lincoln also became a popular name for savings banks. Some cities and towns took the name. As you look through the miscellaneous section of photographs in this book, you will see other examples.

Lincoln and Prohibition

Around the turn of the century and into the Lincoln Centennial, Anti-Saloon Leaguers and prohibitionists used Lincoln as their figurehead. Lincoln was not, publicly, a drinker but apparently had nothing against people who drank. Some prohibitionists, however, claimed that Lincoln intended to tackle the drinking problem after the Civil War and the emancipation of the slaves. They claimed that Lincoln had made a written pledge to abstain from liquor and they encouraged others to sign on to Lincoln's pledge. While not numerous, there are an interesting group of items connecting Lincoln to the Prohibitionists. A popular, newer collecting field, is following the social history movement which includes prohibitionist activities, women's suffrage, labor issues, the Ku Klux Klan (there are a handful of KKK items showing Lincoln), and the rise of black power. Dealers in these materials may also carry items showing Lincoln.

Lincoln and Post-Death Politics

Lincoln's death did not keep him out of politics. After his death, politicians constantly referred to his acts and deeds and often used his statements or his image on their political campaign material, in effect saying, "I am like Lincoln and as such, deserve your vote." There was a Lincoln political party. Lincoln's image was used as an illustration on political ballots to denote, to the illiterate, that this was the Republican or Lincoln party. Some, like Roosevelt in 1938, went so far as to make a speech at Gettysburg, using many references to Lincoln. As you study Lincoln's speeches and writings, you will begin to notice some of Lincoln's words in present day politics. As one political advisor recently said, "Emphasize your humble beginnings and your understanding of the problems of the working man. Act sincere, even if you don't mean it."

AFTERSHAVE, ca. 1976. Two Avon bottles of aftershave. The left one is "Lincoln Aftershave" and the right one, 7 inches tall, is "Wild Country". You had to ask—Lincoln's head is removable. Value $15-$40.

ASHTRAY, ca. 1928. A plaster bust of Lincoln with attached ashtray. 5.5 inches tall. Value $75-$100.

WILLIAM HOWARD TAFT 1912

ASHTRAYS, ca. 1933. Two souvenir ashtrays showing Lincoln. The bust version is unmarked and may be from the 1940s. The flatter style is from the Lincoln exhibit at the Century Of Progress fair in 1933. It is 5 inches wide. *From the Robert DeLorenzo collection.* Value $35-$50.

BADGE, ca. 1912. A Republican National Convention Delegate's badge or medal. It is 5 inches long. *From the Robert DeLorenzo collection.* Value $50-$85.

BADGE, ca. 1913. A 50th anniversary Gettysburg reunion badge or medal for a Massachusetts regiment. It is 3.25 inches long. *From the Robert DeLorenzo collection.* Value $50-$85.

BADGE, ca. 1940. An unmarked (maybe 75th anniversary) badge. The reverse says "Civil War 1861-1865". It is 3 inches long. *From the Robert DeLorenzo collection.*

BADGE, ca. 1930. Award for an insurance agent issued by the Lincoln National Life Insurance Co. of N.Y. 2.5 inches tall. *From the Robert DeLorenzo collection.* Value $35-$45.

BADGE, ca. 1944. A Republican National Convention Alternate Delegate's badge. The metal looking parts are made out of pressed and painted cardboard since brass was a strategic war metal. It is 4.25 inches long. *From the Robert DeLorenzo collection.*

BADGE, ca. 1952. A Republican National Convention honorary assistant Sgt. at Arms' badge. It is 3.5 inches long. *From the Robert DeLorenzo collection.* Value $35-$45.

BALLOT, ca. 1890. A Maryland sample ballot with three parties running for representative in the 52nd Congress of the United States. 9.25 x 12.25 inches. *From the Robert DeLorenzo collection.*

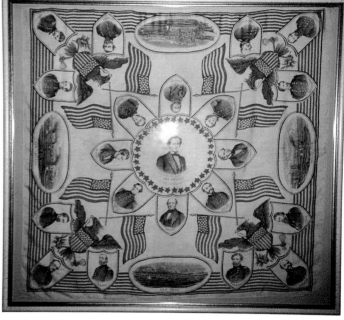

BANDANNA, ca. 1864. A silk bandanna produced in England about 1863-1864 and reproduced again in 1865 after Lincoln's death. It shows Lincoln's cabinet and some Army and Navy generals. 31 x 32.5 inches. Value $1,750-$2,500.

BANK, ca. 1930. A nice painted pot metal bank with the coin slot on the bottom. 6 inches tall. The bottom plate is often missing which greatly reduces value. Value $45-$75.

BANK ca. 1930. This copper plated metal bank is in the shape of Lincoln's log cabin. Size is 4.25 inches x 6.5 inches. Value $45-$60.

BANK, ca. 1932. The back of this 6 inch tall bronzed metal bank is marked "Lincoln National Life Insurance Company". The money is put in through the bottom. Made by Preferred Bank Service Co. Value $85-$110.

BANK, ca. 1940. A bronze toned white metal bust of Lincoln with the coin slot in the bottom. There are probably more different banks showing Lincoln than any other personality. Similar styles were made from the 1920s to the 1960s. It is 5 inches tall. *From the Robert DeLorenzo collection.*

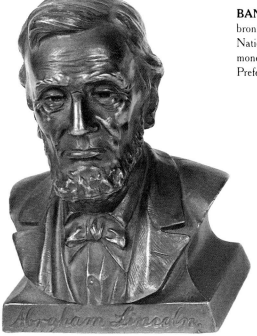

BANK, ca. 1932. The best quality metal bank showing the bust of Lincoln. 5.25 inches tall. This was made by A.C. Rehberger Co., Chicago. Value $100-$150.

BANK, ca. 1950. Metal bank made by B. Anthrico. 5.5 inches tall. Value $35-$45.

BANK, ca. 1950. A bronzed metal bust of Lincoln give out by the Lincoln Savings Bank of Brooklyn, New York. 6 inches tall. Value $35-$45.

BANKS, ca. 1930s to 1970s. These Lincoln bank bottles can be found in several size and shape variations originally containing different products. They are currently fairly easy to find. Value $12-$20.

BOOKENDS, ca. 1909. Heavy cast iron bust of Lincoln bookends. They have the remainder of their bronze coating visible. 6.25 inches tall. Value $75-$90.

BOOKENDS, ca. 1915. A pair of very well made and well finished bookends of the Lincoln statue that stands in front of the Essex County courthouse in Newark, New Jersey. There are no makers markings on these heavy metal pieces. The statue was sculpted in 1910 by Gutzon Borglum who also designed the Mount Rushmore sculpture. 6 inches wide x 6.5 inches tall. The same sculpture, 29 inches tall x 22 inches long, sold at auction in 1994 for $150,000. Value $150-$200.

BOOKENDS, ca. 1909. Bronze bookends marked, "M. Peinlich, Sculp." Cast by the Griffoul Co. of Newark, New Jersey. These can also be found marked "Gorham Foundry". 5.5 inches tall. Value $100-$150.

BOOKENDS, ca. 1920. Bronze bookends showing the Borglum statue, unmarked. 5 inches tall. Value $50-$80.

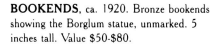

BOOKENDS, ca. 1922. Cast iron profile bust of Lincoln bookends. They are bronze plated. 6 inches tall. Value $55-$70.

BOOKENDS, ca. 1922. Bronzed cast iron bookends showing Lincoln reading to Tad. Marked "1922, O.P. Muller, MetaHaun, MP". 7.25 inches tall. Value $85-$110.

BOOKENDS, ca. 1922. Bronzed metal bookends made by the Nu-Art Company. Nu-Art was a trademark, used during the early 1920s, of the Imperial Glass Co. of Bellaire, Ohio. 6.5 inches tall. Value $75-$100.

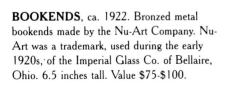

214

215

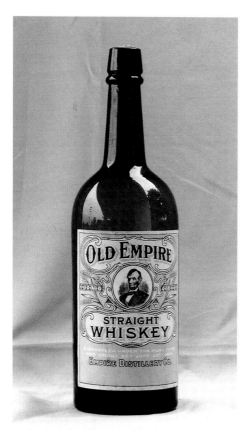

BOTTLE, ca. 1909. Old Empire Whiskey used the image of Lincoln. The Temperance Union people would just die when they saw this. 12 inches tall. Value $25-$40.

BOTTLE, ca. 1976. This is a great ceramic image of a young Lincoln with his dog and it held whiskey. Sold by the McCormick Distilling Co., it stands 13 inches tall.

BOTTLES, MILK, ca. 1938. As you may have guessed by now, the name "Lincoln" was popularly used for many products. Two milk bottles with their "Pogs" intact from the Lincoln Dairy Co. of Hartford. 9.5 and 5.5 inches tall. Value $35-$45.

BOTTLE, ca. 1988. A Lincoln On Democracy bottle of Chardonnay from Woodbury Vineyard, New York. Most likely put out to honor the book by Governor Cuomo and Hal Holzer. Value $14-$18.

BOTTLES, ca. 1976. These flasks were probably made for the Bicentennial. It is very unlikely that any flasks of this style were made during Lincoln's presidency or shortly after his death. The flask style is late 1700s to early 1800s. The blue bottle is 8.5 inches tall and the yellow one is 8 inches tall. Value $10-$15.

BRUSH, ca. 1924. A clothes brush from the Lincoln Trust Co. of Paterson, New Jersey. It is 3.5 inches wide. *From the Robert DeLorenzo collection.* Value $20-$30.

BUBBLE GUM TRADING CARDS, ca. 1956. These were included in bubble gum packs. Value $10-$18.

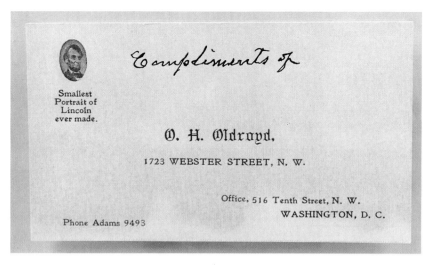

BUSINESS CARD, ca. 1927. Osborn H. Oldroyd's business card.
Value $40-$55.

BUTTONS, ca. 1930s to present. These five celluloid covered buttons
seem to be later than the 1909 centennial. The images are half toned.
From left to right, top to bottom, 1.25 inches, .875 inches, .875 inches,
1.25 inches, and 1.25 inches. Value $12.50-$20.00.

CALENDAR, ca. 1911. An ornate die cut
Lincoln theme calendar. Value (without frame)
$45-$60.

BUTTONS, ca. 1930s to present. These
three celluloid covered buttons seem to be later
than the 1909 centennial. The images are half
toned. From left to right, 1.5 inches, 1.125
inches and 1.5 inches. Value $12.50-$20.00.

CALENDAR, 1931. A Lincoln calendar given out by the Lincoln National Life Insurance Co. About 6 inches long. *From the Robert DeLorenzo collection.* Value $30-$40.

CALENDAR, 1912. Lincoln's image was a popular graphic for calendars. About 9 inches tall. *From the Robert DeLorenzo collection.* Value $35-$50.

CALENDAR, 1920. A Lincoln calendar. Each month has a Lincoln illustration and some words about him and by him. About 9 inches wide. *From the Robert DeLorenzo collection.* Value $35-$50.

CARTOON, ca. 1971. *Will The Real Mr. Lincoln Please Stand Up* by Holland. Lincoln's birthday has lost the stature of years ago and is slowly being phased out. The great president's birthday is now a part of President's Day in February. *From the Frank & Virginia Williams Collection of Lincolniana.*

CATALOG, 1949. An interesting item for Lincoln collectors—A Parke-Bernet Galleries auction catalog wherein the "Bliss" manuscript of the Gettysburg Address in Lincoln's own handwriting was offered for sale. To compliment it, there is a magazine article showing the proud purchaser of the manuscript, Oskar B. Cintas of Cuba, who purchased it for $54,000. *From the Robert DeLorenzo collection.*

CERTIFICATE, ca. 1906. A certificate from The Lincoln Farm Association. The Association was formed to raise money to have the farm where Lincoln was born turned into a national park. Contributors were given this certificate. *From the Joseph Edward Garrera collection.* Value $175-$200.

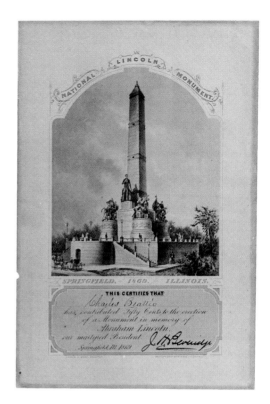

CERTIFICATE, ca. 1869. A certificate, signed by J.H. Beveridge, from National Lincoln Monument in Springfield, Illinois. People giving money (in this case fifty cents) to erect the monument were given this certificate. *From the Joseph Edward Garrera collection.* Value $175-$200.

CHARM, ca. unknown. A tiny Lincoln bust in 18kt gold. It originally had a loop at the back of the head. The loop was removed and it now has a tie tack back. It is .875 inches tall. Value $300-$350.

CIGAR BOX LABEL, ca. 1895. A. Lincoln box end label. 4.5 x 4.5 inches. Value $20-$30.

CIGAR BOX LABEL, ca. 1895. Cigar box label collecting is an entire field unto itself. There are labels for almost any subject, such as portraits of Lincoln. There are not too many Lincoln labels. All are valued here, in mint condition. A nice Lincoln graphic on La Flor De Lincoln. About 8 inches wide. *From the Robert DeLorenzo collection.* Value $40-$50.

CIGAR BOX LABEL, ca. 1900. A great Lincoln graphic on Lincoln Bouquet. About 8 inches wide. *From the Robert DeLorenzo collection.* Value $45-$60.

CIGAR BOX LABEL, ca. 1900. Los Inmortales is tough to find. About 5 inches wide. *From the Robert DeLorenzo collection.* Value $30-$40.

CIGAR BOX LABEL, ca. 1910. Old Honesty Cigars box sample inner label. 6 x 8 inches wide. Made as late as 1920. Value $40-$50.

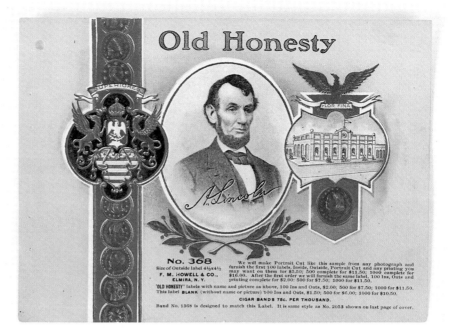

CIGAR BOX LABEL, ca. 1918. Abraham Lincoln box end label. 4.5 x 4.5 inches. Value $20-$30.

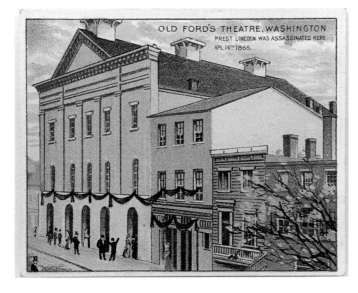

CIGARETTE CARD, ca. 1912. A picture of Lincoln's log cabin with an advertisement for "Helmar" cigarettes on the back. A pack of cigarettes would have held one card. Value $20-$30.

CIGARETTE CARD ca. 1918. A picture of Ford's Theater, with an advertisement for "Between The Acts" cigars on the back. A tin of cigars would have held one or more cards. Value $25-$30.

CIGARETTE LIGHTER, 1934. The Ronson (Art Metal Works) Lincoln striker lighter. The wand in Lincoln's hat pulls out and has a wick and metal striker. It is scraped along the back and sparks light the wick. The original sculpture was done by Gutzon Borglum in 1910. Value $175-$225.

COMIC BOOK, 1959. A Lincoln comic book telling about Lincoln and the railroad. *From the Robert DeLorenzo collection.* Value $10-$12.

CURRENCY, ca. 1861. This is obsolete local currency from the Merchant's Bank of New Jersey and may have been the first piece of currency to contain Lincoln's picture. When there was a money shortage during the Civil War, local banks issued their own currency. Congress outlawed the issuing of private currency in 1862. Value $50-$100.

CURRENCY, ca. 1863. Lincoln's image graces this fifty cent "fractional currency". During the war years, there was a shortage of coins. Merchants issued penny size tokens to use as change and postage stamps, encased in a rigid frame, were also used for currency. The government tried to help by printing bills in denominations under a dollar. *From the Robert DeLorenzo collection.* Value $40-$60.

CURRENCY, 1899. A one dollar 1899 series silver certificate of the large size type notes. Value (in this condition) $25-$35.

CURRENCY, ca. 1914. A Lincoln five dollar bill from the series of 1914. It is larger than our current five dollar bill. *From the Robert DeLorenzo collection.* Value in excellent condition $70-$80.

CURRENCY, ca. 1934. A Lincoln five dollar silver certificate from the series of 1934. *From the Robert DeLorenzo collection.* Value in excellent condition $18-$24.

CURRENCY, ca. 1942. An "Occupation" Lincoln five dollar bill from the series of 1934 that has been overprinted "Hawaii". During the second World War, it was feared that Hawaii would be taken over by the Japanese. The dollars would be devalued to prevent the Japanese from using them if the island fell into enemy hands. *From the Robert DeLorenzo collection.* Value in excellent condition $20-$30.

DOOR KNOCKER, ca. 1950. A brass door knocker showing a young Abe Lincoln reading a book by firelight, unmarked. 2.5 x 3.75 inches. Value $35-$45.

DOLL, ca. 19?. This handmade Lincoln doll is 11.5 inches tall. All of his clothing is finely tailored and he has great personality and detail. This could have been made anytime from the 1940s to 1970s.

DOOR KNOCKER, ca. 1940. A brass door knocker. 2 x 3 inches. Value $40-$50.

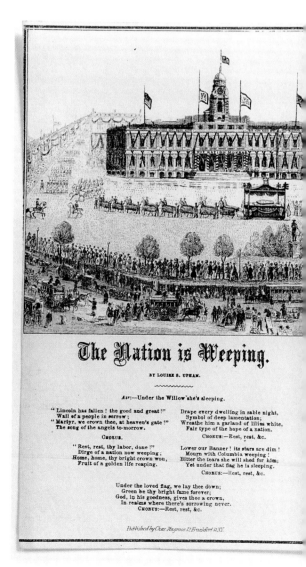

The Nation Mourns.

From all churches
Sad and slow,
Toll the bells
The knell of woe.

Hark! their sad and solemn notes attend
Abraham Lincoln to his last way's end.

Dead silence mutely hovers
Above grave's dreary strand,
With sable pall it covers
The Leader of Our Land.

Despairing men are wringing
In vain their hands here wound,
The Orphan's wail is winning
No solace from its ground.

The nightingales' caroling
Sounds never in its womb;
True Patriots tears are rolling
But on the mossy tomb.

FAN, ca. 1866. A superb hand colored fan of
embossed metal covered wood and paper,
designed by August Edouard Achille Luce.
This is a variation on the uncolored version
and contains a "Booth" dagger built into one
end of the handle. About 18 inches across.
From the Gary Lattimer Family collection.
Value $9,500-$10,500.

EULOGY FLYERS, 1865. Nicely
illustrated sheets that have woodcuts of funeral
or mourning scenes. These may have been
created for use in church services. 5 x 8
inches. Value $75-$100.

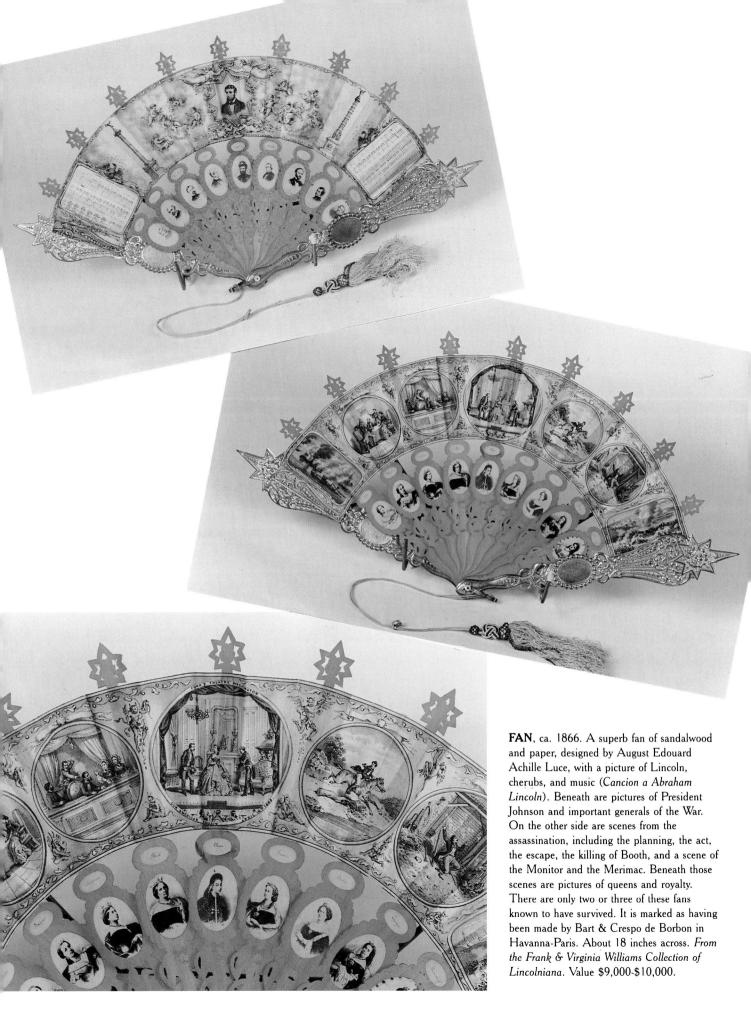

FAN, ca. 1866. A superb fan of sandalwood and paper, designed by August Edouard Achille Luce, with a picture of Lincoln, cherubs, and music (*Cancion a Abraham Lincoln*). Beneath are pictures of President Johnson and important generals of the War. On the other side are scenes from the assassination, including the planning, the act, the escape, the killing of Booth, and a scene of the Monitor and the Merimac. Beneath those scenes are pictures of queens and royalty. There are only two or three of these fans known to have survived. It is marked as having been made by Bart & Crespo de Borbon in Havanna-Paris. About 18 inches across. *From the Frank & Virginia Williams Collection of Lincolniana.* Value $9,000-$10,000.

FOLK ART, ca. 1865. After Lincoln's death, many people felt the need to have a remembrance of the President. A talented carver created two wooden frames and put the President and his wife on their wall. 8 inches tall. *From the Joseph Edward Garrera collection.* Value $400-$500.

FOLK ART, ca. 1909. A talented but folksy sculpture of Lincoln on wood. 5.25 inches tall x 6 inches wide. Value $350-$500.

FOLK ART, ca. 1932. A 6 x 8 inch horseshoe shaped frame with mirrors attached. While it is difficult to date this homemade tribute to Lincoln and it could be as early at the 1880s, it has a Depression era flavor to it and seems to fit into Depression era folk art. Value $65-$100.

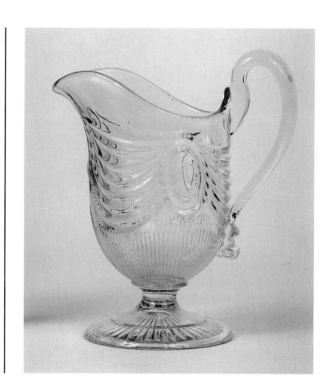

GAME, ca. 1924. The Lincoln's Log Cabin game by "W.H.D." Perhaps it was a spelling and numbers game since the tin lithographed spinner offers both. It is 11 inches wide. *From the Robert DeLorenzo collection.* Value $20-$30.

GLASS, ca. 1862. A popular glass pattern called "Lincoln Drape" in different styles and sizes. Also made with a tassel hanging from the center of the drape. The story that the pattern was allegedly made to commemorate Lincoln's death is probably not true, since Flint glass was popular in the 1850s and stopped being made about 1865, the time of Lincoln's death. 6 inch and 4 inch tall goblets. Value $150-$200 each.

GRAVY BOAT, ca. 1909. A ceramic gravy boat with Lincoln's Gettysburg Address made by the Homer Laughlin China Co. for the firm's Historical America china set. *From the Frank & Virginia Williams Collection of Lincolniana.* Value $150-$200.

HAT, ca. 1930. Lincoln's birthday used to be celebrated with much more enthusiasm in the past. This hat is a Lincoln's birthday party hat. 8 x 11.5 inches. Value $30-$40.

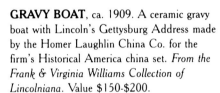

INVITATION, ca. 1865. An engraved invitation to the second inaugural ball on March 4, 1865. It was drawn by Bruff and engraved by Dempsey & O'Toole. 7.5 x 10.5 inches. Value $300-$400.

JIGSAW PUZZLE, ca. 1930. A jigsaw puzzle showing a young Abe Lincoln. 12 x 15.25 inches. *From the Robert DeLorenzo collection.* Value $40-$50.

JIGSAW PUZZLE, ca. 1933. A cardboard puzzle made by the Einson Freeman Co. The artist's name seems to be missing a part. It reads, "Ray Rgan". 14 x 10.5 inches. Value $45-$55.

KNIFE, ca. 1912. A political advertising piece for the Wilson presidency featuring Washington and Lincoln. It is 3.25 inches long. *From the Robert DeLorenzo collection.* Value $90-$125.

KLAN BUTTON, 1925. A celluloid button showing Lincoln and made for a Ku Klux Klan reunion. The Klan at times purportedly revered Lincoln because he really wanted to send freed slaves back to Africa. 1.5 inches. *From the Frank & Virginia Williams Collection of Lincolniana.* Value $100-$150.

LAMP, ca. 1950. An unusual item that is or was most likely available in a souvenir shop. The base is 8 x 5.5 inches. Value $30-$50.

LANTERN SLIDE, ca. 1900. These lantern slides were projected on a screen or wall. They were used in schools to illustrate lectures. Value $75-$100.

LINCOLN

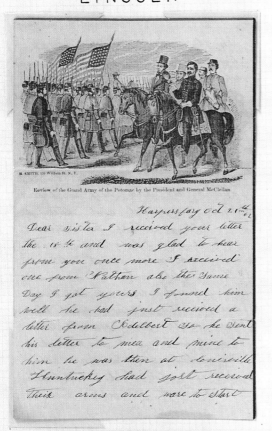

PATRIOTIC LETTER — HARPER'S FERRY- OCT.21'62 PRIVATE D.D. KING WROTE TO HIS SISTER THAT HE HAD SEEN HIS PRESIDENT.

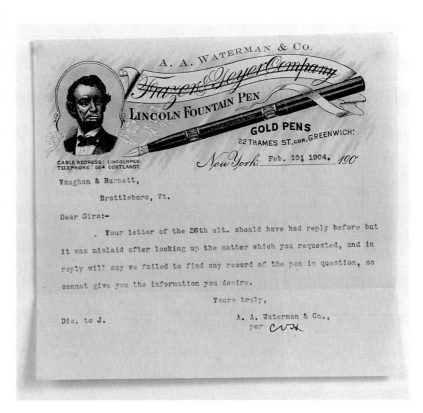

LETTER, 1862. A letter on patriotic letterhead with a great image. A private writes to his sister that he has seen the President. Value $200-$300.

LETTERHEAD, 1904. The Lincoln Fountain Pen was made by the Frazer & Geyer Company. In 1904, they were purchased by the A. A. Waterman Company. Rather than immediately print up new stationary, they recycled the old. Value $35-$50.

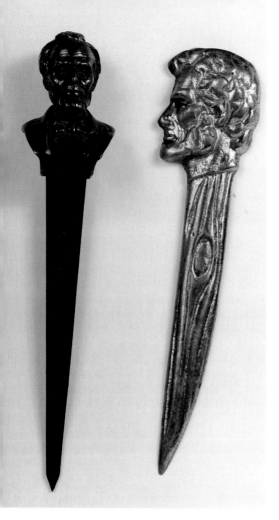

LINCOLN LOGS, ca. 1924. The original Lincoln logs box cover. "Interesting Playthings Typifying The Spirit of America". Value $50-$80.

LETTER OPENERS, ca. 1930. Two souvenir letter openers showing Lincoln. The bust version is marked "souvenir of Washington, DC". The flatter style is unmarked. Both are 7.5 inches long. *From the Robert DeLorenzo collection.* Value $35-$50.

LOG CABIN, ca. 1930. This replica of Lincoln's birthplace was made for Valentine Bjorkman. It is shown in the 1939 photo being held by Dr. Lawson (President of Upsala College) and Carl Sandburg who had come to visit the Bjorkman collection. Size is 15 inches tall.

LETTER OPENER, ca. 1930. A Lincoln letter opener in copper. The bust is unmarked. 6.5 inches long. Value $35-$50.

LOG CABIN, ca. 1935. This is a model of Lincoln's log cabin birthplace made by an unknown maker. Size is 8 inches tall. *From the Robert DeLorenzo collection.*

LOG CABIN, ca. 1937. This replica of Lincoln's birthplace was given to Valentine Bjorkman for his collection. Size is 6 inches tall.

DR. LAWSON AND CARL SANDBURG

MATCHBOOK COVERS, 1930s to 1950s. A grouping of matchbook covers, most put out by the Lincoln National Life Insurance Company. Local agents would have their agency names imprinted. Value $6-$9 each.

MOURNING BANNER ca. 1865. This is a mourning print on board that would have been hung in a window along the Lincoln funeral procession route. Very few of these have survived due to the brittleness of the paper, lack of wording, and the large size of the print. 21 x 22 inches. Value $400-$500.

MEMORIAL CARDS, 1865. A 2.4 x 4 inch mourning card that would fit into the typical CDV album pages. The card on the left is tougher to find. Value $150-$250.

NEEDLEPOINT, ca. 1876. A framed needlepoint piece done for the country's centennial in 1876. These pieces were sold with a silk-screened image on stiff paper. The person would then do the needlepoint work in colors according to the print. The person in this case either did not finish this work or felt that they could not do justice to the illustration of Lincoln. Value $45-$60.

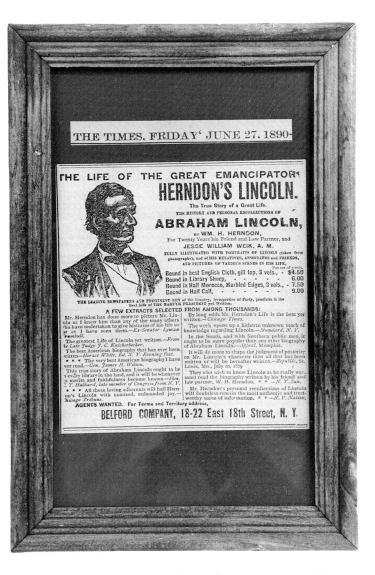

NEWSPAPER AD, 1890. An illustrated ad announcing the publication and sale of Herndon's *Lincoln*. Value $35-$45.

PAPERWEIGHT, ca. 1909. A 4.75 inch tall cast steel image of Lincoln made by Kraeuter &. Co., Inc., Newark, New Jersey. Value $80-$125.

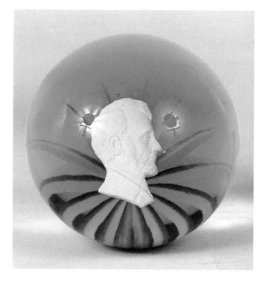

PAPERWEIGHT, ca. 1909. Commemorative cast glass paperweight. Similar pieces were made in 1876 for the nation's centennial. 4 inches. *From the Robert DeLorenzo collection.* Value $65-$100.

PAPERWEIGHT, ca. 1972. Baccarat sulfide image paperweight. This is one of a Presidential series. 3 inches. *From the Robert DeLorenzo collection.* Value $135-$175.

PAPERWEIGHT, ca. 1970. A Baccarat sulfide Lincoln embedded in blue glass. 3.5 inches wide. *From the Frank & Virginia Williams Collection of Lincolniana.* Value $400-$550.

PIN, ca. 1908. This button was sold and worn at the 50th anniversary of the Lincoln-Douglas debate at Freeport, Illinois, held in conjunction with the "Old Settlers' Days " celebration. Value $45-$60.

PIPE, ca. 1935. A high quality carved meerschaum pipe with Lincoln's portrait. Value $375-$450.

PEN, 1976. This plastic pen, 6 inches tall and made by the Locke Co. of St. Charles, Illinois, for the nation's bicentennial, is a piece of kitsch that tells the world that you like Lincoln. Value $15-$20.

PIN, ca. 1939. A silver three-dimensional bust coin pin from the 1939 Worlds Fair. 1 inch wide. *From the Robert DeLorenzo collection.*

PLATE, ca. 1901. "Our Martyrs". This plate shows the three assassinated presidents, Lincoln, Garfield, and McKinley. "Compliments of the Buffalo Supply Co." 9.25 inches. Value $90-$125.

PLATE, ca. 1909. Commemorative or souvenir plate marked "Warwick". 8.75 inches. *From the Robert DeLorenzo collection.* Value $50-$90.

PLATE, ca. 1909. Commemorative or souvenir plate. 9.5 inches. *From the Robert DeLorenzo collection.* Value $50-$90.

PLATE, ca. 1909. A plate with the Gardner photo pose. Made in Germany. 7.5 inches. Value $50-$80.

PLATE, ca. 1909. A Homer Laughlin China Co. dish, 5.75 inches wide, showing Abe the rail splitter. *From the Frank & Virginia Williams Collection of Lincolniana.* Value $100-$125.

PLATE, ca. 1916. An 8.5 inch plate made as a souvenir of a 1915-1916 tour of places where Lincoln appeared. Researching the group that made this tour would be an interesting project. Was it a private group, a GAR group, or a foreign group? Value $65-$90.

PLATE, ca. 1909. A Lincoln homestead memorial plate, probably made for the centennial, 9.5 inches wide. It was made by the Petrus Rocout & Co. of Mastricht, Holland. *From the Frank & Virginia Williams Collection of Lincolniana.* Value $50-$75.

PRESIDENTIAL CHINA, Mary Lincoln bought new china for the White House. This is a reproduction of the pattern. The cup alone is 3.25 inches tall. The reproduction plate (7 inches in diameter) is marked on the back, "Woodmere White House Collection, Abraham Lincoln." The cup just says, "Woodmere". It is important to know what the reproduction looks like so that the cup is not bought by a collector who believes that it is the real thing. The collector should be suspicious of an alleged original that has the back side polished down below the glaze.

PROGRAM, 1907. A dinner program for The Lincoln Club of Philadelphia. *From the Robert DeLorenzo collection.* Value $35-$45.

RECORD, ca. 1940. A Comedy Dialogue called "Mike & Ike in Politics" by Murray & Silver on the Lincoln Record Corp., New York, label. It is a two sided 33 rpm record. *From the Robert DeLorenzo collection.* Value $20-$30.

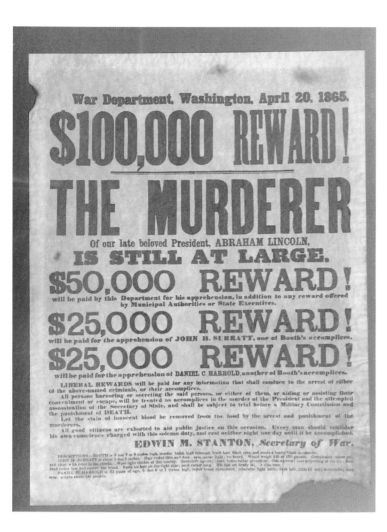

REWARD POSTER, 1865. This is a reproduction of one of the reward posters created after the assassination. Tips to telling a reproduction from the original are 1) thickness of the paper—most early posters were created on a thin paper stock, 2) forced signs of aging—note the burned edges of the paper. The real thing might contain rips or missing pieces, but not usually burns, 3) toning—the color looks like someone has soaked the whole thing in a slurry of wet tea leaves, 4) evenness of printing—printing presses did not always print each letter so evenly and 5) posting holes and folds—most wanted posters were nailed up in public places and when taken down and saved, were often folded. 11.125 x 14.25 inches. Value if original $7,000-$10,000.

RIBBON, 1865. A 2.75 x 7 inch mourning ribbon that would have been pinned to the uniforms of soldiers marching in Lincoln's funeral procession. Value $150-$250.

RIBBON, ca. 1865. A large mourning ribbon with an paper photograph of the President. About 11 inches long. *From the Howard Hazelcorn Collection.* Value $850-$1,000.

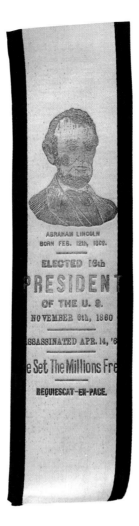

RIBBON, ca. 1865. A black bordered mourning ribbon worn just after Lincoln's death. 2.5 x 9 inches. *From the Frank & Virginia Williams Collection of Lincolniana.* Value $600-$800.

RIBBON, 1865. A large mourning ribbon probably worn by officials marching in the parade with the Lincoln catafalque. Lincoln's image is in the center of the top of the ribbon and the material is similar to the material actually used on the catafalque. 3 x 8 inches. Value $850-$1,000.

RIBBON, ca. 1865. A silk ribbon showing Lincoln. 2.375 x 10.875 inches. *From the Robert DeLorenzo collection.* Value $350-$500.

RIBBON, ca. 1865. This is a beautiful woven silk ribbon that was made to honor the memory of Lincoln. This same ribbon was made for Lincoln's second inauguration and can be found with the words "President" instead of "The Late Lamented President" 9.5 inches long. Made by Thomas Stevens of Covetry, England. *From the Joseph Edward Garrera collection.* Value $350-$500 (inauguration version $650-$700).

RIBBON, ca. 1865. A variation of a memorial ribbon. 2.25 x 9.25 inches.

RIBBON, 1890. A silk ribbon created for a civil war reunion group. 6 inches long. *From the Robert DeLorenzo collection*. Value $60-$100.

RIBBON, ca. 1865. This is a large and beautiful type silk piece made to honor the memory of Lincoln. This is a very hard ribbon to find. 5.125 x 9.5 inches long. *From the Joseph Edward Garrera collection*. Value $850-$1,000.

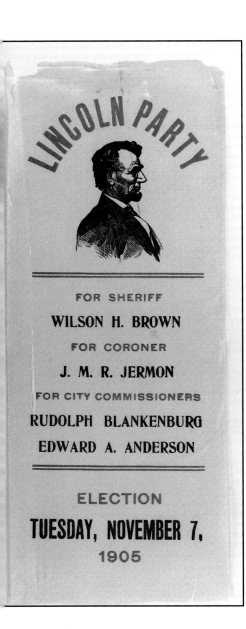

RIBBON, 1905. A silk ribbon showing the candidates running under the Lincoln Party. 8.5 inches long. *From the Robert DeLorenzo collection.* Value $50-$85.

RIBBON, ca. 1916. A "cigarette silk" ribbon showing Lincoln and his autograph. These were included with a pack of Mogul cigarettes. There were many different series of these types of ribbons. 3.25 inches long. *From the Robert DeLorenzo collection.* Value $60-$100.

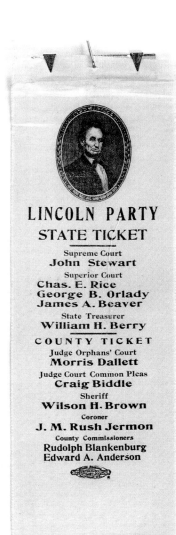

RIBBON, ca. 1905. A silk ribbon showing the candidates running under the Lincoln Party. 3 x 8.75 inches. Value $50-$85.

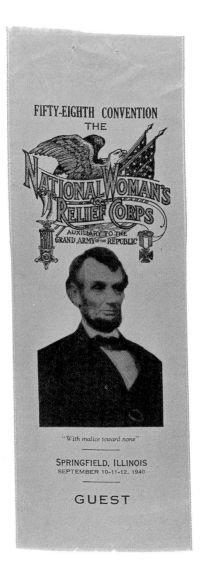

RIBBON, ca. 1940. A silk ribbon for a guest at the 58th convention of the National Woman's Relief Corps. 3.25 x 9 inches. Value $30-$45.

RING, ca. 1930. A 10kt gold school ring from the Lincoln University. *From the Robert DeLorenzo collection.*

SALT & PEPPER, ca. 1950. A pair of souvenir salt & pepper shakers in the shape of a bust of Lincoln. They are marked "Made in Japan". 2.5 inches tall. *From the Robert DeLorenzo collection.*

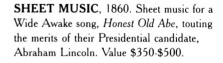

SHEET MUSIC, 1860. Sheet music for a Wide Awake song, *Honest Old Abe*, touting the merits of their Presidential candidate, Abraham Lincoln. Value $350-$500.

SHEET MUSIC, ca. 1862. A very colorful piece of sheet music entitled *President Lincoln's Grand March* by F.B. Helmsmuller. *From the Howard Hazelcorn Collection.* Value $400-$500.

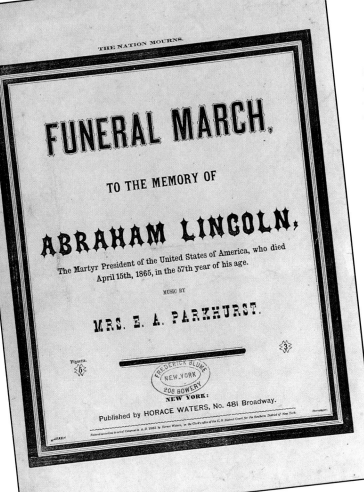

SHEET MUSIC, 1865. After Lincoln was assassinated, song writers tackled the subject and created music for the funeral. This one is called *Funeral March*. Value $125-$150.

SHEET MUSIC, 1865. A Lincoln funeral march called *Abraham Lincoln's Funeral March*. Value $125-$150.

SONG SHEET, ca. 1863. An interesting song called *Hold On Abraham* about the North's moving against the South. 9.25 x 6 inches. Value $50-$75.

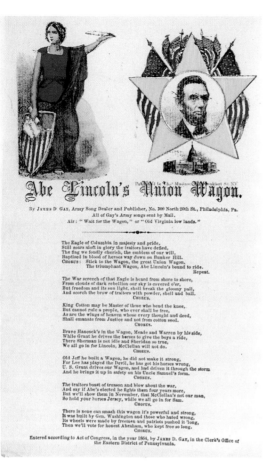

SONG SHEET, ca. 1864. A military song sheet produced and sold by James D. Gay. 5 x 8.25 inches. Value $60-$85.

SOUVENIR SPOONS, ca. 1909. Four enameled silver spoons probably issued during the centennial. One shows the president, another his birthplace, another his first store and first love, Ann Rutledge, and the last, his return home from the Douglas debates. *From the Frank & Virginia Williams Collection of Lincolniana.* Value $135-$175 each.

STAINED GLASS WINDOW, contemporary. Collectors personalize their collection in many ways. This stained glass window designed and created by Diane Garrera greets visitors to the Garrera collection of Lincolniana.

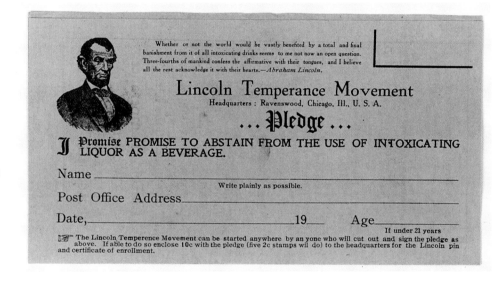

TEMPERANCE CARD, 1906. A pledge card from The Lincoln Temperance Movement. Value $20-$25.

TEMPERANCE CARD, 1909. A pledge card from The Lincoln Legion, a temperance group. Value $20-$25.

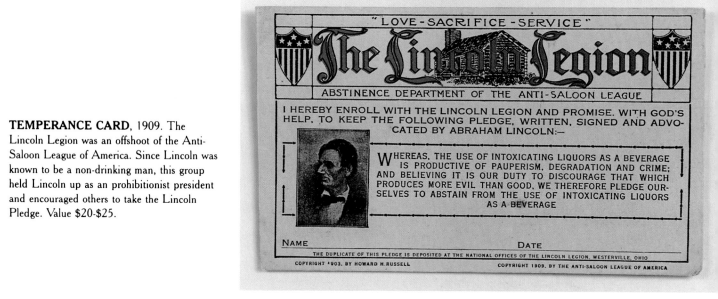

TEMPERANCE CARD, 1909. The Lincoln Legion was an offshoot of the Anti-Saloon League of America. Since Lincoln was known to be a non-drinking man, this group held Lincoln up as an prohibitionist president and encouraged others to take the Lincoln Pledge. Value $20-$25.

TICKET, ca. 1890. A ticket of admission to Col. O.H. Oldroyd's Lincoln museum in the house where Lincoln died. Value $50-$65.

TEMPERANCE MEDAL, ca. 1906. Lincoln temperance medal. Brass, 63 mm. There were allegedly only twenty-five examples made in brass and four in silver. Made by C.H. Hanson and sculpted by H. Ryden. Value $100-$150 in brass, $400-$500 in silver.

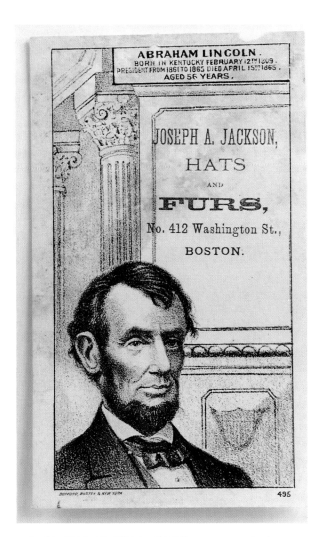

TRADE CARD, ca. 1880. Trade cards were given out by merchants and manufacturers as a point of purchase trade stimulator. Many people collected them in albums. Lincoln's image is on a stock card—one printed without a specific company or merchant's name—but room is left to stamp the name on the card. *From the Robert DeLorenzo collection.* Value $15-$20.

TRADE CARD, ca. 1880. Lincoln's image on a Larkin's Soap Company card. *From the Robert DeLorenzo collection.* Value $15-$20.

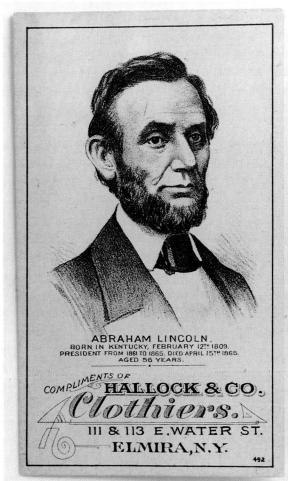

TRADE CARD, ca. 1880. Lincoln's image on a Hallock & Co. clothing store card. *From the Robert DeLorenzo collection.* Value $15-$20.

TREE ORNAMENT, ca. 1909. An 3.5 x 3.5 inch hand sewn ornament of cotton and silk. Perhaps a Christmas tree ornament for the Centennial year. Value $125-$175.

VISITOR'S BOOK, ca. 1930. Valentine Bjorkman had this book hand made to record the visitors who came to visit his Lincoln's collection. The cover, showing young Abe Lincoln sitting under a tree and reading is carved of wood. There is a good chance that the wood was obtained from Lincoln's birthplace. Also shown is part of the page that Ida Tarbell signed. Other visitors were most of the leading Lincoln scholars, Babe Ruth and Carl Sandburg. *From the Joseph Edward Garrera collection.* Size is 12 inches tall.

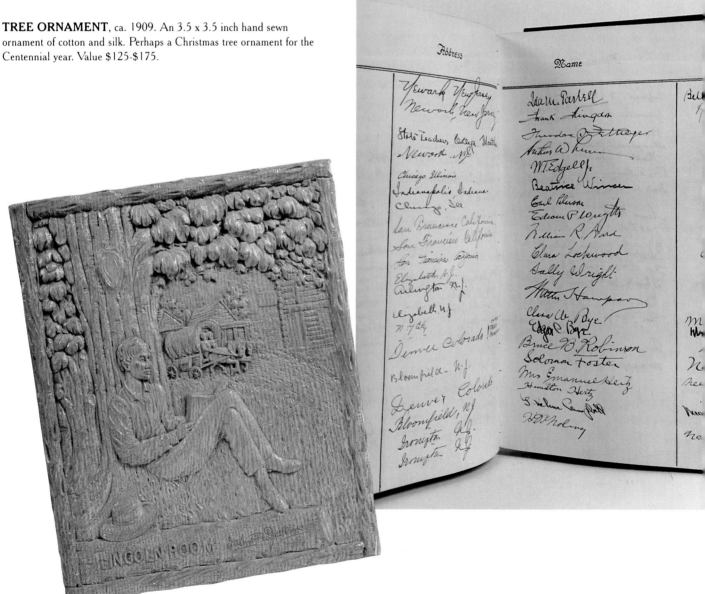

WATCH FOB, ca. 1920. A 1.25 inch brass or bronze watch fob advertising the Lincoln Life Insurance Company of Fort Wayne, Indiana. Value $30-$45.

WATCH FOB, ca. 1922. A 1.25 inch brass or bronze watch fob awarded by the Pittsburgh Press for a Lincoln story contest. Value $30-$45.

WOODEN PLATE, ca. 1909. An 8.5 inch wooden plate or plaque with a hand carving of Lincoln. The size of the head in relation to the plate suggests that this was not a commercially made piece. Value $50-$75.

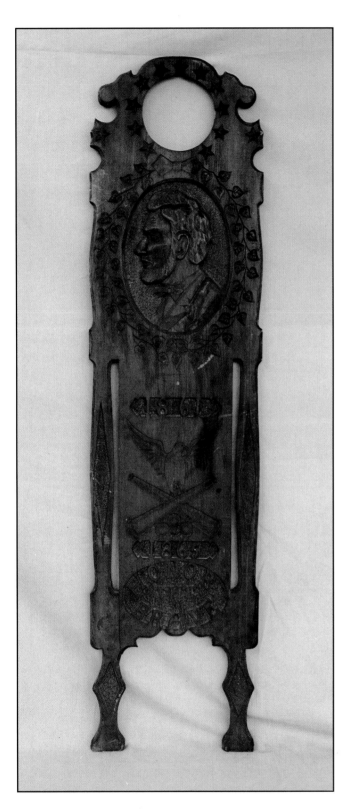

WOODEN PLAQUE, ca. 1909. A 14.5 x 16.5 inch wooden plaque with a hand carving of Lincoln. The piece is signed "C.H." Value $150-$250.

WOODEN PLAQUE, ca. 1880. A piece of regimental art probably made for or during a GAR encampment of Ohio veterans. This type of pyrography was popular in the 1880s. The design is burned into the wood. It says, "1861-1865 Honor The Brave". 49 inches tall and 12.5 inches wide. Value $225-$300.

17. LINCOLN IN THE MOVIES, TELEVISION, THEATER, & MUSIC

Lincoln's life has had a profound impact on the theatrical arts—he was at the theater the night he was assassinated, and his assassin was an actor. His words and deeds have been acted in plays and movies. There is a group of Lincoln collectors who seek out Lincoln memorabilia related to the theater. Items sought are photos of Lincoln actors; broadsides advertising *Our American Cousin* (watch out for the numerous reprints and copies), the play that Lincoln was watching on the night of his assassination; correspondence from the members of the cast of *Our American Cousin*; scripts; play books (pamphlets that give all the lines for the actors and staging directions); movie lobby cards (11 x 14 inch cards that hung in lobbies, showing scenes from the movie); and movie posters. Many Lincoln theatre collectors also actively seek Booth memorabilia or anything to do with Ford's Theatre and its players before and after the assassination. Interestingly, the ticket taker and the ticket seller at Ford's Theatre both later made a business of selling artifacts and lecturing on personal recollections of the events leading up to the assassination and the night of the assassination.

After Lincoln's death, plays began to appear showing many aspects of his life. There are productions about his youth, his alleged romance with Ann Rutledge, his legal trials, the Lincoln-Douglas debates, his run for the presidency, his time in office, the emancipation of the slaves, his involvement in the Civil War, his assassination and offshoots such as productions about John Wilkes Booth and Dr. Mudd. The number is quite large and the variety of items available is seemingly endless.

The earliest plays were stories about Lincoln produced for schools and local theatre groups. Soon, commercial plays appeared. One was called *The Rivalry*, starring Richard Boone. It portrayed the Lincoln-Douglass debates. *Abe Lincoln in Illinois*, staring Raymond Massey, appeared in 1938 and one, called *The Last Days of Lincoln*, was written for the stage in 1959.

The first silent motion picture of Lincoln's life, *The Son of Democracy—A Call To Arms*, starring Benjamin Chapin, was produced about 1924. D.W. Griffith produced *Birth Of A Nation* which showed Lincoln freeing the slaves. He also produced the first Lincoln sound movie in 1930, called *Abraham Lincoln*. John Ford's film, *Young Mr. Lincoln*, starring Henry Fonda, appeared in 1939. *Abe Lincoln in Illinois*, a film, staring Raymond Massey, presented events leading up to the presidency.

In 1953, Abe Lincoln appeared on television in *Abraham Lincoln—The Early Years*. 1959 television viewers were treated to *Meet Mr. Lincoln*. In 1974, Hal Holbrook starred in *Sandberg's Lincoln*. In 1991, millions of viewers watched Ken Burn's *Civil War* with a section devoted to Lincoln and in a similar style of production, a show called *Lincoln* appeared in 1992 using the photos from the famous Kunhardt collection.

Lincoln was no stranger to music. Throughout his presidential campaign, Wide Awake groups sang songs praising his coming presidency. During the Civil War, songs told about his beating the South or riding the Union wagon. After his death, funeral marches were created in his honor. Aaron Copland wrote a patriotic symphony in 1942 called *A Lincoln Portrait*.

Possibly, the most interesting actors are the Lincoln impersonators or "presenters" or "re-enactors" as they prefer to be called. They grow beards, dress and gesture as they believe Lincoln might have and have turned Lincoln's speeches and stories into living history. The history of Lincoln presenters goes back to shortly after he died. Some look-a-likes appeared on stage and recited the Gettysburg address. Some of these presenters are almost exact duplicates of Lincoln while others resemble him (lots of variety here, as is the case with Elvis impersonators). To compliment the Lincoln reenactors, there is also a small contingent of Mary Lincoln impersonators. The Lincoln reenactor's motto could be "Don't just collect Lincoln, be Lincoln".

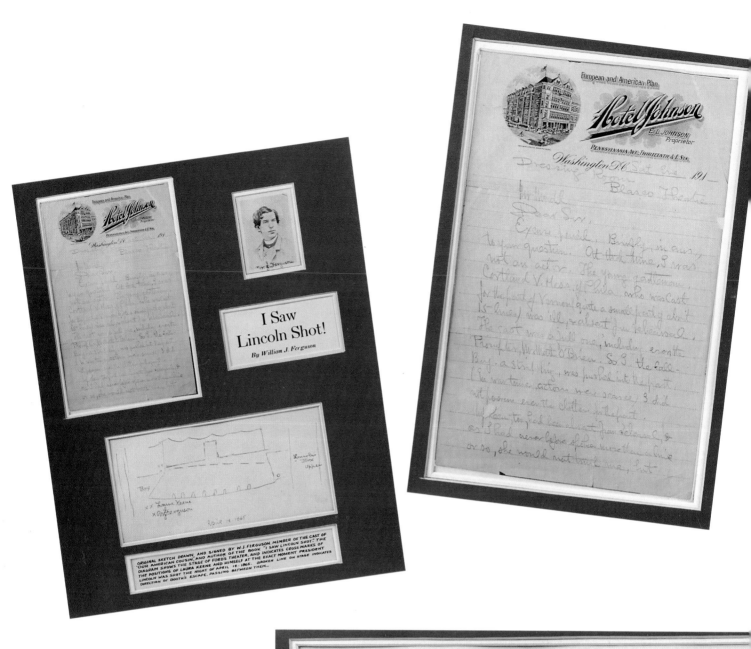

AUTOGRAPH LETTER, PHOTO & SKETCH. William J. Ferguson was an actor in the cast of *Our American Cousin* the night that Lincoln was shot. His letter, written in pencil, details the events surrounding the shooting. The autographed photo shows Ferguson in 1865. His thumbnail sketch, dated April 14, 1865, shows Booth's path across the stage and where he and actress Laura Keene were standing at the time. Value $8,000-$10,000.

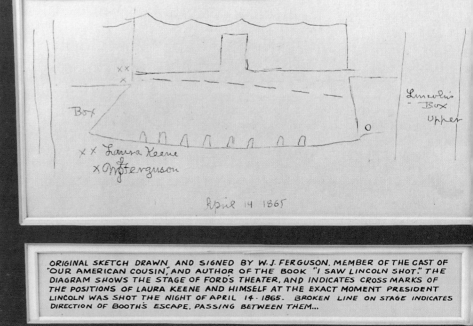

ORIGINAL SKETCH DRAWN, AND SIGNED BY W.J. FERGUSON, MEMBER OF THE CAST OF "OUR AMERICAN COUSIN," AND AUTHOR OF THE BOOK "I SAW LINCOLN SHOT." THE DIAGRAM SHOWS THE STAGE OF FORD'S THEATER, AND INDICATES CROSS MARKS OF THE POSITIONS OF LAURA KEENE AND HIMSELF AT THE EXACT MOMENT PRESIDENT LINCOLN WAS SHOT THE NIGHT OF APRIL 14·1865. BROKEN LINE ON STAGE INDICATES DIRECTION OF BOOTH'S ESCAPE, PASSING BETWEEN THEM...

AUTOGRAPH LETTERS. Autographed letters from Laura Keene and Jennie Gourlay (Struthers) with a reproduction of the playbill from the night Lincoln was shot. Miss Keene's letter refers to engaging a children's acting troupe at her own New York City theater in 1857. Jennie Gourlay was a member of the troupe at the time. Eight years later, they were both in *Our American Cousin* the night that the President was shot. Jennie Gourlay's letter, written in 1923 from her daughter's home in New Jersey, refers her correspondent to Oldroyd's book on the subject. Value (Keene) $750-$900, (Gourlay) $1,250-$1,500.

STAGE PHOTOGRAPH, 1865. A very rare and large photograph of the stage at Ford's theater taken shortly after the assassination. The photo is credited to Mathew Brady's studio and is actually three photos fitted together to create a panorama of the entire scene. Value $3,000-$4,000.

BROADSIDE, ca. 1865. An original broadside advertising the last night of *Our American Cousin* playing at Ford's Theater. This is the rare last minute printing as it contains a reference to the William Whither's piece that was to be played in honor of the President's attendance. 5.5 x 19 inches. *From the Frank & Virginia Williams Collection of Lincolniana.* Value $8,000-$10,000.

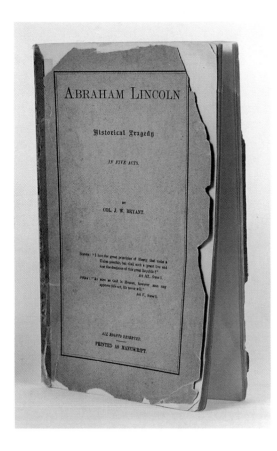

PLAY BOOK, 1886. *Abraham Lincoln—Historical Tragedy*, by J.W. Bryant. A play about Lincoln and Booth. 45 pages. This copy was formerly owned by John T. Ford, owner of the theater where Lincoln was shot. Value $100-$125.

MOVIE LOBBY CARD, 1915. A scene showing Joseph Henabery as Lincoln in the epic film, *The Birth Of A Nation*, by D.W. Griffith. The movie was loosely based upon the book, *The Clansman*, by Thomas Dixon. A reproduction of the original.

CABINET CARD, ca. 1890. Elmer Grandin was an actor who portrayed Lincoln. Here he is as himself and as Lincoln. *From the Frank & Virginia Williams Collection of Lincolniana.* Value $200-$250.

LOBBY CARDS, ca. 1918. *The Son of Democracy—A Call To Arms* a silent movie about Lincoln and the Civil War starring Benjamin Chapin. Chapin began playing Lincoln parts about 1904. 11 inches x 14 inches. Value $325-$400.

PHOTO, ca. 1920. Lincoln actor, Meyer Stroell, with the Doris and Lionel Barrymore on the set of *The Copperhead*. *From the Dan Bassuk Collection.*

PHOTO, ca. 1923. George Chester Billings portrayed Lincoln in the 1924-1925 Rockett Brothers' Lincoln film, *The Dramatic Life of Abe Lincoln. From the Frank & Virginia Williams Collection of Lincolniana.* Value $50-$75.

PHOTO, ca. 1922. Edwin Carroll of Lawrenceville, Indiana, portrayed Lincoln. *From the Frank & Virginia Williams Collection of Lincolniana.* Value $50-$75.

Wm HARRIS J^r presents
John Drinkwater's
ABRAHAM LINCOLN
with Frank McGlynn

OHIO THEATRE
CLEVELAND
COMMENCING
Mon., NOV. 21
Matinee Wednesday & Saturday
Special Matinee, Thursday, Thanksgiving Day

THEATER, 1923. A photograph of the leading actors in a play called *Lincoln Memories. From the Robert DeLorenzo collection.*

PLAY ADVERTISEMENT, 1924. John Drinkwater's play, *Abraham Lincoln,* starring Frank McGlynn (1866-1951). The play, with McGlynn as Lincoln, was originally produced in 1919-1924 and revived in 1929-1930. McGlynn became a lawyer in 1894 and in 1896 left the profession to became a professional actor. Value $20-$30.

MOVIE LOBBY CARDS, 1924. *The Dramatic Life of Abraham Lincoln*, an early silent movie about Lincoln produced by the Rockett Brothers for First National Pictures. 11 inches x 14 inches. Value $175-$225.

PHOTO, ca. 1925 and 1928. Judge Charles Bull (1881-1971) portrayed Lincoln in *The Iron Horse (1924)*, directed by John Ford and later in *The Heart of Maryland*. Between the two, he became a Justice of the Peace in Nevada. He performed at the Chicago World's Fair in 1933-34. Two autographed photos. *From the Frank & Virginia Williams Collection of Lincolniana.* Value $60-$85 each.

BROCHURE, ca. 1925. A brochure advertising Lincoln Caswell as Abraham Lincoln. He was an early Lincoln actor/impersonator. His portrayals included a day with Lincoln, Lincoln's stories and humor, memorable sayings, and more. Appeared in *Lincoln's Gettysburg Address*, a 1927 Warner Bros./Vitaphone film. He was the pastor of the Crawford Methodist Church of White Plains, New York.

"*And, that government of the people, by the people, for the people, shall not perish from the earth.*"

MOVIE LOBBY CARD, 1935. The short film, *A. Lincoln—The Perfect Tribute*, starring Charles "Chic" Sale. Sale had obtained the rights to produce a Lincoln movie from Ida Tarbell's writings. Value $30-$50.

MOVIE LOBBY CARDS, 1930. *Abraham Lincoln*, D.W. Griffith's first "talkie" movie starring Walter Huston (1884-1950). 11 inches x 14 inches. Value $200-$300.

MOVIE LOBBY CARD, 1936. *The Prisoner of Shark Island*, starring Warner Baxter as Dr. Mudd, was directed by John Ford. Value $400-$500.

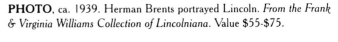

PHOTO, ca. 1939. Herman Brents portrayed Lincoln. *From the Frank & Virginia Williams Collection of Lincolniana.* Value $55-$75.

THEATER, 1938. Life magazine's cover showing Raymond Massey (1896-1983) as Lincoln. *From the Robert DeLorenzo collection.* Value $20-$30.

MOVIE LOBBY CARD, 1939. *Young Mr. Lincoln*, starring Henry
Fonda (1905-1982) and directed by John Ford. 11 inches x 14 inches.
Value $75-$100.

MOVIES, 1939. Two "stills", one showing a scene from the movie
Young Mr. Lincoln and the other showing Henry Fonda as that young
Mr. Lincoln. *From the Robert DeLorenzo collection.* Value $35-$45.

THEATER, 1939. A Playbill from the Plymouth Theater where Raymond Massey was playing Lincoln in *Abe Lincoln In Illinois. From the Robert DeLorenzo collection.* Value $35-$45.

PROGRAM, 1939. *Abe Lincoln in Illinois* theater program for the Robert Sherwood play starring Raymond Massey. Value $35-$45.

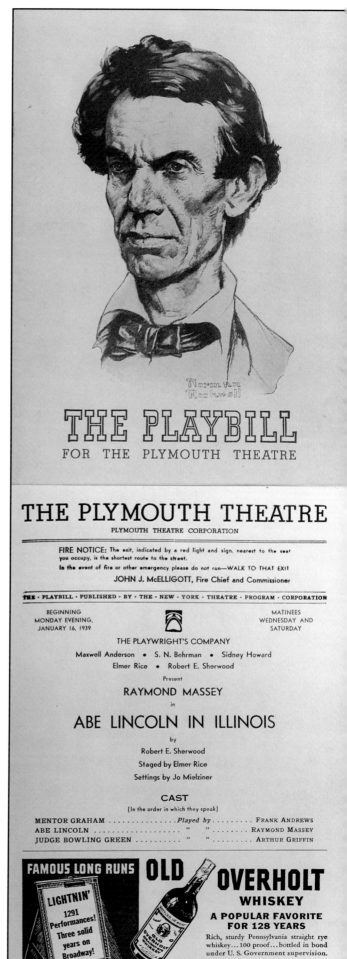

STAGE MAGAZINE, 1939. *Abe Lincoln in Illinois* is featured in this issue. Value $6-$8.

PLAYBILL COVER, 1939. Lincoln actor, Richard Gaines, as Abe Lincoln in *Abe Lincoln In Illinois* playing at the Plymouth Theater in New York in the latter half of 1939. *From the Dan Bassuk Collection.*

MOVIE LOBBY CARD, 1940. The movie *Abe Lincoln in Illinois*, starring Raymond Massey. Value $75-$100.

MOVIE POSTER, 1940. *Abe Lincoln in Illinois*, starring Raymond Massey. Value $40-$65.

PLAYBILL, 1940. *The Man Who Killed Lincoln*, by Philip Van Doren Stern. A play about J. Wilkes Booth starring Richard Waring as the assassin. Value $25-$40.

PLAY BOOKS, 1940-1950s. A group of plays about Lincoln. Value $10-$15 each.

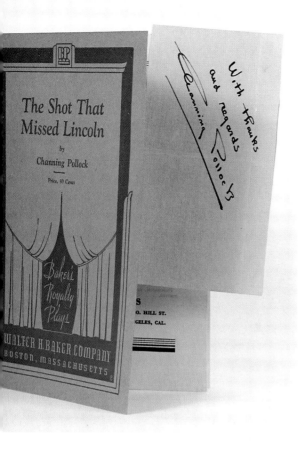

PLAY BOOK, 1959. *The Shot That Missed Lincoln*, by Channing Pollock. A one-act play about J. Wilkes Booth. Value $25-$40.

LINCOLN PRESENTERS, ca. 1995. A portion of The Association of Lincoln Presenters with Mary Lincolns.

PLAY BOOK, 1966. *I Married Irene Because She Had Eyes Like Lincoln*, by Joseph Baldwin. A one-act comedy about a man who likes to stay at home and try beards on his wife because she has eyes like Lincoln. Value $5-$10.

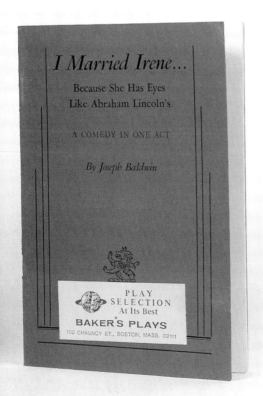

LINCOLN PRESENTERS, ca. 1996. A group portrait of The Association of Lincoln Presenters.

18. POSTCARDS

Postcard collecting is one of the fastest growing hobbies in the country. Prices for rare cards have reached thousands of dollars. Luckily for Lincoln collectors, postcards with a Lincoln theme are a very reasonable Lincoln "collectible". There were hundreds made and they range from simple cards with one or two colors to elaborate cards with five colors, embossing, and gilding. Picture postcards began appearing about 1890 and by the early 1900s, millions were being produced every year. 1909, Lincoln's birth centennial, is considered to be the height of the golden age of postcards. Many were commissioned from the leading artists and publishers of the day. Names to look for are Chapman, C. Bunnell, Gibson, Tuck, and others.

Germany was the center of the world's postcard printing until the first World War. Almost all colorful, heavily embossed and gilded Lincoln Centennial cards were printed in Germany. Some nice cards, especially photographic styles, were produced in America.

One of the rarer series of cards that can be found was produced by Buckingham & Harley Publishing. Buckingham was the ticket taker at Ford's Theatre the night that Lincoln was shot. He produced and sold postcards of scenes and people from Lincoln's life and death.

Postcard collecting can be as expensive or as inexpensive a hobby as one cares to have. Prices for post cards in mint condition have been escalating, but a wonderful Lincoln postcard collection can be assembled very reasonably if you will accept cards showing some wear or lacking the name of a known publisher.

PETERSON HOUSE
In which President Lincoln Died, April 15, 1865

THE HANGING OF PRESIDENT LINCOLN'S ASSASSINS

POSTCARDS, ca. 1909. Postcard variety is vast. These are "Lincoln Medallion" style cards. *From the Robert DeLorenzo collection.* Value $8-$12.

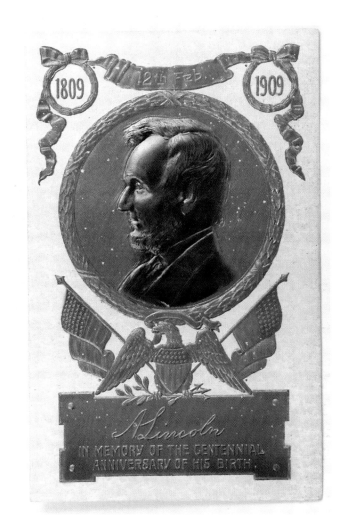

POSTCARDS, ca. 1907. Three postcards published by Buckingham & Harley showing 1) the A. Gardner's 1865 photo of the hanging of the conspirators., 2) the Petersen House in which Lincoln died, and 3) Boston Corbett, who shot John Wilkes Booth. Buckingham was the ticket taker at Ford's Theater the night Lincoln was shot. Value $20-$30.

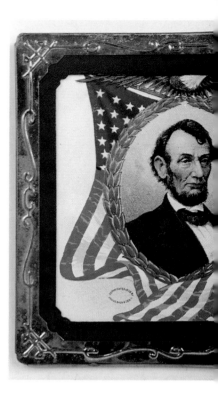

POSTCARD, ca. 1909. A Majestic Publishing colored photo postcard showing Abe Lincoln's horse, Old Bob. The photo was taken about 1865. Value $6-$8.

POSTCARDS, ca. 1909. Two similar postcards, but one is printed on leather. *From the Robert DeLorenzo collection.* Value $5-$12.

POSTCARD, ca. 1909. A nice Lincoln Centennial postcard in a metal frame that was sent through the mails. *From the Robert DeLorenzo collection.* Value $12-$18.

POSTCARD, ca. 1909. A very simple Lincoln Centennial postcard. *From the Robert DeLorenzo collection.* Value $5-$8.

POSTCARDS, ca. 1909. These are the "Lincoln Scenes" type of card. The first is a reproduction. From *the Robert DeLorenzo collection.* Value $8-$12.

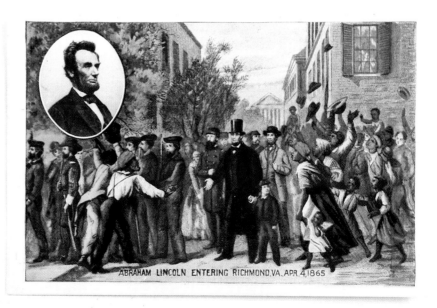

POSTCARDS, ca. 1909. A card sold by the Veteran Art Co. *From the Robert DeLorenzo collection.* Value $8-$12.

POSTCARDS, ca. 1909. A series of cards, copyright by E. Nash. *From the Robert DeLorenzo collection.* Value $8-$12.

POSTCARDS, ca. 1909. These are the "Assassination" type of cards. Copyright by P. Sander. Value $8-$12.

POSTCARDS, ca. 1909. These are "In Memory of the Centennial" cards. Value $8-$12.

POSTCARD, ca. 1909. Centennial card. Value $8-$12.

POSTCARD, ca. 1909. The rail splitter Centennial card. Copyright by P. Sander. Value $8-$12.

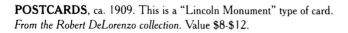

POSTCARD, ca. 1909. Centennial card. Value $8-$12.

POSTCARDS, ca. 1909. This is a "Lincoln Monument" type of card. *From the Robert DeLorenzo collection.* Value $8-$12.

POSTCARDS, ca. 1909. These are the "Lincoln Scenes" type of card.
From the Robert DeLorenzo collection. Value $8-$12.

POSTCARDS, ca. 1909. A card published by Wolf & Co. *From the
Robert DeLorenzo collection.* Value $8-$12.

POSTCARDS, ca. 1909. A three card series. *From the Robert DeLorenzo collection*. Value $8-$12.

POSTCARDS, ca. 1909. An unusual card from a G.A.R. gathering, showing the Lincoln funeral car. *From the Robert DeLorenzo collection.* Value $12-$18.

POSTCARD, ca. 1911. A colored photo postcard showing the house (turned into a museum by O.H. Oldroyd) in which Lincoln died. Value $7-$10.

POSTCARD, ca. 1911. A colored photo postcard showing the room in which Lincoln died. Value $7-$10.

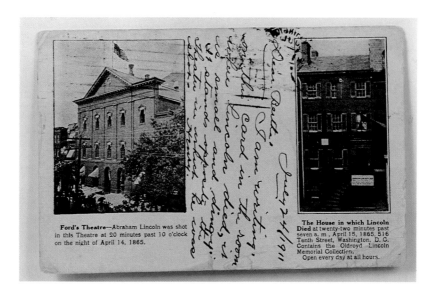

POSTCARD, ca. 1911. A photo postcard, published by O.H. Oldroyd, showing the house where Lincoln died and Ford's Theater. The more interesting feature of this card is the writer's comment about seeing "the small and dingy room" where Lincoln died. Value $7-$10.

POSTCARD, ca. 1912. A colored photo postcard showing the seated Lincoln statue by Borglum, in front of the Essex County Court House in Newark, New Jersey. Value $4-$6.

POSTCARD, ca. 1911. A colored photo postcard showing Ford's Theater. Value $6-$8.

BIBLIOGRAPHY

Darrah, Wm. *Stereo Views*. Gettysburg, PA: Times & News Pub., 1964.

Donald, David H. *Lincoln*. Simon & Schuster, 1995. (I believe this is one of the best and most readable books about Lincoln.)

Ebert, J., and K. Ebert. *Old American Prints For Collectors*. New York: Charles Scribner Sons, 1974.

Fuld, G., and M. Fuld. *Patriotic Civil War Tokens*. Iola, WI: Krause Publications, reprinted 1991.

Gores, Stan. *Presidential and Campaign Memorabilia*. Des Moines, Iowa: Wallace-Homestead, 1982.

Hake, Ted. *Political Buttons-Book III*. York, PA: Hake Americana Press, 1978.

Hamilton, Charles. *Great Forgers and Famous Fakes*. Lakewood, CO: Glenbridge Publishing, 1980, 1996.

Hamilton, Charles, and Lloyd Ostendorf. *Lincoln In Photographs*. Morningside House, revised edition, 1985.

Holzer, Boritt, and Neely. *The Lincoln Image*. NY: Scribners, 1984.

_____. *Changing The Lincoln Image*. Ft. Wayne, IN: Louis A. Warren Lincoln Library and Museum, 1985.

Horan, J. *Mathew Brady—Historian With A Camera*. NY: Bonanza Books, 1955.

Julian, R.W. *Medals of the United States Mint—The First Century*. The Token & Medal Society.

Katz, D. Mark. *Witness To An Era—Alexander Gardner*. NYC: Viking, 1991.

Kunhardt, D., and P. Kunhardt. *Twenty Days*. NJ: Castle Books, 1965.

Kunhardt, Philip, Philip Kunhardt, Jr., and Peter Kunhardt. *Lincoln*. NY: Alfred J. Knopf, 1992.

Lorrant, S. *Lincoln: A Picture Story Of His Life*. NY: Harper & Bros., 1952.

_____. *Lincoln: His Life In Photographs*. NY: Duell, Sloan & Pierce, 1941.

Mellon, J. *The Face of Lincoln*. NY: Viking Press, 1979.

Meredith, R. *Mr. Lincoln's Cameraman-Mathew B. Brady*. NY: Dover, 1974.

Peterson, M.D. *Lincoln in American Memory*. Oxford University Press, 1994.

Sullivan, E.B. *Collecting Political Americana*. Christopher Publ., 1991.

_____. *American Political Badges and Medalets, 1789-1892*. Lawrence, MA: Quarterman Publ., 1981.

Resources

The Abraham Lincoln Book Shop, 357 West Chicago Ave., Chicago, IL 60610. Mail order catalog and store carrying books, photos, prints, documents, etc. relating to Lincoln and the Civil War.

American Political Items Collectors, P.O. Box 340339, San Antonio, TX 78234. $30/yr, a must for political item collectors.

American Photographic Historical Society, 1150 Ave. of the Americas, New York, NY 10036. Good organization for photo collectors.

Association of Lincoln Presenters, c/o Dan Bassuk, 1143 River Rd., Neshanic, NJ 08853. A re-enactment group (about 175 members) devoted to dressing, looking, and acting like Abe Lincoln with a subgroup of Mary Lincolns. Newsletter is *Lincarnations*, dues $20/yr.

Christie Manson & Woods, 502 Park Ave., New York, NY 10022. Auction house handling fine Lincoln documents and autographs.

Civil War Token Society, c/o Mark Greenspan, P.O. Box 532, Burlington, VT 05401. $10/yr dues.

Currency Auctions of America, Inc., P.O. Box 573, Milwaukee, WI 53201. Mail auctions of fine currency.

Charles G. Moore Americana, 32 East 57th St., New York, NY 10022. Mail order auctions of Americana. Good service.

Coin World, P.O. Box 150, Sidney, OH 45365. Publishes a weekly newspaper for the coin collecting community.

Hakes Americana, P.O. Box 1444, York, PA 17405. Mail order auctions of political and other pins & collectibles.

Tony Hyman, P.O. Box 3028, Pismo Beach, CA 93448. Author of *Handbook of American Cigar Boxes* and dealer in cigar box art.

The Lincoln Group of New York, c/o George Craig, 83-12 St. James St., Elmhurst, NY 11373. Group dedicated to the study of all aspects of Lincoln.

The Lincoln Museum, P.O. Box 7838, Fort Wayne, IN 46801.

The Old Print Shop, 150 Lexington Ave., New York, NY 10016. Source for vintage prints.

The Rail Splitter, P.O. Box 275, New York, NY 10044. $12.00 per year. Lincoln political collector's newsletter.

Rex Stark, Box 1029, Gardner, MA 01440. Mail order catalog and auction of high quality political and historical material and ephemera. $10/4 issues.

Token and Medal Society, P.O. Box 951988, Lake Mary, FL 32795. $20/yr dues. Good source for token and medal collectors.

University Archives, 600 Summer St., Stamford, CT 06901. Autograph dealer.

Additional resources

Al Anderson, P.O. Box 644, Troy, OH 45373. Mail auctions, political items.

Bob Coup, P.O. Box 348, Leola, PA 17540. Mail auctions, political items.

C. Wesley Cowan, 747 Park Ave., Terrace Park, OH 45174. Auction of historic collectibles.

The Political Gallery, 5335 North Tacoma, #24, Indianapolis, IN 46220. Mail auctions, political items.

Robert Siegel Auctions, 65 E. 55th St., New York, NY 10022. Postal items auctions.

Swan Galleries, 104 E. 25th St., New York, NY. Auction house for books, autographs, and photographs.

INDEX

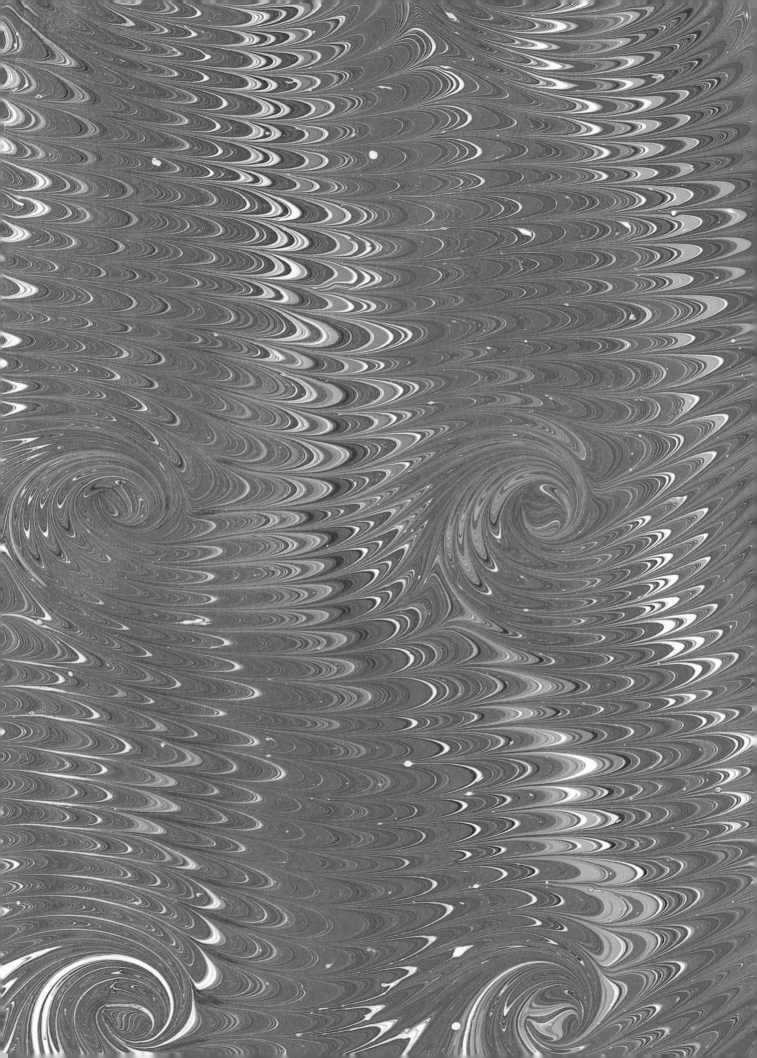